⌂THE NOTHING LEFT OUT HOME IMPROVEMENT BOOK ⌂

Also by Tom Philbin / HOME REPAIRS ANY WOMAN CAN DO

THE NOTHING LEFT OUT HOME IMPROVEMENT BOOK

by *TOM PHILBIN* and *Professional Home Remodeler* *FRITZ KOELBEL*

With Illustrations by Joseph G. Koelbel, Jr.

PRENTICE-HALL, INC., Englewood Cliffs, New Jersey

The Nothing Left Out Home Improvement Book
by Tom Philbin and Fritz Koelbel
Copyright © 1976 by Tom Philbin and Fritz Koelbel
All rights reserved. No part of this book may be
reproduced in any form or by any means, except
for the inclusion of brief quotations in a review,
without permission in writing from the publisher.
Printed in the United States of America
Prentice-Hall International, Inc., London
Prentice-Hall of Australia, Pty. Ltd., Sydney
Prentice-Hall of Canada, Ltd., Toronto
Prentice-Hall of India Private Ltd., New Delhi
Prentice-Hall of Japan, Inc., Tokyo
Prentice-Hall of Southeast Asia Pte. Ltd., Singapore
Whitehall Books Limited, Wellington, New Zealand

10 9 8 7 6 5 4 3 2 1

Library of Congress Cataloging in Publication Data
Philbin, Thomas.
    The nothing left out home improvement book.
    1. Dwellings—Remodeling—Amateurs' manuals.
I. Koelbel, Fritz. joint author.
II. Title.
TH4816.P5   643'.7   76-16515
ISBN 0-13-624353-3

Introduction

In the dozen or so years that I've been an editor and writer of how-to material for the do-it-yourselfer, I've seen many a book on home improvement projects. To varying degrees, usually more than less, these books have been characterized by glibness: They make every do-it-yourself project seem like the easiest thing in the world. Want to add a room? Simple. Just read these four pages and follow the handy sketch. Want to install Sheetrock? Simple. Find the studs, cut panels to fit, nail in place, tape. Simple. Very simple.

It all seems simple until the poor do-it-yourselfer tries to do-it himself (or herself). Then he finds that he doesn't have nearly enough information to do the job. He's not really told, ironically, *how to*. Oh, there might be some information there, but not for the specific situation that the do-it-yourselfer faces on his or her particular house. You may find out how to install flashing under clapboard siding. Fine—but your house is covered with aluminum siding.

This book attempts to fill that information gap. To get down to the nitty gritty, to provide all steps, all details, for many different kinds of situations that do-it-yourselfers face. And it attempts to be realistic, telling you how to circumnavigate problems—because problems do crop up on many jobs. They must when you consider that walls are never plumb, rooms never perfect rectangles, ceilings never perfectly flat. And before you begin a project this book will help you decide whether or not you should attempt it, based on your own skills. (See Contents for "Rating the Jobs.")

The book is organized to be read completely through before you select a particular project for doing. For two reasons. First, it will give you in-depth knowledge of how your house is constructed. Second, the various chapters complement one another. For example, Chapter 3 has information on how to install a header in a bearing wall. This will help you in the later project on installing a window: You'll know everything you're up against.

Of necessity the book is not glib. Indeed, it is meant to be studied rather than read, because some of the concepts are not simon-simple to understand, and it is heavily detailed. But stick with it—you'll be rewarded. And armed with the information you'll be able to attempt projects not detailed in the book.

The information in the book (except for the chapter on painting) is from Frederick J. "Fritz" Koelbel, a professional home remodeler for twenty-five years on Long Island, New York, and the finest and most knowledgeable craftsman I have ever known. We lived with the book for two and one-half years and at times it seemed like an endless project. Fritz's storehouse of knowledge is so great that he could always think of one more situation that we didn't cover—and then we always covered it.

The drawings are by Joe Koelbel, Fritz's brother, and we both owe him an enormous debt of gratitude. He spent hundreds of hours preparing the meticulous drawings, and was always willing to go that one step further with us. Joe shares with Fritz something that seems to run in the Koelbel family: pride. Pride that says if you're going to do a job, do it right.

When Fritz and I started to do the book, we vowed to make it the best how-to book on home improvement projects ever. I don't mean to boast, but in my heart I think we've done that. And I hope you do, too.

Tom Philbin

Rating the Job

The home improvement projects described in this book range from very easy to very difficult. To help you determine if a job is for you we've rated the jobs according to their mechanical complexity. We've assumed that you have a beginning handyman's skills, time, muscle, diligence, and will give the job T.L.C. (Tender Loving Care).

We've rated them as follows:

Fairly Easy
Easy
Difficult
Very Difficult
Extremely Difficult

Before you attempt any job, you should research it until you understand all aspects of it thoroughly. The more you know about a job the easier it will be and the more confidence you'll have.

Contents

🏠THE NOTHING LEFT OUT HOME IMPROVEMENT BOOK 🏠

Chapter 1

How Your House Is Framed

Essential to making many home improvements is a knowledge of how your house is framed. The frame is the wooden skeleton of your house—the main structure which rests on the masonry foundation. There are three main sections—floors, walls, and roof. Two types of framing predominate: box framing and balloon framing, popular in older homes.

Basic differences are these. In balloon framing studs (vertical boards in walls) run from the bottom of the house to the top in one continuous line no matter how tall the house is. When these tall studs are in the floors are added. In box framing each floor is built like a shallow box with walls added a story at a time. This has a big advantage: It's not as susceptible to serious damage by fire. In balloon framing a fire starting in the basement can burn up to the roof because the continuous frame spaces act as flues, so fire can go right up through the walls unless there are fire stops (horizontal boards between studs).

THE SILL

The first member installed in framing a house is the sill. The sill is commonly made of 2 by 6's nailed together to form 4 by 6's and secured to the top of the foundation with anchor bolts that protrude up from the foundation. Corners are connected with half-lap joints (Fig. A). The sill goes around the entire perimeter of the house.

The girder is the main supporting beam of the house. It is installed across the foundation in the middle of the house with ends resting on notches made in the foundation and the top flush with the

1

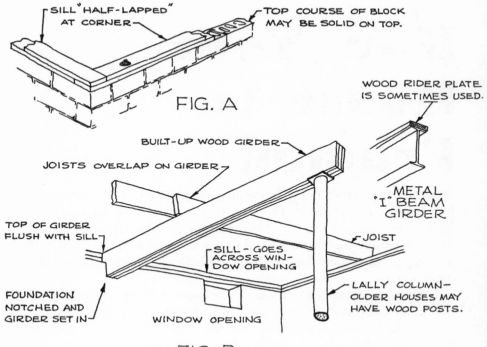

FIG. A

FIG. B.

top of the sill (Fig. B). It may be a steel I-beam (in cross section shaped like the letter "I") or it may be made from three members of 2-inch thick boards nailed together to form a 6 by 8 usually; 10 and 12 inches are also common. The girder will also rest on Lally columns, cement-filled steel pipes with steel plates welded on both ends. If the girder is a 6 by 8, the Lallys will be about seven feet apart. In older houses locust posts may be used instead of Lally columns; these are made of a hard, extremely durable wood impervious to decay and termites.

JOISTS

On the top of the sill and girder are the joists. These are installed across the foundation with other joists butted against the end. These abutting joists are commonly known as the box. Joists are usually 2 by 8's, although for longer spans over fourteen feet 3 by 8's and 2 by 10's are used (Fig. B).

When the sill boards are installed they are squared up (located at right angles) on top of the foundation even if the foundation itself is out-of-square. It's not always possible to get the sill boards exactly square so further correction is made when the joists are laid and the box is built around them. The box is made as square as possible. If this box isn't square the whole house will be unsquared.

Very seldom is a piece of wood absolutely straight; it usually has a slight curve down it in both directions. Joists are no exceptions. So, when laid, they are put with the high part, or crown, up so that they will straighten as the house settles.

Joists are laid to accommodate, or allow space for, plumbing; they must also support the weight of the plumbing pipes; extra ones are put in where necessary. In addition to joists on sixteen-inch centers (sixteen inches apart from center of one to center of adjacent ones) there ought to be a double joist beneath wall partitions.

Bridging (short pieces of wood or metal) is nailed between joists to help distribute loads on floor and keep joists from tripping (falling over) under extreme loads. Most building codes require either wood or steel bridging. (Codes, incidentally, are not updated as often as they should be.) A government study shows that bridging, as it is commonly done lends very little to strength of the house. Green lumber is used and, as it dries it becomes loose. If joists dry out bridging also becomes ineffective. However, houses thus framed seem to survive.

On top of the box and joists subflooring, also called the deck, is nailed on. In some cases it's laid diagonally and the finished flooring is installed across it at right angles to the joists. So installed it will not come loose and squeak, as it can when it is parallel to the finished flooring. In modern homes builders use plywood for subflooring. This eliminates the problem of diagonal versus parallel flooring.

The walls go on top of the subflooring. Each is composed of a shoe, or 2 by 4 bottom board, studs which rest on the shoe, and a plate, two 2 by 4 boards nailed together and to the tops of the studs (Fig. C).

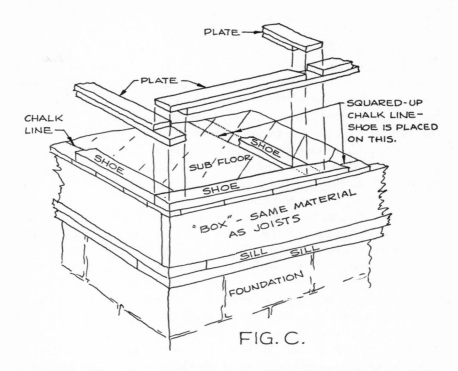

FIG. C.

To install each wall the location of its shoe is first carefully marked out on the subfloor with chalk line and square. The shoe is nailed to the subflooring with nails going through into the joists. Wherever there is a doorway the shoe is cut away to allow for it. After all the shoes are in place, the plates, each consisting of nailed together 2 by 4's, are prefabricated on top of the shoes; that is, each shoe is used as a template or pattern for cutting its corresponding plate. The first member of the plate is temporarily toenailed (nails driven at angle through side of board) in place and a second is made fast to the first. Corners are half lapped.

After the plate is nailed to the shoe, location of regular studs and jack studs are marked on it. Studs go from the shoe to the plate to form a wall; jack studs are short studs that go up to some other member such as a windowsill or header—a double board—over a door. Cripple studs are short studs that start at the plate and go down to some other member such as a header. Then all of the studs are cut to length (they can also be obtained precut) and are toenailed to the plate while it's on the deck. Jack studs are usually nailed to regular studs and then these "assemblies" are nailed in place. Whenever two studs are nailed together the crowns are placed in opposite directions, then are pulled straight when nailed. The whole wall is then stood up and braced temporarily while the bottom ends of the studs are toenailed to the marks on the shoe. Each wall is done in this way until all are in place. Small headers are made up and nailed in place on the deck and cripple studs put in place. Large headers are made after the wall is in simply because it would make the wall too heavy to lift. For various views of erected walls, and door and window framing, see Figs. D, E, and F.

Corner studs are also part of a wall. These are made of three studs and blocks nailed together to form inside and outside corner nailing surfaces. Sometimes they are nailed to the wall as it is being made on the deck and sometimes after it is up. It is up to the individual carpenter.

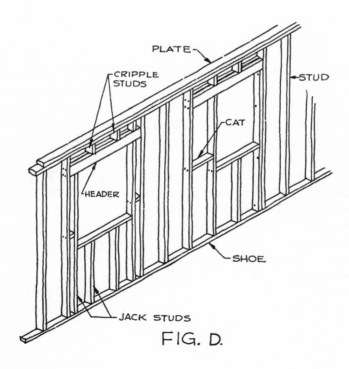

FIG. D.

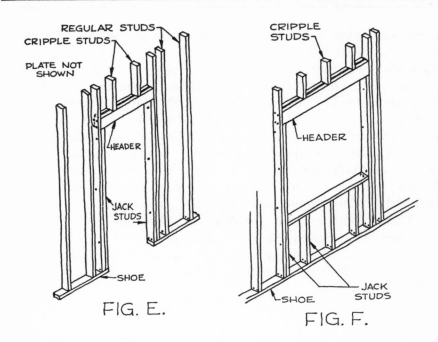

FIG. E.

FIG. F.

After walls are in the whole structure is leveled and plumbed, and walls are straightened and braced because this is the only chance to make the house straight. Often builders neglect to do a thorough job and consequently the house is unsquared forever. It's not difficult to do. First, a bar is driven between sill and foundation and pried up at low points, and slate shims installed (or any material hard enough to bear weight until the mason is able to shove grout in under the sill). Walls are straightened by nailing pieces of 2 by 4 or 1 by 4 diagonally to corner studs. Also, the girder is leveled. This can be raised or lowered with an A-frame (this is shown in Chapter 3). If you try to level a floor before any weight is on it, the weight will make it out-of-level later.

Second floor framework is simpler. Joists are spaced to allow for plumbing and to support walls that might be above them. They should be doubled up where walls are located but this is not always done. One wall is constructed so it is directly above another wall

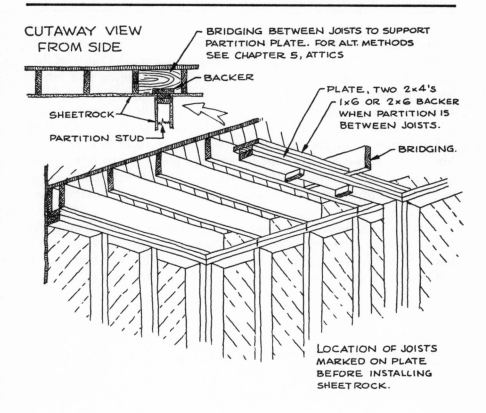

CUTAWAY VIEW FROM SIDE

BRIDGING BETWEEN JOISTS TO SUPPORT PARTITION PLATE. FOR ALT. METHODS SEE CHAPTER 5, ATTICS

BACKER

SHEETROCK

PARTITION STUD

PLATE, TWO 2×4'S 1×6 OR 2×6 BACKER WHEN PARTITION IS BETWEEN JOISTS.

BRIDGING.

LOCATION OF JOISTS MARKED ON PLATE BEFORE INSTALLING SHEETROCK.

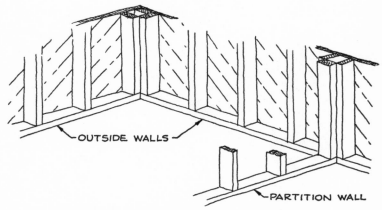

OUTSIDE WALLS

PARTITION WALL

FRAMING FOR SHEETROCK

FIG. F1.

directly above the girder. This wall is called load-bearing because it helps support all structure above it; it is, in effect, the spine of the house. Outside walls are also load-bearing. Subflooring and other walls are laid out the same as the first floor. Ceiling beams, which aren't intended to support anything but just provide a nailing surface for ceiling material, go in next. When in place, partition walls that fall between them are capped (see Chapter 5) to form nailers for Sheetrock. This is usually done by nailing a piece of 2 by 6 or 2 by 8 or "1 by—" right on top of the partition wall so it extends in both directions. How a room is framed out for Sheetrock is shown in Fig. F1.

   Rafters are next. These may rest right on the second floor plate (Fig. G) or on a special shoe on top of the ceiling beam. Rafters are cut to fit and lie flat against ridge rafter (the spine of the house) and notched to fit (given a "bird's mouth" at the plate) Fig. H.

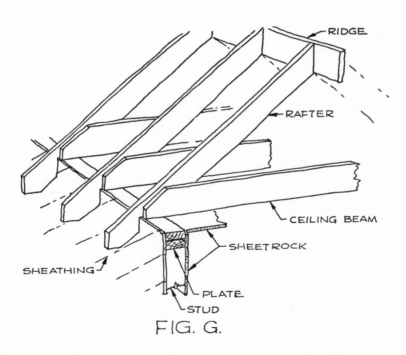

FIG. G.

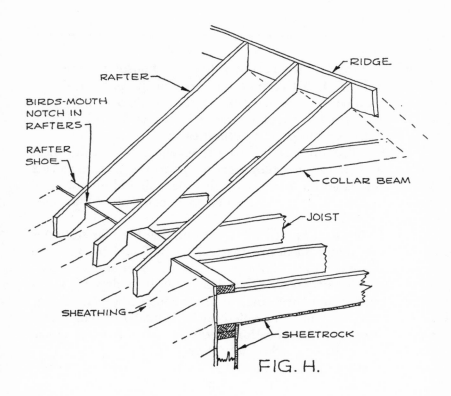

RAFTER

RIDGE

BIRDS-MOUTH NOTCH IN RAFTERS

RAFTER SHOE

COLLAR BEAM

JOIST

SHEATHING

SHEETROCK

FIG. H.

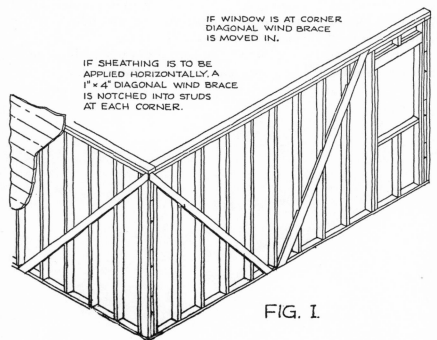

IF WINDOW IS AT CORNER DIAGONAL WIND BRACE IS MOVED IN.

IF SHEATHING IS TO BE APPLIED HORIZONTALLY, A 1" × 4" DIAGONAL WIND BRACE IS NOTCHED INTO STUDS AT EACH CORNER.

FIG. I.

Gable end (usually the narrow side of the house) is formed by nailing cut-to-fit studs between two rafters and the plate below. A carefully framed house will have gable studs directly over wall studs from the story below instead of in random locations. This gives extra support and makes nailing on sheathing easier.

The gable studs are installed so they extend half their thickness inside the rafter. In this way they form an opportune place to nail a 2 by 4 to make a nailer for Sheetrock. All nailers should be put in all necessary places at this time. It's much more convenient than after the house is built.

After the house is framed the sheathing (the base for siding) is nailed to the framing. Sheathing is usually 1 by 6 or 1 by 8 tongue and groove boards or 1 by 8 shiplap (boards with overlapping edges) or sheathing-grade plywood (either 1/2 or 3/8 inch depending on building code) gypsum sheathing, or other composition sheathing. The 1 by 6 or 1 by 8 may be nailed on horizontally or diagonally. Horizontal or composition sheathing requires wind braces (diagonal boards under sheathing notched into studs) Fig. I.

Roof sheathing usually must be wood—plywood or boards; other materials won't hold shingles down.

On top of the sheathing are 15-pound felt sheets, commonly called tar paper. Its purpose is to moisture-proof the house. It is installed with staples or large-head galvanized nails.

Finally, siding and roofing are applied. Exactly how these materials are secured will become clear in subsequent chapters.

Chapter 2

Measuring

Accurate measuring begins with using the right measuring tools. There are a variety of these each with virtues and drawbacks. Following are ones I recommend and how to use them.

For long measurements, I use a 12-foot steel tape. This is nice and compact and very seldom do you have to lay it out more than twice on one measurement since very few rooms run more than 24 feet long. In cases where you are measuring something very large you can use a 50- or 100-foot tape and measure it all in one shot.

With a tape you have less chance of building up an error. Suppose you use a 1-foot ruler. If you can hold it within 1/32 inch of a true foot each time you mark you're close. But that 1/32 inch error can build up on something like a 16 foot wall so all you end up with is an approximation.

For small carpentry work such as marking off boards up to 8 feet long, or molding, a folding wood ruler is convenient and has certain advantages over a tape; it's stiffer and will brace against a wall. I don't recommend a yardstick when accuracy is important. They wear on the edges just hanging around the house; also, the yardstick may be only 35-7/8 inches long to begin with. But it's all right for measuring curtains or for shim purposes, and it makes a nice paint stirrer, too.

Before using a tape check its length with your partner's if you're fortunate enough to have one. As a shop foreman I insisted that everyone buy a Lufkin ruler. Lufkin is no better than Stanley but the two brands were different lengths. If one man used a Stanley ruler and another a Lufkin ruler there was a continual discrepancy. All companies try to make an accurate ruler and I don't know why this discrepancy exists. But it is there.

SQUARES

There are three different kinds of squares used in carpentry. The framing square is an L-shaped piece of flat steel 16 inches on one leg and 24 inches on the other. It's made to this size for convenience in laying out 16 inch centers, a common distance between frame members, in laying out roof rafters as mentioned in Chapter 1. Its large size is an advantage for various other kinds of layout work.

Another kind of square is the tri-square (Fig. A). It comes in various small sizes up to about 12 inches and consists of a metal blade and a wooden section with a 45-degree end—you can use it for a quick 45-degree or a 90-degree angle check. It's also good for checking the end of a board to see if it's square. It's easier to hold it tight against the edge of the board to mark than a framing square which you must hold down at a little angle and thus risk not being exact.

Finally, there is the adjustable square. This is similar to the tri-square in use in that you can check 90- and 45-degree angles, but the blade can be slid back and forth. You can set the blade for an exact size: set a pencil on the end of it, and by moving the square along the board edge make a line exactly parallel to it (Fig. B).

For marking accurate 45-degree angles on big pieces of wood the framing square is better than the adjustable. To use the adjustable you have to lay the non-blade section on the edge of the board; a bit of grit or sawdust could throw it off. The error might not be noticeable over a short span but over a long span it would be. With a framing square you just align numbers on opposite legs of the square with the board edge and draw your angle (Fig. C). As long as those numbers are accurately aligned on the edge you can't go wrong.

CHALK LINE

This is the tool for marking straight lines. It consists of a string coiled in a chalk box. To mark a straight line you pull the string out, place the end over one mark you've made, the other end over another mark, pull it tight in place and snap the string. A perfectly straight line is marked.

LEVEL

This is another essential tool. There are wood and metal levels. I have no particular preference. Some have the bubble vials fixed;

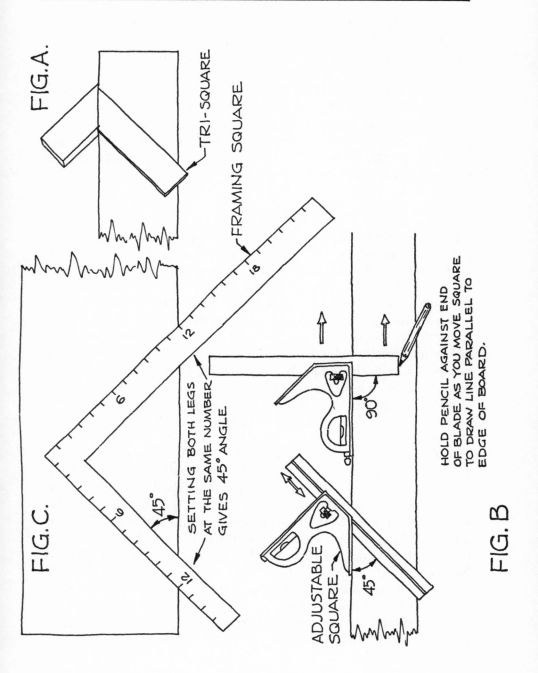

FIG. A.

TRI-SQUARE

FRAMING SQUARE

FIG. C.

45°

SETTING BOTH LEGS
AT THE SAME NUMBER
GIVES 45° ANGLE

ADJUSTABLE
SQUARE

45°

90°

HOLD PENCIL AGAINST END
OF BLADE AS YOU MOVE SQUARE
TO DRAW LINE PARALLEL TO
EDGE OF BOARD.

FIG. B

more expensive ones have adjustable bubble vials. I don't know if that's necessarily an advantage except that you can correct the level when it's wrong, which can happen if it gets jarred.

When leveling, place the level horizontally on the piece, turning it once end for end. You should view the same bubble. It should read correctly in both directions with the bubble perfectly centered. If it doesn't the work isn't level or your level is inaccurate. The same procedure is used when checking something for plumb-verticality. Always wipe the surface of the level clean before placing—even a speck of sawdust can throw it off.

PLUMB BOB

Another needed tool is a plumb bob. This is a teardrop shaped, pointed weight on a string. One of its major uses is to help you mark perfectly vertical lines on a wall. To use it in this application, hang it with a nail from the ceiling, or have a helper hold the end, so that the bob is just clear of the wall at the floor. The string shouldn't touch anything, either. A bump on the wall can throw it off. When it's perfectly still stand directly in front of the string, look at the wall and mark directly behind the string—one mark close to the ceiling and one close to the floor. Then stand back, close one eye and sight the two marks behind the string; the string must obscure both marks simultaneously. If this is the case one mark is directly below the other. Then simply draw a chalk line across the two marks and snap it (Fig. D).

You can also use the plumb bob for extra long distances, such as establishing plumb down a second floor stairwell. Also, you can use it to check if a wall itself is plumb. Just hold the line an inch or so away from the wall from the ceiling. If there is a bow or bump the string will pass closer there than on either end and the wall is not plumb. Other good uses: lining up wallpaper or paneling strips. One caution: there is danger that some force will cause the plumb bob to hang cockeyed, such as a slight wind which may not let it settle down, or the impatience of the user who will just mark an approximate spot where it may stop.

For short distances you needn't necessarily use a plumb bob. I recommend using a long (four foot) level. You can also use a straight-

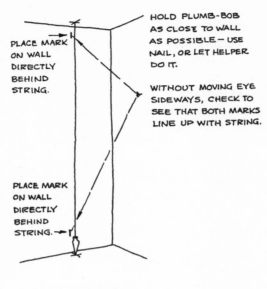

PLACE MARK
ON WALL
DIRECTLY
BEHIND
STRING.

HOLD PLUMB-BOB
AS CLOSE TO WALL
AS POSSIBLE — USE
NAIL, OR LET HELPER
DO IT.

WITHOUT MOVING EYE
SIDEWAYS, CHECK TO
SEE THAT BOTH MARKS
LINE UP WITH STRING.

PLACE MARK
ON WALL
DIRECTLY
BEHIND
STRING. ➔

FIG. D.

edge and a level. For example, if you have a nice straight 2 by 4 for laying out stud walls in a basement you can use this in conjunction with a level and be able to mark from the floor to the ceiling: Just lay the 2 by 4 on the wall and the level on the 2 by 4.

MEASURING IN GENERAL

When measuring anything you should always take overall measurements. Figure out two ways to measure and see if you get the same answer twice. This is particularly important on something like kitchen cabinets. You wait a month until they're delivered, try to install them and they don't fit! You then have to rip the kitchen apart—an awful problem that careful measuring could have avoided.

When you're building something that requires precise measuring such as a cabinet, a good way to avoid problems is to lay things out so all the openings come out in even inches, making up the odd amounts on the widths of the wood members. You can't always do that, but it's good to keep it in mind.

It's also a good idea to know the exact sizes of components

before you start to build. For example, if you're going to use ready-made shutters as doors on a cabinet, find out just what size the shutters will be before you buy. That way you can adjust your cabinet to the shutter.

On some jobs no tape or ruler is needed. Knowing component size allows this. For instance, you can measure roof shingles from the ground by just counting them. Shingles are 5 inches to the weather which means that each shingle course is exposed 5 inches. Just count across the edge of the roof, multiply by 5 and divide by 12 to know how many feet of width you have. Since tabs are 1-foot long, you count them across the face of the roof to know how long it is. If you are measuring for ceiling or floor tiles you can do the same thing. When ordering the material you just add so much for waste.

NOMINAL VERSUS ACTUAL SIZE

Be aware, though, that some materials differ in nominal, or named size versus actual size. For example, a 12 inch by 12 inch tile covers 12 inches by 12 inches. But many kinds of wood paneling don't cover what they are supposed to. For example, a 1 by 6 tongue and groove decorative finished paneling covers 5 inches. There's an inch loss in the size. Three-inch flooring nets about 2-1/4 inches. Lumber is always less in actual size; a 2 by 4 now measures 1-9/16 by 3-9/16, a 2 by 6 is 1-9/16 by 5-1/2. You must have a knowledge of the material, something you can get by visiting the lumberyard before you begin.

AVOID MEASURING WHEN POSSIBLE

Whenever possible fit things together without measuring. Just cut it to workable lengths. For instance, for casing around a door you could cut your piece seven feet (or even buy it 7 feet), stand it up where it is to be installed, then mark where it needs to be cut. The less you work with measuring tools, the less the chances of errors.

A FEW MEASURING TIPS

If you want to mark a board or panel to a certain length, draw the tape down along the edge, sight along it and hold the tape exactly

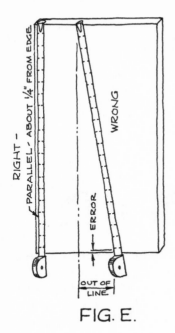

FIG. E.

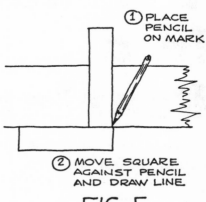

① PLACE PENCIL ON MARK

② MOVE SQUARE AGAINST PENCIL AND DRAW LINE

FIG. F.

parallel but about 1/4-inch away (Fig. E). Make your mark right on the edge of your board. Hold your square on the mark and mark it across the board. If you're working with narrow pieces the possibility of error is very slight. If you're working with a wide board you can get your tape slightly out of parallel and create error. So be sure to use the square.

When making any marks it pays to keep the pencil sharp. If you put a mark that you want to square from place the point of the pencil on the mark, move the square up to it, then draw the line (Fig. E).

The way to avoid measuring mistakes is, as mentioned, to double check every measurement you make. The most common mistake is to be exactly one inch wrong. What happens is that a person reads the fraction, then the printed number next to it. Instead of reading 78 and 3/4, you read 3/4 and then you read 79 and write down 79-3/4. If you are standing so that you look at the tape from the wrong direction you might read the tape as 80-3/4 when it is 79-1/4. This happens more frequently in the evening when you're tired.

Chapter 3

Installing A Header In a Bearing Wall

There are two types of walls in the average home: partition and bearing. The first simply sits between floor and ceiling supporting nothing. A bearing wall, however, supports a portion of the house above it. If you are going to install anything in a bearing wall—say a window, archway, or door—either from scratch or by enlarging an existing opening, you have to install a header. As noted previously, this is a double thickness of boards that runs horizontally at the top of a particular opening with the ends of the boards resting on jack (short) studs.

Before working on a bearing wall you have to build a temporary wall to replace its supporting function. Since it is best to locate this temporary wall about 30 inches from the bearing wall, you won't have much room for working. Hence, it's a good idea to remove all the surface material you can from the bearing wall first. That is, siding, plasterboard, sheathing, whatever. Go right down to bare studs. This won't affect its supporting ability in the slightest.

BUILDING THE TEMPORARY WALL

The temporary wall simply consists of a shoe at the bottom and a plate against the ceiling, and wedged-in angled studs between the two.

Following Fig. A, cut the shoe and plate lengths needed for the structure. A 2 by 4 can serve as your shoe. (This can be laid right on

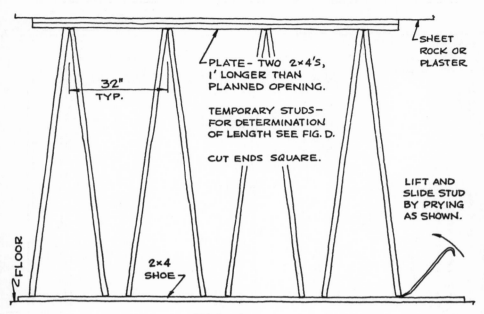

FIG. A.

wall-to-wall carpet if necessary) and a double 2 by 4 nailed together as a plate, just as in regular house framing.

With these parts prepared, lay the shoe in place, then lay the plate (nailed together 2 by 4's) on the shoe and measure for the stud lengths as indicated in Fig. B—between the top of the plate and the ceiling.

To install the wall, have a helper hold the plate in position on the ceiling while you set the first pair of studs under it in the middle of the plate. Wedge one leg in place (tap with a hammer) then wedge the second in next to it right away. Then use a flat bar (see Fig. A) at the bottom of the legs to bring them together in the form of the letter "A" and force the plate tight against the ceiling.

Follow the same procedure for putting the rest of the A's in place, spacing them 32 inches on center. When they're all tightly in place use tenpenny nails to secure them to one another and plate or shoe as the case may be. Leave enough of the nail heads out so you can pull them easily later.

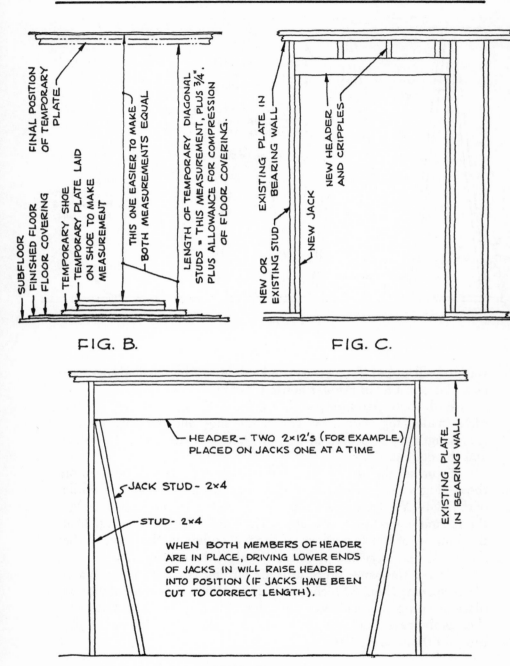

FIG. B.

SUBFLOOR
FINISHED FLOOR
FLOOR COVERING
TEMPORARY SHOE
TEMPORARY PLATE LAID ON SHOE TO MAKE MEASUREMENT
FINAL POSITION OF TEMPORARY PLATE
THIS ONE EASIER TO MAKE — BOTH MEASUREMENTS EQUAL
LENGTH OF TEMPORARY DIAGONAL STUDS = THIS MEASUREMENT, PLUS 3/4", PLUS ALLOWANCE FOR COMPRESSION OF FLOOR COVERING.

FIG. C.

EXISTING PLATE IN BEARING WALL
NEW HEADER AND CRIPPLES
NEW OR EXISTING STUD
NEW JACK

FIG. D.

HEADER — TWO 2×12's (FOR EXAMPLE) PLACED ON JACKS ONE AT A TIME

JACK STUD — 2×4

STUD — 2×4

WHEN BOTH MEMBERS OF HEADER ARE IN PLACE, DRIVING LOWER ENDS OF JACKS IN WILL RAISE HEADER INTO POSITION (IF JACKS HAVE BEEN CUT TO CORRECT LENGTH).

EXISTING PLATE IN BEARING WALL

With temporary wall in place, remove studs and existing header, if any, from the bearing wall. Install the new jack studs and header immediately. If the header is especially large it is best to install it in two pieces. If the construction dictates that the header is to be tight against the plate (such as a 4 by 12 in an 8-foot wall), follow this procedure: Lean the jack studs against their respective studs. Rest one member of the header on them and tack in place. Put the second header member next to the first and nail together temporarily with tenpenny nails. Then drive the jacks in place to force the header to the plate, and nail everything up solid (Fig. C).

For narrower headers install the jacks right away and put the header on top of them, then cut cripple studs and nail them in place 16 inches on centers (Fig. D). With header in, you can remove your temporary wall and install window, door, or archway as called for. See other chapters for details.

Chapter 4

Installing A Window

There are various reasons why you may want to install a new window, or windows. Some houses have inferior windows. For example, steel casements are not very practical. There is no good way to put a storm window on them and they do represent a certain fire hazard—if you can't open one wide enough to get your body through, you're in trouble. You can always operate on a wooden window with an ax or chair and get out. Aluminum windows are frequently very bad—I've seen ones where the panels wouldn't even stay in the frames. Or the window may simply be rotted out. Or you may need one or more for a new addition.

First thing to consider is how your house is covered. If covered with brick veneer, solid masonry, cement, or stucco, you'll probably be able to put in only the exact kind and size of window you took out. You can't remove these materials easily to accommodate a larger window. You could install a smaller one by building framework up inside.

On the other hand, if you have any kind of wooden shingle, or siding, clapboard, or asbestos siding, you won't have too much trouble because you can remove pieces of the siding fairly easily to make the new window fit in.

There are, as known in the trade, "before sheathing" (Fig. A) and "after sheathing" (Fig. B) windows. The former has an extra strip of wood along each side that you nail through directly to the studs. To secure the latter you nail through the casing and the sheathing into the jack studs. There is no special reason for this. Both types are good but your best bet is to install an "after" type.

DETERMINING WHAT SIZE YOU NEED

Before ordering a window and installing it there are a few terms to understand.

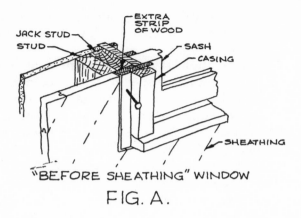

"BEFORE SHEATHING" WINDOW
FIG. A.

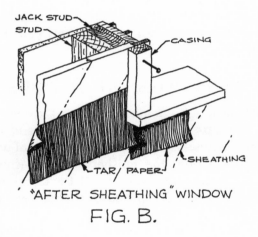

"AFTER SHEATHING" WINDOW
FIG. B.

Rough Opening. This refers to the framework of boards that the window fits into.

Nominal size. This refers to the size of the sash—the window panels the glass is in.

Actual or overall size. This is the size of the sash plus the framework around it—the three jambs at sides and top and the sill.

Window catalogues at lumberyards commonly list nominal and rough opening size and the figure you give the dealer is the nominal size.

To determine these sizes for modern double-hung windows refer to Fig. C. To get rough opening width you measure from jamb to jamb, then add two inches. To get height just measure glass in one sash disregarding any wood "framework" over it, double it and add six inches to get the nominal size; add another four inches to get rough opening. If sash pieces on the bottom and top are different sizes, measure both pieces of glass separately. Add them together, then continue as above.

As mentioned, this is for measuring rough opening of modern windows. Suppose you have an existing old-fashioned window with sash weights? The height can be obtained the same way but for the width the only way is to remove the panels that cover the sash weight recesses. Then you can measure between studs to get the rough opening.

MEASURING FOR CASEMENT WINDOWS

To determine the rough opening width on a casement window in plaster walls, measure as shown in Fig. D and add 1-1/2 inches to compensate for thickness of plaster on each side of window. To get the height measure from the finished opening (from the stool—inside ledge mistakenly called the sill—to the top of the opening the window sits in) and add 1-3/4 inches for the plaster and thickness of stool and the shim beneath it.

For a casement in Sheetrock use the same method but add 3/8 inch to the height plus stool-shim thickness and 3/4 inch to the width. This system is usually correct. However, the rough opening may be slightly larger.

Once you have the rough opening you can order the window. It is possible to order a window that is longer than your rough opening without running into construction problems; you may want to do so because the existing window is too short—a firetrap. (You should make sure the bottom of the window is at least six inches above any radiator or convector that might be there.) However, you can't order

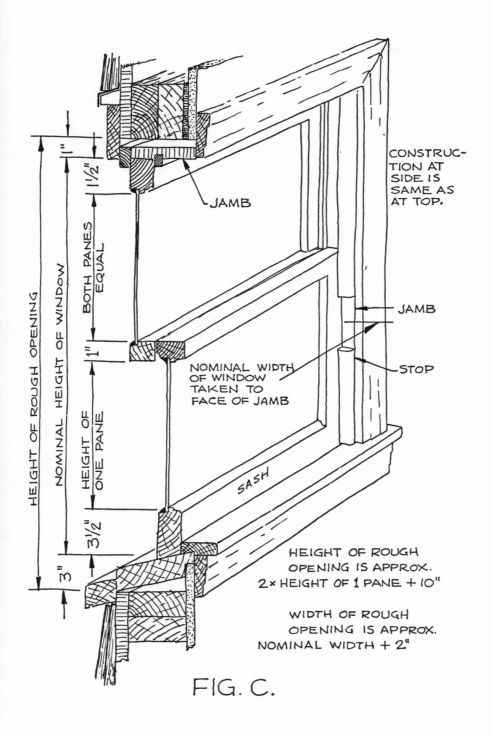

HEIGHT OF ROUGH OPENING

NOMINAL HEIGHT OF WINDOW

BOTH PANES EQUAL

HEIGHT OF ONE PANE

1"

1 1/2"

1"

3 1/2"

3"

JAMB

CONSTRUC-
TION AT
SIDE IS
SAME AS
AT TOP.

JAMB

STOP

NOMINAL WIDTH
OF WINDOW
TAKEN TO
FACE OF JAMB

SASH

HEIGHT OF ROUGH
OPENING IS APPROX.
2 × HEIGHT OF 1 PANE + 10"

WIDTH OF ROUGH
OPENING IS APPROX.
NOMINAL WIDTH + 2"

FIG. C.

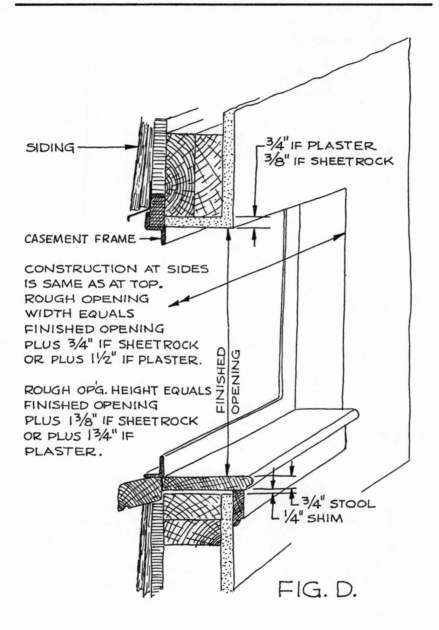

SIDING

¾" IF PLASTER
⅜" IF SHEETROCK

CASEMENT FRAME

CONSTRUCTION AT SIDES
IS SAME AS AT TOP.
ROUGH OPENING
WIDTH EQUALS
FINISHED OPENING
PLUS ¾" IF SHEETROCK
OR PLUS 1½" IF PLASTER.

ROUGH OP'G. HEIGHT EQUALS
FINISHED OPENING
PLUS 1⅜" IF SHEETROCK
OR PLUS 1¾" IF
PLASTER.

FINISHED OPENING

¾" STOOL
¼" SHIM

FIG. D.

one larger in width than your rough opening without installing a new header, a 4 by 6 (two 2 by 6's nailed together) or larger, and this involves opening the walls up and rearranging the framing. It's a big job, but if you want to do it see Chapter 3 for information.

You can order any window whose rough opening width is narrower than on the house down to any small size you want because it just involves adding framing members inside the larger opening. An example of this might be when you want to put in a small bathroom window.

To order, take the rough opening size down to your lumberyard. The dealer will show you catalogues of windows. In terms of width just select the rough opening that's narrower, read the nominal size next to it and give that figure to your dealer. For example, if rough opening width for double-hung window is 3 feet 2 inches the nominal size would be 3 feet 0 inches.

GENERAL TIPS ON PICKING A WINDOW

The kind of window you pick will depend on the purpose you have in mind. Beyond that, however, here are some general tips for buying windows:

Buying a window is not a place to save money. A good window costs.

Wood windows generally are better than metal windows. They seal better and don't warp as much as metal.

Many millwork companies (these supply finished wood products to lumberyards) provide good quality wooden windows.

Good windows of wood with metal weather stripping work out well. These are practically draft proof. If you want to go all the way on quality buy the type that have double-insulated glass and are clad with vinyl. These never require painting and no storm windows are needed.

Have the windows delivered. If you have to carry the window in your car, lay it flat on the top of the car putty side up; this lets the glass rest on the wooden frame rather than the little glazier's points that hold it in place under the putty.

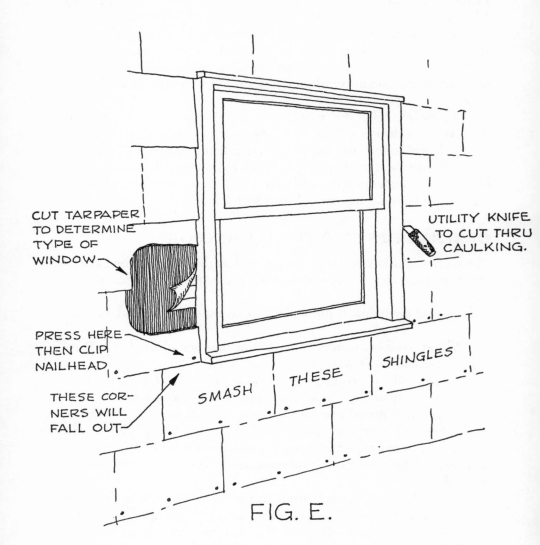

CUT TARPAPER
TO DETERMINE
TYPE OF
WINDOW

UTILITY KNIFE
TO CUT THRU
CAULKING.

PRESS HERE
THEN CLIP
NAILHEAD

THESE COR-
NERS WILL
FALL OUT

SMASH THESE SHINGLES

FIG. E.

PREPARATORY WORK

First, get rid of the old window. Remove all inside trim around the window. A claw hammer or pry bar comes in handy. It's not too important to be careful here because you're going to have to mess things up anyway.

Next, go to the outside and start to remove materials around the window there. What you do depends on the type of siding you have. If you have asbestos shingles (Fig. E), take a hammer and smash all the shingles immediately below the window. The corners of shingles that are under the course immediately above it should fall out.

Next, depress one shingle on either side of the window directly above the ones you smashed. This will make the heads of nails holding it on the bottom accessible. Use snips, carpenter's shears, or the like to clip heads off. Then use a utility knife, penknife, or old chisel to cut the caulk between that shingle and the window frame. With this cut you should be able to slip the shingle out and reuse it. Then cut the exposed tar paper and observe what kind of a window it is. If it is an "after sheathing" window go inside the house and push the window out intact. First, though, cut it free from all the caulk around it; you may also have to pry off the drip cap on the top of the window. Forget about salvaging the drip cap—you won't be able to reuse it (anyway, a 10-foot piece will cost under a dollar). By "push it out," I mean with a pry bar. Figure F shows where to pry. It would

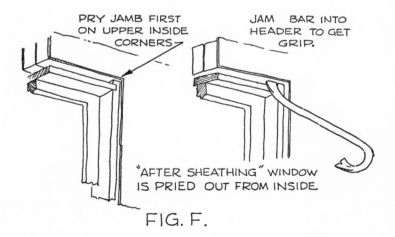

PRY JAMB FIRST
ON UPPER INSIDE
CORNERS

JAM BAR INTO
HEADER TO GET
GRIP.

"AFTER SHEATHING" WINDOW
IS PRIED OUT FROM INSIDE.

FIG. F.

be a good idea to have someone on the outside to see that the window doesn't fall out. If you're working alone you can pry it out to a certain point from the inside, then pry it out from the outside.

BEFORE SHEATHING TYPE

If it's the "before sheathing" type, or any one of the metal types with a flange (lip that extends from sides of window), you have to remove all shingles around the window before pulling it out. The big idea is to remove these shingles without breaking them or adjacent ones. Take out one shingle to the side on the bottom. Depress the shingle, clip off the nailheads, cut the caulk, and slip the shingle out. Proceed like this all around the window.

It's likely that you'll break some of these shingles when taking them out. But you should at least try to get them out unbroken, so you can reuse them. When shingles are out pry the window out from the outside (Fig. G).

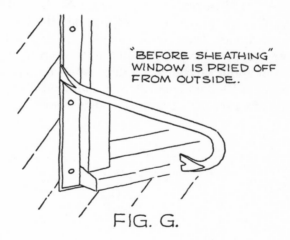

"BEFORE SHEATHING" WINDOW IS PRIED OFF FROM OUTSIDE.

FIG. G.

REMOVING CEDAR SHINGLES

If you have cedar shingles removal depends on the way they are laid. Some cedar shingles are face-nailed. If you have this situation see Fig. H for removal method. It involves pulling certain nails out and cutting off others to clear an area all the way around the window.

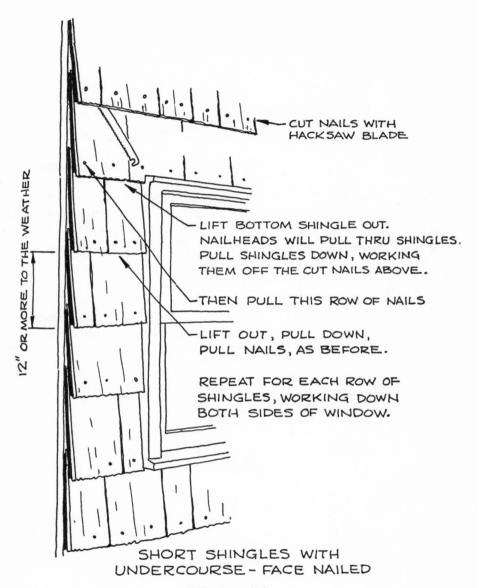

CUT NAILS WITH
HACKSAW BLADE

LIFT BOTTOM SHINGLE OUT.
NAILHEADS WILL PULL THRU SHINGLES.
PULL SHINGLES DOWN, WORKING
THEM OFF THE CUT NAILS ABOVE.

THEN PULL THIS ROW OF NAILS

LIFT OUT, PULL DOWN,
PULL NAILS, AS BEFORE.

REPEAT FOR EACH ROW OF
SHINGLES, WORKING DOWN
BOTH SIDES OF WINDOW.

12" OR MORE TO THE WEATHER

SHORT SHINGLES WITH
UNDERCOURSE - FACE NAILED

FIG. H.

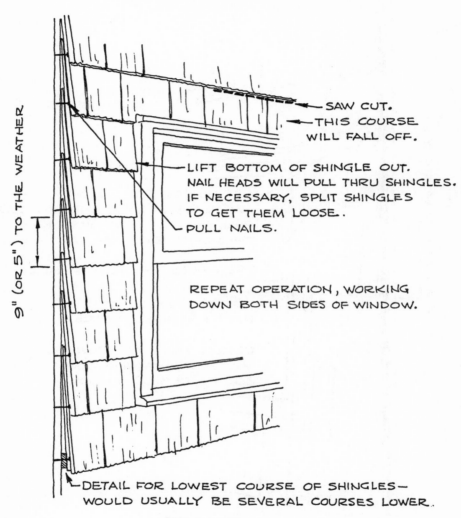

9" (OR 5") TO THE WEATHER

SAW CUT.

THIS COURSE
WILL FALL OFF.

LIFT BOTTOM OF SHINGLE OUT.
NAIL HEADS WILL PULL THRU SHINGLES.
IF NECESSARY, SPLIT SHINGLES
TO GET THEM LOOSE.
PULL NAILS.

REPEAT OPERATION, WORKING
DOWN BOTH SIDES OF WINDOW.

DETAIL FOR LOWEST COURSE OF SHINGLES—
WOULD USUALLY BE SEVERAL COURSES LOWER.

FIG. I.

The other way is used when they are nailed "five inches to the weather" and the nails don't show at all. This means that five (or nine) inches of each shingle is exposed to the weather. Here the parts that are exposed have no nails in them, but the overlapped portions of shingles do. To remove these see Fig. I.

If you have aluminum siding it's not a good idea to replace a window yourself. It involves much cutting and is a job for a professional. Any windows that need replacing should be installed before the siding is installed.

When removing clapboard you may just be able to take out short boards that flank the window; for example, where windows are close together.

Clapboard is either cedar or pine boards. It comes 3/4 inch thick on one side tapering to 0 inch on the other and in nominal 6 inch, 8 inch and 10 inch widths. However, regular 3/4 inch boards are sometimes used. When applied clapboard is face-nailed through the bottom edge; the same nails also secure the tops of courses below.

To remove a portion of this siding you first remove nails. You can pry the boards out slightly to pull the nails out a bit, then pull the nails out all the way. If this doesn't work, use a hacksaw blade to sever nails. Or, finally, drive the nails through the board with a large nail set. Try to take the boards out intact. If they split, you'll have to get new boards to match.

One other way to remove a window is simply to demolish it in place. But I don't recommend this because it makes too much of a mess, although it may be necessary if your house is brick.

INSTALLATION

I'm going to describe how to put a long, narrow window into a wide and short rough opening. I think this will cover everything for any installation eventuality.

Let's assume that the window frame is covered by plaster on the inside. First, referring to Fig. J, measure the overall height of the new window exclusive of the trim—that is, from the bottom of the sill to the top of the jamb. Then add two inches to this. Then meas-

EXISTING WINDOW
OPENING –
SASH REMOVED.

OVERALL
HEIGHT OF
NEW WIN-
DOW UNIT
PLUS 2".

◄ BREAK PLASTER OUT
TO INSIDE EDGE
OF JACK STUDS. ►

STRIKE
LINE ON
WALL.

POSSIBLE
OUTLET.

DOUBLE CHECK
TO BE SURE
LINE IS LEVEL.

SAW CUT
THRU
PLASTER

FIG. J.

ure this amount down from the bottom of the header and draw a level line on the wall the width of the old window. Make a mark and use a level to get this line. Then use a keyhole saw and hammer to break out the plaster to the jack studs; also cut away the sheathing. If you find wires they must be rerouted, but it's unusual to find them there. Of course if you have pipes in the way, you'll have to get them rerouted or build around them. You probably won't find pipes in any room but the kitchen.

Next, cut the studs off at the same height. Then use a hammer to tap out the sill of the rough opening. Renail the sill to the tops of the just-cut 2 by 4's. Use two tenpenny nails to secure the sill to the tops of the studs, and three tenpenny nails on each side to toenail the sill into the jack studs. Next add two short studs that fit between the sill and header to serve as the sides of the new rough opening. These studs should be placed so that the distance between them is equal to the overall (actual) width of the window plus a half inch. This allows space for plumbing the window if the rough opening isn't perfectly square. Make certain the sill is level and the new jack studs are true. The above steps are shown in Figs. K and L.

WINDOW TO ONE SIDE?

This stud placement assumes that you want the window centered in the rough opening. If you want to move it to one side or the other in the rough opening you can use one stud, placing it so that the distance between it and the face of the existing jack stud is equal to the width of the window, plus a half inch. If there is only a small amount of distance between the edges of the new window and existing jack studs you can get away with nailing one or two furring strips, as needed, to the studs.

Now go outside and fill in the sheathing. You may or may not have boards or a "nailer" to nail the sheathing to. If you don't have one see Fig. M. Cover the sheathing with tar paper (15-pound felt), a strip down each side. Wherever you have sheathing you put felt. Use large-head galvanized nails to secure the tar paper.

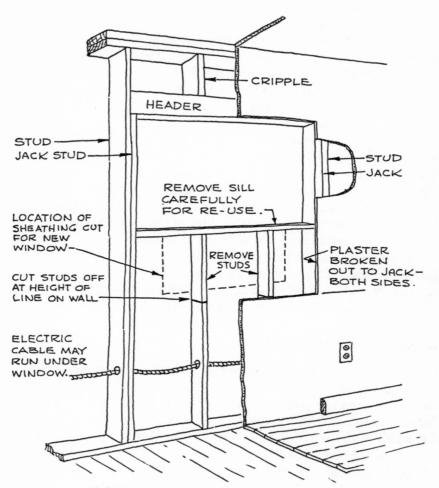

CRIPPLE

HEADER

STUD
JACK STUD

STUD
JACK

REMOVE SILL
CAREFULLY
FOR RE-USE.

LOCATION OF
SHEATHING CUT
FOR NEW
WINDOW

REMOVE
STUDS

PLASTER
BROKEN
OUT TO JACK-
BOTH SIDES.

CUT STUDS OFF
AT HEIGHT OF
LINE ON WALL

ELECTRIC
CABLE MAY
RUN UNDER
WINDOW.

PLASTER SHOWN CUTAWAY TO SHOW
STRUCTURE AROUND EXISTING WINDOW.

FIG. K.

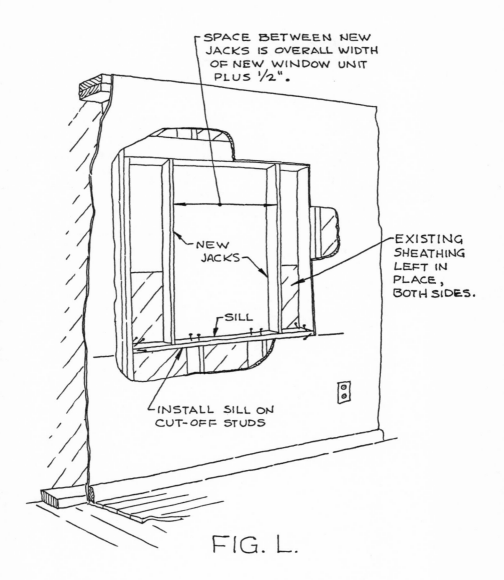

SPACE BETWEEN NEW JACKS IS OVERALL WIDTH OF NEW WINDOW UNIT PLUS 1/2".

NEW JACKS

EXISTING SHEATHING LEFT IN PLACE, BOTH SIDES.

SILL

INSTALL SILL ON CUT-OFF STUDS

FIG. L.

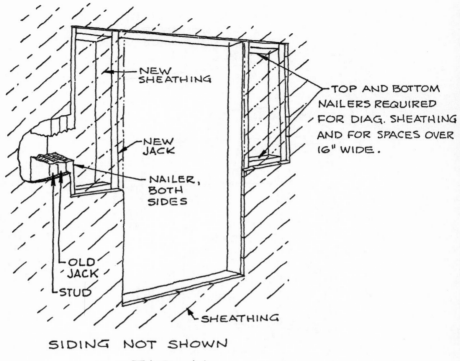

NEW SHEATHING

TOP AND BOTTOM NAILERS REQUIRED FOR DIAG. SHEATHING AND FOR SPACES OVER 16" WIDE.

NEW JACK

NAILER, BOTH SIDES

OLD JACK

STUD

SHEATHING

SIDING NOT SHOWN

FIG. M.

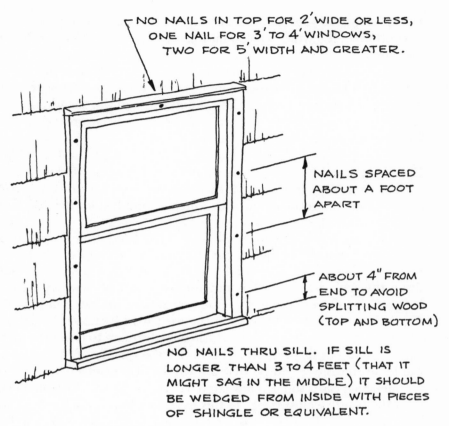

NO NAILS IN TOP FOR 2' WIDE OR LESS,
ONE NAIL FOR 3' TO 4' WINDOWS,
TWO FOR 5' WIDTH AND GREATER.

NAILS SPACED
ABOUT A FOOT
APART

ABOUT 4" FROM
END TO AVOID
SPLITTING WOOD
(TOP AND BOTTOM)

NO NAILS THRU SILL. IF SILL IS
LONGER THAN 3 TO 4 FEET (THAT IT
MIGHT SAG IN THE MIDDLE) IT SHOULD
BE WEDGED FROM INSIDE WITH PIECES
OF SHINGLE OR EQUIVALENT.

FIG. N.

PUTTING WINDOW IN

Now you're ready to put the window in (Fig. N). The window goes in from the outside. Simply lift it up and slip it in place. For this you need a helper on the inside. When in, check with your eye to see that you have a quarter inch space on both sides (that extra half inch of measurement). Then put the level on the back edge of the sill.

The sill slopes so you want to make certain that the level is parallel to the bottom of the window. You may need someone to help you level the window.

Look at the level. One side will likely be higher than the other. On the high side drive one tenpenny common nail through the casing 4 to 5 inches up from the sill and through the sheathing and into the jack studs. Don't drive it in all the way—leave enough of the head out so you can remove the nail if necessary.

Place the level against the side of the window on the high side. Check for plumb. Use a pry bar to get it plumb (the window is not rigid at corners), and holding it that way with the bar drive another nail into the top of the casing 4 to 5 inches from header through the sheathing into the jack stud.

Put the level back on the sill, level the sill and drive a nail 4 to 5 inches up from sill through the casing on the other side. After this nail is in check again for plumb and level. If it is plumb and level drive the nails home. If it is not remove the nails and try again. When O.K., drive more nails, equally spaced as indicated in Fig. N. But before doing this be certain the sash works easily. It may be necessary to leave the window a little out-of-square to make the sash run smoothly or fit properly. The better the quality of the window the less probable it will be that the window is out-of-square.

In some cases the window jamb will be too narrow to come flush with the inside wall surface. In this case, nail large enough strips of wood to the inside edge of the jamb to make up the difference. If the jamb projects beyond the wall, shim out behind the casing. For the complete story on trimming the inside of a window, see Chapter 14.

Chapter 5

How to Install Plasterboard

Learning to install plaster, or wet wall, takes a long time. Far better for the home owner is plasterboard (also known as dry wall and Sheetrock) which comes 4 feet wide in 6-, 7-, 8-, 10-, 12-, and 16-foot lengths and 3/8-, 1/2- and 5/8-inch thicknesses. The 5/8-inch thickness is used mainly to fireproof walls and comes only in 4 by 8 foot sizes for an obvious reason—obvious when you try to pick it up! As building materials go plasterboard is very uniform in quality, regardless of manufacturer. There are no hidden defects; it is visibly good or broken. And it's cheap.

Plasterboard's primary use is as a new wall material. It's also very good for covering up heavily cracked walls and ceilings. If you don't like the look of ceiling tile this will also cover it nicely.

SHEETROCKING A NEW ROOM

Before you start to Sheetrock a room there are some general things to know. You should think about how to do it with the least amount of joints—it will minimize the taping that must be done over joints. The mistake most people make is applying Sheetrock vertically; it's much easier to tape a horizontal seam at shoulder height or lower than to tape from floor to ceiling.

You should install the material on the ceiling first. Ninety percent of the time it works out better to run the Sheetrock at right angles to the joist, butting the ends on the joists. If possible, get Sheetrock long enough to span the ceiling in one piece. Butt joints, which occur when end pieces go together, are harder to tape than edge joints; edges are tapered (depressed) to accept joint compound and tape. Also, use pieces as long as you can get them for the walls.

41

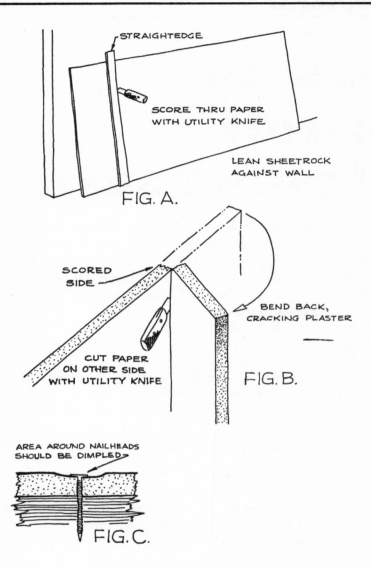

STRAIGHTEDGE

SCORE THRU PAPER
WITH UTILITY KNIFE

LEAN SHEETROCK
AGAINST WALL

FIG. A.

SCORED
SIDE

BEND BACK,
CRACKING PLASTER

CUT PAPER
ON OTHER SIDE
WITH UTILITY KNIFE

FIG. B.

AREA AROUND NAILHEADS
SHOULD BE DIMPLED

FIG. C.

Sheetrock is cut with a utility knife rather than a saw. First you score it using a straightedge as a guide (Fig. A). Or consider getting a 4-foot T-square made especially for cutting. You stand the Sheetrock against the wall, put the top of the T-square on the top edge and cut right down next to the metal part. After scoring, bend it toward the back, then cut the back on the fold (Fig. B). Cut this way the end of the panel will always be a little bit rough so always cut 1/4 inch shorter than the actual space you want to fill. This will allow rough ends of pieces to fit together.

When nailing Sheetrock to the ceiling you must have a helper. You also need something to stand on, relative to the height of the workers. A professional Sheetrocker has a wood horse built to his size so that his head will be three inches from the ceiling. When a tall man works with a short man they have different size horses.

Before starting the job mark where the joists fall on the plate. As you nail ceiling panels in place you can refer to the marks and know where the joists are.

Use dry wall nails. These are 1-3/8 inch, blued, large head nails with a ringed shank for better holding. Drive them 7 to 8 inches apart. Each spot where a nail is driven should show a slight hammer mark or dimple, but the paper should not be broken (Fig. C). If you break the paper you can patch it with a piece of tape.

INSTALLATION

Start in a corner. Lift Sheetrock with partner and butt it tight in the corner. Have one man hold Sheetrock in place (or use T braces as shown in Fig. D) while the other drives a few nails in all the edges to hold it temporarily. After the first few nails are in, nail all the way across one joist and continue this way. Nail the ends of each panel in place last. You'll have to work fast because, as mentioned, Sheetrock is heavy and it can pull through the nails and come down.

Butt the second panel against the first piece with the beveled (tapered) edges meeting. To make it easier to hold the panel, first nail a few 1 by 6 blocks as shown in Fig. E, forming a ledge that the panel can rest on until you have it nailed in securely. Use eightpenny common nails to secure the blocks. Continue installing panels as described.

HANDLING ELECTRICAL BOX

In the average room, when you're securing the second panel you'll encounter the electrical box for the light fixture. Before putting the

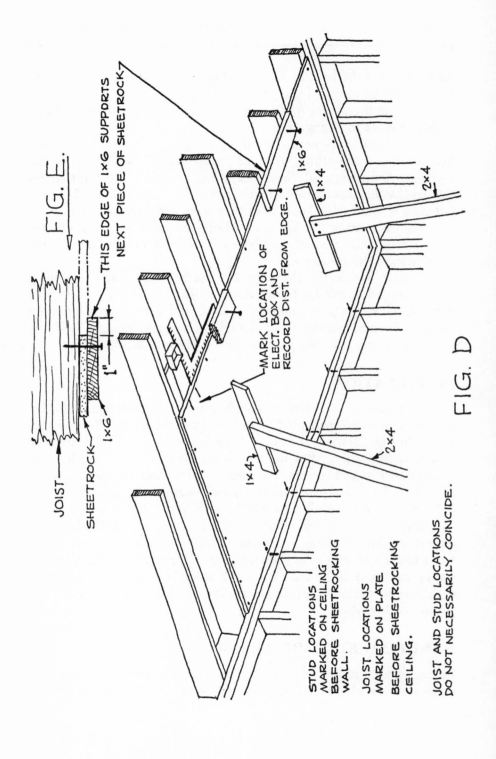

FIG. E.

JOIST

SHEETROCK

1×6

1"

THIS EDGE OF 1×6 SUPPORTS
NEXT PIECE OF SHEETROCK

MARK LOCATION OF
ELECT. BOX AND
RECORD DIST. FROM EDGE.

1×6

1×4

2×4

1×4

2×4

FIG. D

STUD LOCATIONS
MARKED ON CEILING
BEFORE SHEETROCKING
WALL.

JOIST LOCATIONS
MARKED ON PLATE
BEFORE SHEETROCKING
CEILING.

JOIST AND STUD LOCATIONS
DO NOT NECESSARILY COINCIDE.

panel in place proceed as follows. Using a square (detail in Fig. D) measure distance from the last installed panel where the box will fall; mark the dimensions on the first panel. Then, when the second panel is up, refer to your dimensions and you'll know where to break out the hole for the box. Do this with a hammer, enlarging it neatly with a utility knife.

When cutting panels to length cut them to different sizes so the ends are staggered and will fall on different joists. If you let all the ends fall on one joist taping will be difficult. The ends aren't tapered like the sides and don't accommodate tape and compound nicely.

One caution: Don't assume the room is square. The room can be as much as 2 inches out of square, shaped like a parallelogram. So before you trim pieces to fit in next to the wall, measure at various spots along the last installed piece to the wall so you can trim the last piece to the exact angle needed.

SHEETROCKING WALLS

In general work from the top down. A good place to butt panels is next to or above a window or door. This cuts down the amount of taping required; you'll have a short joint instead of a long one. If any wall area is shorter than four feet long, apply Sheetrock vertically and you'll have no seams at all, saving a spackling (taping) job on all but the corners. It's usually better to throw away small pieces. However, if you wind up with a lot of 3- or 4-foot pieces you can probably use them in a closet.

Before starting on walls mark the stud locations on the ceiling; you'll know where they are for nailing even as you cover them with panels (as with the joists).

Start at any end. Hike a panel tight up in the corner. To hold it there you can tack it in place, then nail to studs and plate (Fig. F). Then put in the bottom sheet and proceed around the room.

That's for the average wall, 8 feet high. If the wall is higher, say 8 feet 2 inches, the best procedure is to install the top piece up tight against the ceiling, then rest the bottom piece on the floor and nail it in place. This will leave a small gap between the two pieces. Just fill

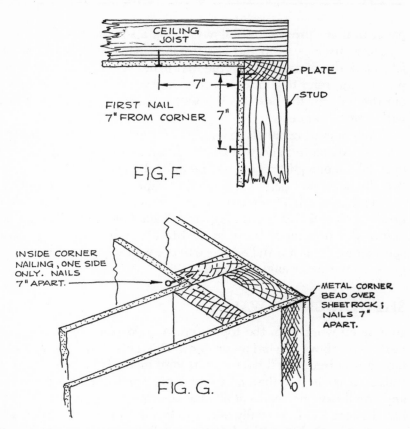

FIG. F

FIG. G.

this with a narrow strip of Sheetrock as detailed in Fig. K. Later, when you tape, you will be doing it at a convenient height rather than if you butted the bottom against the top piece, because you'd then have to fill the gap between the bottom panel and the floor. Of course if you are using wide baseboard molding you may be able to butt the pieces and cover the big 2-inch gap on the bottom with the molding.

When nailing Sheetrock at the corners you neen't secure both abutting sheets. Just one is sufficient. A detail of this is shown in Fig. G.

After all Sheetrock has been installed put on outside metal corner beads as needed. (You buy these when you buy the Sheetrock.) Any outside corner is vulnerable to chipping and the beading protects these. It should be pressed snugly in place (not hammered) and nailed on (use the same nails as on Sheetrock). See Fig. G.

TAPING

A professional not only has to be good but very fast. Given a little time and care though, a do-it-yourselfer can come up with a job that is even better. In the trade a two- or three-coat job is usual: three coats if painting and two for when the plasterboard will be covered by wallpaper or Sanitas. Doing it yourself, you can apply as many coats as needed to make joints invisible. Sometimes four coats are necessary. One tip: It's much easier to get a smooth job by spackling than sandpapering. If you have a difficult area that needs to be built up with layers of compound, the main thing is not to leave any spots that have to be sanded.

WHAT TO TAPE

Vertical corners must be taped. The corners between ceiling and walls are optional; you can use tape, or cove, or crown molding. You generally tend to get openings between molding and plasterboard which would have to be filled on a subsequent paint job (the cracks occur because the molding contracts slightly). On the other hand, this doesn't occur with taping. Of the two moldings, cove is easier to install because there's less matching at corners.

The tape itself is a 2-inch wide paper that comes in rolls up to 250 feet long. There are two kinds. One has a rough texture and perforations that are so small they're practically invisible. The other has holes that are large by comparison. It's not nearly as good to use because the spackle keeps coming through the holes and making bumps. In an emergency you can use a piece of kraft paper.

There are two kinds of joint compound. One is mixed with water, the other comes premixed in 1 or 5 gallon pails. I like the common premixed. (There is a vinyl type that is more expensive.) It is always at the proper consistency and keeps longer than the kind you mix yourself from a powder.

TOOLS

For the job you'll need a hawk, which is a rectangular piece of metal, usually aluminum or stainless steel, 14 inches square, mounted on a wooden handle. This is used to hold the compound while you're working. It's essential for any kind of proficiency in taping. You'll also need a broad knife; this is sort of an oversized putty knife, 4 to 5 inches wide and flexible. There is also a taping knife made for taping, but I prefer the broad kind. A 5 by 11 steel trowel is also needed. A corner knife is a tool that makes corner taping much easier, but it's not essential. Fig. H shows the basic tools.

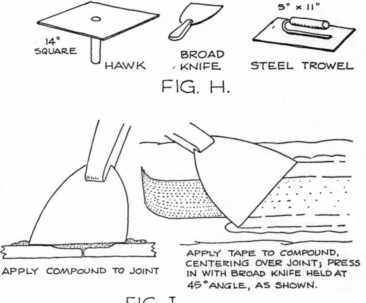

FIG. H.

FIG. I.

Tape the flat areas first for practice rather than corner joints. Put a glob of compound about the size of a grapefruit on the hawk. Take the broad knife, scoop it off the hawk and apply liberally to joint no more than 1/8 inches thick and about 6 inches wide. Apply to full length of joint; it doesn't have to be evenly applied but every spot of wall must be covered. Strip off tape to proper length and press it in the compound with your fingers, making certain it's centered over the joint. Use the broad knife to press it more firmly into the compound, at the same time remove all excess compound (Fig. I). Be careful that there are no lumps, and concentrate on stretching the tape slightly with the knife as you go. Work from the middle of the tape toward ends.

Continue around the room. When you come to a corner the tape must be folded before application. It is made to fold easily. First, apply the compound to both edges of the corner. The easiest technique is to lay a blob on the side of the broad knife, hold knife vertically, set on wall and spread on in a downward motion. Be sure to fill completely any space between Sheetrock and corner. Then repeat for other side of corner. Then press tape into corners with fingers and embed it as for flat joint, except do both sides separately. With a corner knife you can do both sides at once. The corner knife leaves a bead of compound beyond its reach on each wall which has to be removed with broad knife. If the tape is loose at any point it means insufficient compound has been applied.

LET FIRST COAT DRY

Allow first coat and additional coat to dry thoroughly before applying subsequent ones. Each coat should be three inches wider on each

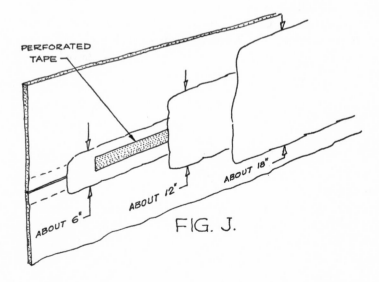

PERFORATED TAPE

ABOUT 6"

ABOUT 12"

ABOUT 18"

FIG. J.

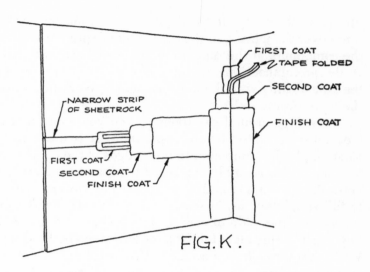

FIG. K .

side than the preceding one (Fig. J). You end up with a total spackle width of eighteen inches for three coats. Also, each coat has to be carefully feathered or blended in; use more pressure on trowel with each coat. The second coat fills in tapered edges and goes past them a little. The final coat is really for smoothness. Apply this coat liberally with a trowel and scrape it off, keeping the leading edge up. Collectively, all coats should be about 1/16 inch thick and level with surrounding wall area. For an overall view of taping see Fig. K.

As mentioned, don't leave bumps. Holes are okay. When dry you can fill them in. Also, use broad knife to knock off any little particles which will cause problems.

Compound drying time varies according to the kind you use, temperature, and humidity. It's usually from two to forty-eight hours. The edges dry first. When the color is uniform, the compound is dry.

Cover the nail heads with two coats and the metal lip portions of any outside corner beading. Use as many coats as are necessary to get a smooth job.

If you do a thorough taping job sanding will not be necessary. If it is, sand after priming. The paint will cover slight irregularities and there will be less to sand. Also, if you sand raw Sheetrock it will become fuzzy. For the job use grade 80 sandpaper or the equivalent.

Chapter 6

Basics of Converting an Attic Into Living Area

The attic is a good place to turn to if you're looking to make extra rooms in your home. If you wish it can serve well as a storage area.

There are a number of things to plan before you begin the job. The first is accessibility. If you intend the attic to be a full-time or even part-time living area, a permanent set of stairs is required. You could build the stairs yourself from scratch, but it is a bit complicated for the do-it-yourselfer, and I'd advise you to leave it to a professional. He will not only build them for you, but help you decide where they should be placed, based on what you plan for the room. Of course, if the attic was earmarked for future expansion when the house was built, stair location was probably figured out. Indeed, the stairs may already be there. One option, if you have only a small space in which to place the stairs, is a circular staircase. If you intend to use the area only for storage, stairs that fold into the ceiling are good. If the hall below is cramped you may gain space for stairs by removing the hall closet—if there is one—below the attic.

Another thing to consider is the size of the things you intend to install there. If large pieces of furniture or fixtures for a bath, make sure that you'll be able to get them up through the access and into the room or rooms you create.

LAYOUT

There are many different ways one can lay out an attic for living, and this will depend on your individual needs. It's best to work it all out carefully with pencil and paper first. If you plan to have a bath up

51

there try to locate it over a bath on the lower floors. In this way the plumbing will be accessible, and easier and less expensive to hook up.

If you are planning two rooms, it's best to plan a central hall that leads from the stairs and provides private entrances for each of the rooms. This hall should be wide enough—at least three feet—so you can move furniture and the like through it after the rooms are finished. It should be long enough so that if there is a door at the head of the stairs it can swing 180 degrees to clear the passageway.

SUPPORTING JOISTS

Another consideration is the strength of the attic joists. These must be beefy enough to support what you intend to have up there. If you're simply finishing the area for storage it's okay to build on 2 by 6's. If you're going to convert the area to a full living area—perhaps with kids tussling up there—there ought to be 2 by 8 joists on 16-inch centers (from the center of one to the centers of adjacent ones, and they should not extend unsupported more than 14 feet). If the 2 by 8 foot boards span between 14 and 16 feet and are on 16-inch centers, they should be beefed up. Using 2 by 8 on 12-inch centers would be fine. Or nail a new 2 by 8 joist to every other joist.

INSTALLING SUBFLOORING

First step in finishing the attic for living is to install subflooring. For this you can use 1/2-inch or thicker sheathing grade plywood, 1 by 4 boards made for the purpose, or 1 by 6 tongue and groove boards. If you can't get the plywood sheets into the attic simply pick one of the other materials. One good way to get long boards into a room is through a window. Protect the windowsill by securing a piece of sheathing to it with a couple of nails. One-half-inch plywood sub-flooring should be installed at right angles to the joists, never parallel. For boards, use two eightpenny common nails into every joist. For plywood, sixpenny common nails about 6 to 8 inches apart.

CONSTRUCTING KNEE WALLS

Making rooms in the attic always involves making knee walls. These are the short walls built under the roof on the long sides of the house, as opposed to the gable, or short ends.

You can make them any height you wish but four feet is usually best. In this way you can use standard 4 by 8 foot prefinished paneling or plasterboard without waste. You just cut the prefinished panels in half; the plasterboard is 4 feet high and can be laid on its side. If you were to make a larger wall, say 5 feet, you could end up with three feet of waste per panel.

There are two ways to build knee walls. One way is to nail a shoe across the floor and have all the studs standing on it and nailed to the shoes of the rafters without any plate between. However, unless there is some pressing reason, such as the house being very badly out of shape, this is not the preferred method. The best way is securing studs between a shoe and a plate. One benefit, in addition to its solidity as wall structure, is that as you nail the knee wall studs in place you can take the sag out of a roof—and roofs always sag. In an older house that has Sheetrocked ceilings below, this method can result in a few popped nails in the ceiling but it's nothing to be concerned about. The same thing, incidentally, can happen when finish flooring is nailed down.

For an easier, more accurate job when making knee wall studs, it's best to make a pattern, or template, with which you can cut all knee wall studs to size. To do this, follow the steps in Fig. A. Use this to mark the rafters and the floor (hold stud plumb while doing this). Snap a chalk line across the rafters and on the floor to the length of the room you're doing. It's a good idea to install knee walls across entire attic even if room doesn't extend that far. Use tenpenny common nails to nail the 2 by 4 plate to the rafters and 2 by 4 shoe to the floor. With these in you're ready to start installing the studs which you precut using the pattern.

NAILING STUDS

Start nailing the studs on from either end (16 inches center to center) of the wall using tenpenny nails. Go through the angled ends

1. MARK HEIGHT OF WALL ON PIECE OF 2×4; THAT IS, HEIGHT OF SHEETROCK PLUS 1" (SEE FIG. B.)

2. STAND PLUMB AGAINST RAFTER; MARK OUT-LINE OF RAFTER ON 2×4.

3. USE SCRAP PIECE OF 2×4 TO DEDUCT THICKNESS OF PLATE AND MARK ITS UPPER EDGE.

4. REMOVE EXCESS MATERIAL FROM TOP OF 2×4 SO PATTERN MAY BE USED TO MARK FLOOR AND RAFTERS.

5. REMOVE THICKNESS OF PLATE AND SHOE TO PRODUCE FINAL PATTERN FOR STUDS.

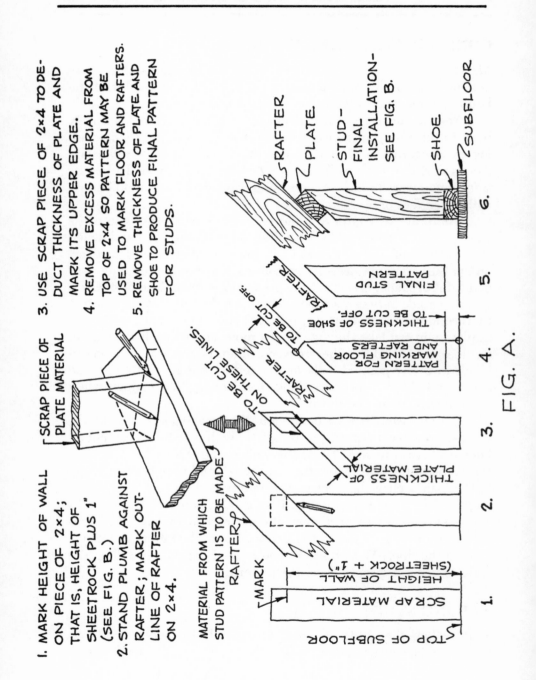

FIG. A.

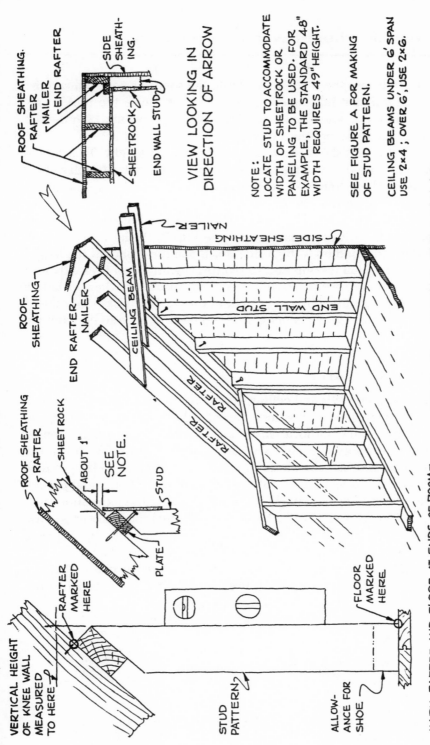

ROOF SHEATHING.
RAFTER
END RAFTER

SIDE SHEATH- ING.

SHEETROCK
END WALL STUD

VIEW LOOKING IN DIRECTION OF ARROW

NOTE:
LOCATE STUD TO ACCOMMODATE WIDTH OF SHEETROCK OR PANELING TO BE USED. FOR EXAMPLE, THE STANDARD 48" WIDTH REQUIRES 49" HEIGHT.

SEE FIGURE A FOR MAKING OF STUD PATTERN.

CEILING BEAMS UNDER 6' SPAN USE 2×4; OVER 6', USE 2×6.

NAILER
SIDE SHEATHING
ROOF SHEATHING
END RAFTER NAILER
CEILING BEAM
END WALL STUD
RAFTER
RAFTER

FIG. B. ATTIC FRAMING.

ROOF SHEATHING
RAFTER
SHEET ROCK
ABOUT 1"
SEE NOTE.
STUD
PLATE

VERTICAL HEIGHT OF KNEE WALL MEASURED TO HERE

RAFTER MARKED HERE

FLOOR MARKED HERE

STUD PATTERN

ALLOW- ANCE FOR SHOE

MARK RAFTER AND FLOOR AT ENDS OF ROOM— SNAP CHALK LINE FOR INTERMEDIATE MARKS.

of the studs into the plate; toenail into the shoe. As you go down the line you'll find it takes more effort—that's because the roof is sagging. After the knee walls are in, install the ceiling beams—the boards that go across the rafters.

First establish where you want the ceiling height. This should be a minimum of seven feet and a maximum of eight. Stretch a chalk line along the rafters on one side at this height and snap the mark. Do the same on the other side.

Next, cut and nail beams in place with the bottom edge of the boards even with your chalk marks (see Fig. B). Make sure that each beam is "crowned up"—high side up. If you can work out the height so the horizontal (as opposed to slanting) ceiling span is exactly four feet, you'll save work. It will mean less spackling when installing Sheetrock and it will be easier to fit in tiles (assuming you use these) which come in 12-inch square sizes—none will have to be trimmed to fit.

REGULAR WALLS

After the knee walls and ceiling beams are in place, make your final layout of partitions on the floor. Strike a chalk line for either edge of each shoe. Mark the locations of all doorways—the rough opening for interior doors is 2 inches wider than the nominal width of the door. Cut and nail the shoes in place. Cut single 2 inch by 4 inch plates for those sections of wall that are under the horizontal portion of the ceiling. Lay out (mark) all the studs and jacks on the shoe only. The framing is basically like the framing in any room, except you use only a single 2 by 4 for the plate and it must be made up in place, and you need only a single 2 by 4 for headers over doors.

Next, install the horizontal plates. Nail those plates that run crosswise to the ceiling beams directly to them. Use a straight stud,

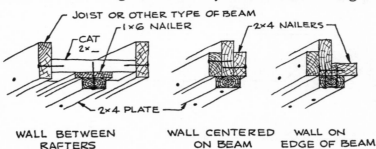

WALL BETWEEN
RAFTERS

WALL CENTERED
ON BEAM

WALL ON
EDGE OF BEAM

FIG. C.

3 inches or so longer than the distance between the shoe and the plate, and a level to make sure the plate is plumb over the shoe. To install a plate that falls between the ceiling beams, nail two 2 by 4 boards in place between the ceiling beams, near the ends of the plate. These boards should be 3/4 inch above the bottom edge of the ceiling beams. This is to allow room for a nailer. Cap the plate with a 1 by 6 to be the nailer, that is, nail the 1 by 6 to the top of the plate with eightpenny common nails. Then install both plate and nailer. Plumb plate above the shoe and nail to the cats. If the plate comes in the way of the ceiling beam just nail it to the ceiling beam and add nailers above it. After the horizontal plates are in place follow the same procedure for the plates in the sloping ceilings. See Fig. C for examples. Like gable studs, the studs in the walls with sloping tops are on 16-inch centers and have a common difference in length. Follow framing tips given in Chapter 1.

To install studs in wall, proceed as follows: install one stud in each wall taking care to plumb it. Then lay out all the studs on the plate from these studs. For examples of walls that run parallel and transverse, see Figs. D, E, and F.

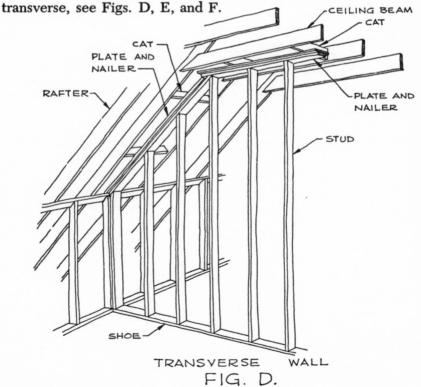

CEILING BEAM
CAT
CAT
PLATE AND NAILER
RAFTER
PLATE AND NAILER
STUD
SHOE

TRANSVERSE   WALL

FIG. D.

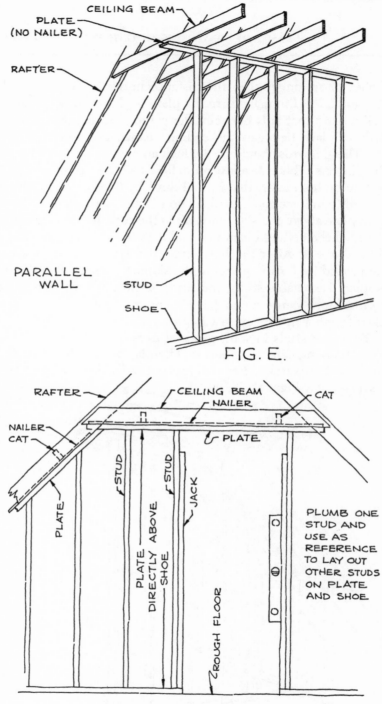

CEILING BEAM

PLATE
(NO NAILER)

RAFTER

PARALLEL
WALL

STUD

SHOE

FIG. E.

RAFTER

CEILING BEAM

NAILER

CAT

NAILER
CAT

PLATE

PLATE

STUD

PLATE DIRECTLY ABOVE

STUD

SHOE

JACK

ROUGH FLOOR

PLUMB ONE
STUD AND
USE AS
REFERENCE
TO LAY OUT
OTHER STUDS
ON PLATE
AND SHOE

PLUMBING AND
LAYING OUT STUDS

FIG. F.

Also necessary will be a nailer for the Sheetrock on the gable ends of the house. Following Fig. B, just cut a 2 by 4 to fit on top of the gable-end studs and nail it up through the studs. As you do this, the nailer will be drawn down tight.

ELECTRICAL WORK

After the attic is framed out is the time to install electrical wiring. Here, I recommend that you hire a licensed electrician rather than do it yourself, but a few suggestions might be helpful.

One thing you should insist on is a duplex outlet every twelve feet. Another handy thing is a three-way switch. This lets you turn on a hall light at the bottom of the attic stairs, and turn it off from upstairs. Switch location upstairs should be determined by the way the door upstairs swings. As you enter the room the switch should be on the wall near the doorknob side. If on the hinged side you won't be able to get at it.

In closets don't use exposed incandescent bulbs. These are a fire hazard. Use fluorescent strips or circular fixtures. The switch for the closet light should be on the outside of the door. A special light should be installed at the switch that stays lit when closet light is on. This will help you keep the closet light from staying on when the door is closed.

VENTILATION

Another thing to consider while the framing is exposed is ventilation. Without proper ventilation heat will rise and collect in the highest parts of the attic and raise the temperature considerably, making the attic unlivable in the summer.

Installing louvers, either in the roof or gable ends of the house is necessary. A motorized fan with a thermostat is also very good. When heat gets high the fan kicks on, sucking warm air out of the attic and cool air in through the louvers. When the attic temperature declines to a certain point the fan goes off. There are a number of variables to consider when installing a fan and it is really a job for a professional. A fan is a good idea even if you have air conditioning. It makes the air conditioner more effective because it doesn't have to work as hard.

HEATING

This is the next step you should take and you should seek the advice of professionals on it. Your present system may be able to supply enough heat. If it can't you may want to install a new system. No matter what kind of heating you have now it makes sense to consider gas, electric, and oil heating. Check with professionals. Learning what each system has to offer can be an education in itself and help you decide what's best for you.

You needn't heat all rooms from one system. For example, if your attic plans included only an occasionally used guest room, you could heat this with electric baseboard heating, and the rest of the rooms with oil heat. Be aware, also, that you can equip rooms with individual thermostats. This can be a great fuel saver.

INSULATION

This is the material used to keep heat in or out of your home. When finishing an attic for a living area, it's best to insulate both the walls and the roof. How much you use will depend on the climate in your area and is something to consult with your dealer on. Local utilities also have information.

There are various kinds of insulation. One of the best kind is blankets. These come in long lengths and specified widths designed to make them fit neatly between studs. They have lipped edges that you staple easily to the studs. When doing this make sure that the lip edge is flush with the stud edge rather than overlapping it. Also, the vapor barrier—the printed side of the insulation—should be facing the inside of the room.

SHEETROCK

Installing Sheetrock on ceilings and walls comes next. For this, follow the instructions for installing Sheetrock in Chapter 5. Start from the ceiling, nailing the material in place there. Cut pieces to fit and install them on the rafters, then do the walls.

When the Sheetrock is up, the area is ready for final finishing.

There are any number of materials that can be applied. For ceilings, there are tiles (see Chapter 10); walls can be either painted (see Chapter 30), papered, or paneled (see Chapter 9). If you panel, don't use paneling that is less than 3/16-inch thick. There have been cases where very thin paneling installed directly on studs have almost literally exploded into flame because of a small fire.

FLOORING

Here, too, there are a variety of materials available. For example, resilient flooring (Chapter 12). I would not recommend installing solid wood flooring (Chapter 23) if there is a finished ceiling below. It may have escaped unscathed from hammering the knee walls, but the amount of hammering involved in putting in the flooring could damage it.

Chapter 7

Furring

Furring is the name given to 1 by 2 boards used to provide a level surface when installing wall material, such as paneling, or ceiling tiles. You should make an attempt to get straight pieces of furring. A board may look straight until you sight down it. To check, place another board against it as shown in Fig. A.

TWO BOARDS SIDE BY SIDE.

MAY APPEAR TO BE STRAIGHT —
TURN ONE OVER TO CHECK.

CHECKING BOARDS FOR STRAIGHTNESS.
FIG. A.

On walls, furring is placed horizontally on about one-foot centers; spacing is not critical. Under ceiling tile, however, spacing is very important.

INSTALLING FURRING ON CEILINGS

There is one method in common use for placing furring on a ceiling that is likely to give trouble. This involves using a length of furring as a spacer between strips. Here there is usually a slight error with each measurement and it builds up to a cumulatively significant one.

It is better to mark one-foot centers on joists (or ceiling if joists aren't exposed), then mark the joists at three or four intervals all the way across. Temporarily secure furring to joists at these points, sighting down each strip as you do to make sure it's straight. You should not drive nails (6 penny common nails are used) all the way home at this time.

Next, tie a string to one end of a furring strip nearest the wall.

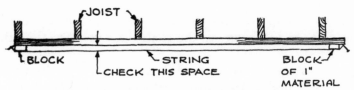

SHIM FIRRING STRIP DOWN AS REQUIRED.

FIG. B

Stretch it tight and tie it to the other end of the strip. At each end, force a block of furring between the string and the strip. Use another block of furring to measure the space between the string and the furring at each joist (Fig. B). At any point along its length where the space is less than the thickness of the measuring block, drive shims (cedar shingle points) under the furring strip at the ends to lower them enough to fit the block in at the closest (least amount of space) point. Then drive shims, as necessary, at each joist to make the space between the string and strip the same and drive all the nails home. If the ends of the furring are closest to the string, nail them home and shim as above.

Follow the same procedure along the adjacent walls (Fig. C). In this case the string will go across the ends of all the furring instead of

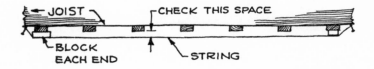

CHECKING FURRING
FOR STRAIGHTNESS
(BOTH DIRECTIONS)
FIG. C.

along the length, but the rest of the procedure is the same. Do the same thing to the strip on the other walls. This done, the perimeter furring around the room will be level.

Next, use the string and blocks to check how much the center of the ceiling is sagging. Since most ceilings sag and we are used to seeing them this way, it is not necessary to get the whole thing perfectly flat. In an average-sized room if the ceiling sags 3/4 inch it is acceptable, and you can use the center as a guide to shim the rest of the furring.

Use a straight piece of furring that spans half the room as a guide. Lay one end on the center of the ceiling and proceed to shim the strips between one end of the straightedge and the other. Make sure you keep the straightedge tight against strips as you go.

If the center of the ceiling sags more than 3/4 inch you can drop all the furring down an extra 3/4 inch around the entire room. To do this, double the end furring, then drop each strip individually at the ends with another piece of furring under it and use a straightedge to finish the job as above.

If the ceiling does not sag use the string and block method to level all the furring and you'll get a nearly perfect job.

The same general rules apply to furring walls. However, with masonry walls, where furring is attached with masonry nails, adjustment is impossible. Therefore furring masonry walls is only practical where the walls are reasonably flat.

Chapter 8

Finishing
A Basement

If you are thinking about finishing your basement the first thing to consider is the presence of dampness or water. It may show up on the walls or the floor. If it is showing up only on the floor it means that the water table (natural water in the ground) is higher than the floor. This height varies with the amount of rainfall, hence the floor may stay dry for long periods and then suddenly become wet. The only thing that can be done for this condition is to install a sump pump and, unfortunately, forget about finishing the basement.

If the water comes from above—it's on the walls—in all likelihood it can be traced to bad grading of soil around the house. In order to keep a basement dry the ground must pitch enough to make all water run away freely. Also, all gutters and leaders must be installed to make the water run away from the house, and areaways around basement windows must be high enough to keep any surface water from running over the top. If you see that all these things are in proper order, ninety-nine times out of a hundred that is all that will be necessary to make the basement dry.

If these things don't cure the problem the job calls for professional waterproofing done from the outside. I have very little faith in coatings applied inside the foundation walls being permanently waterproof.

All aspects of finishing a basement are discussed in other chapters, but the framing is different enough to warrant further discussion.

The foundation walls are never straight or plumb (indeed, no wall is ever straight or plumb). Because of this, in most cases it is better to frame a whole new wall than to try to install furring. If there is some important reason for furring, like room at the side or foot of a stairwell where you don't want framing lumber to eat up space, you can use masonry nails (1-1/2 inch nails for 3/4 inch furring), but the results are somewhat unpredictable. The concrete may crack and the nails become loose while you are working on it.

Frame the outside (foundation) walls with 2 inch by 3 inch's and any partitions that will be finished on both sides with 2 inch by 4 inch's. To frame outside walls strike chalk lines 5 inches away from the concrete walls as a guide to where the inside of the studding will fall. Strike lines for the other partition walls as you need them. Because a concrete floor is inclined to be wavy the studs usually have to be cut to fit individually.

Work on one wall at a time. Nail a 2 inch by 3 inch shoe to the floor with 2-1/2 inch masonry nails. Don't expect to get the shoe to hold tightly; when the studs are in place they will keep it from sliding around. The studs will force the shoe tight and the nail points in the concrete will also prevent it from sliding. Plumb up from each end of the shoe to get the location of the plate. Where the plate runs at right angles to the joist strike a chalk line across them, then nail the plate on with tenpenny common nails. If the plate is parallel to the joists the construction is the same as in an attic between the ceiling beams. See Chapter 6.

After the shoe and plate are in place cut one end stud to fit. Stand it in place, plumb it, and toenail each end with three tenpenny common nails. Next, mark off 16 inch centers from this stud on both shoe and plate. Make the second stud 15-1/4 inches center to center from the first stud; this will make the edges of 48 inches (4 feet) wide paneling fall on stud centers; otherwise the edges would miss.

To fit the remaining studs follow this procedure. Take a stud slightly longer than needed and stand it up with one end on the shoe, the other end next to the plate. Make sure that the ends are aligned with their marks. Then stand on the shoe to insure that it is tight to the floor and mark the top of the stud at the plate. Cut the stud at this line but don't obliterate the line as you do—leave it on. Then nail the stud in place.

Before the wall is fully erected, lay a 2 inch by 3 inch stringer on the floor behind it. (After the wall is erected you won't be able to get it in.) When all the studs are in place, hold the stringer tight to the back of the studs about halfway up the wall (studs) and toenail it through the studs in place (Fig. A). As you do, make sure that each

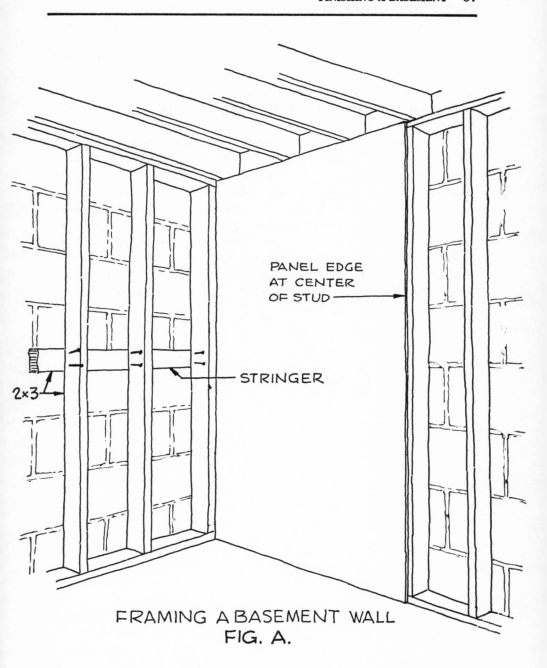

FRAMING A BASEMENT WALL
FIG. A.

stud is straight top to bottom and tight to the stringer. This will hold the middle line of the wall as straight as it can be made. Frame the rest of the 2 inch by 3 inch walls in the same manner. The 2 inch by 4 inch walls are framed the same except that there is no center stringer used.

Keep in mind as you frame a basement that you have to provide access panels to all valves, fuse boxes, circuit breakers, junction boxes, telephone connecting blocks, and cleanout plugs in the plumbing. You can make a simple access panel by constructing a box in the wall framing, then simply cut out the section of the paneling to form a door that covers the opening. Mount this piece of paneling on a piece of 1/2 inch or 3/4 inch plywood or flakeboard. Trim the edges with mullion strip and mount the door on decorative hinges. Another way is to cut a piece of paneling with matching grooves larger than the opening, mount on plywood and hinge with over-lay hinges (hinges for slab doors).

Chapter 9

How to Get A Better Paneling Job

If you are one of those "I never want to paint again people," paneling may be the way for you to finish one or more rooms. You might also use it simply because you like the way it looks. If you are reasonably good with tools, take a little time and patience and you will get a respectable finished job. Following are some tips and techniques for doing it.

Select the right panel. The quality of a panel is not necessarily proportional to the price. Exotic woods run up the cost but not the quality. Keep in mind the surface that the panels will be applied to. If it is going to be applied directly to studs or furring strips it must be at least 1/4 inch thick. On the other hand, you can glue thinner panels to plaster walls using an adhesive from a caulking gun, with some better success than heavier panels. On Sheetrock, 1/4 inch panels nailed through the Sheetrock to the studs makes the best job.

Hardboard panels have simulated wood grains, are difficult to cut, chip easily when worked with hand tools, but have good resistance to impact.

Wood paneling, on the other hand, may be vinyl covered and have simulated wood grain, or it may have real wood veneer with a high quality finish. It may be made with a hardwood core (inside layers of wood) and be difficult to cut or it may be made with a softwood core which you can cut with a knife. Its resistance to impact varies according to its thickness and hardness. There is a wide variety of 3/16 inch thick luan (softwood) vinyl-covered simulated woodgrain panels that are moderately priced and easily worked. One of these is a good choice for use over Sheetrock, especially for a first attempt at paneling.

Take some time to plan where panels (each is 4 by 8) will go to make sure the edges land on studs. Avoid a situation where it will be necessary to use a narrow (say less than 6 inch wide) strip of paneling to finish a wall. (It's difficult to make a narrow strip lay in flat.) For example, if you are framing a wall that is 12 feet 3 inches long, plan to make the first panel from 32 inches to 36 inches wide. Other things, like a door or window, could determine on which stud you butt the panels. Avoid a narrow strip next to a window or door.

The way to cut out a panel to fit around a window, or doorway if the jamb is already there, is with a router with a plastic laminate trim bit. This is a straight, two flute carbide bit with a ball bearing guide on the bottom end (Fig. A).

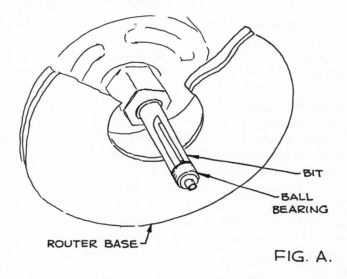

FIG. A.

Set the panel right over the window frame or door after removing the molding (casing stool, stop whatever) and nail it to all the studs. For large windows drive one or two nails carefully through the panel into the middle of the jamb to hold it straight while you trim the paneling with the router. You needn't do this on small windows. Then just run router against jamb (maybe starting hole if necessary) and cut out piece inside window. Make sure the router bit doesn't hit a nail—it'll ruin the bit.

When paneling over Sheetrock find the studs first. Locate them by tapping the wall with your hammer to find where it feels solid. Then drive a nail to make sure. Try 16-inch centers from the first stud you find. Keep trying until you have located all of them. Then plan the positions of all the panels so that all edges fall on studs. If this is not possible secure unnailed edges with panel adhesive.

On plaster walls in very good condition glue 3/16 inch paneling directly to the surface panel adhesive. This is a form of contact cement that comes in a caulking cartridge and is applied with a caulking gun. Apply 1 inch by 2 inch furring horizontally to plaster walls that are in bad condition. See Chapter 7 for furring instructions.

The router is a good tool (rather than a saw and plane) to cut panels, especially hardboard. To do this prepare a straightedge, using a 3/4 inch by 12 inch by 96 inch piece of flakeboard with strips of plastic laminate glued to the edges. Measure and mark the panel to be cut on each end and clamp it to the board with marks aligning with edge of straightedge, then cut it with the router. The router will cut in one direction only. If you go the wrong way it will pull away from the guide.

When cutting for electrical outlets it is usually easy to measure accurately for the horizontal location, but the vertical measurement is more difficult because the floor is seldom level. Therefore plan to keep the panel 1/4 inch above the floor and lower than the ceiling to allow room to raise or lower it. First, measure up from the floor to the bottom of the box and cut the panel for the box (3-1/2 inches high) 1/4 inch less than this measurement. This opening is shorter than the box but it can be enlarged by a utility knife to expose the box screw holes after it is in place. In this way, if you have to move the panel up or down to clear the floor or ceiling, the cutout for the box will still be covered by the outlet plate.

One thing that makes a paneling job look good is inside corners that fit right without molding. This is not difficult if you plan ahead.

If you have framed the wall yourself and you can get behind the wall (you can't do it unless you can get behind it) the thing to do is cut one panel to fit in the corner but do not nail it to the corner stud. Butt the second panel to the first. Check it for plumb, and nail it in place. Now drive wood shingle tips between the first panel and the stud to bring it tight to the second panel. This gives you a straight, plumb, tight corner.

If you are paneling over Sheetrock or plaster and the panel doesn't fit flat, take an old chisel and "clear out" the corner to make sure that it is square all the way from the floor to the ceiling.

Before you panel into a corner check the wall with a straight-edge to look for irregularities. If the corner is firm but has some "waves" in it you can still make a straight corner.

Fit the first panel to the corner (remember that you have the thickness of the panel to cover a poor fit). Put this panel aside. Stand the second panel in place in the corner and tack it with two nails to hold it so its outer edge is plumb. Check the edge of the panel against the corner. If the corner is more than 1/4 inch out of plumb, mark the ends of the panel an equal distance—say 1/2 inch—from the corner. Remove the panel, then trim it to these marks with a router and straightedge. Now stand the panel in the corner again. Plumb it and tack it again. Next, cut shingle points (Fig. B) to fit between the edge of the first panel and the corner; six tips are usually enough. Tack them in place as indicated in the sketch.

Take the panel down and run heavy bead of panel adhesive down the first wall, near the corner. Install the first panel but don't nail in the corner. Install the second panel nailing the corner. The shims and heavy bead of glue will hold the first panel tight to the second, giving a straight, if not plumb, tight corner. This procedure is easier than planing the edge of the panel to fit a very irregular wall.

With Sheetrock walls you can cut the Sheetrock away to allow the panel to fit closer to the corner. This too can be easier than planing a panel to fit. Very often there is a gap between pieces of Sheetrock butted at the corner and you slip the panel edge in the gap.

When cutting for more than one electrical outlet in the same panel, it is very important that the cutouts be located accurately in relation to each other, because if you have to move the panel up or down, all the holes move together. To do this, draw a level line from the bottom of one outlet extending over or under the other. This will

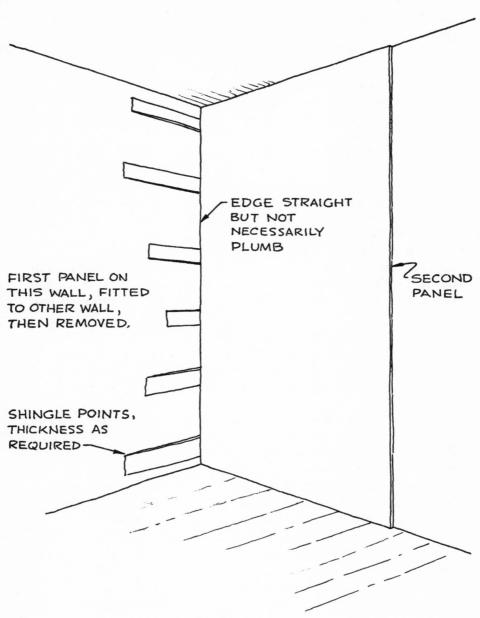

EDGE STRAIGHT
BUT NOT
NECESSARILY
PLUMB

SECOND
PANEL

FIRST PANEL ON
THIS WALL, FITTED
TO OTHER WALL,
THEN REMOVED.

SHINGLE POINTS,
THICKNESS AS
REQUIRED

FIG. B.

enable you to measure up from the floor for all outlets from the same point. If you cut an outlet in the wrong place, before you cut another panel, it is very often possible to move the box to coincide with the hole in the panel, especially up or down on open studs. Sideways you have a fifty-fifty chance.

To scribe a panel to a very irregular surface such as the edge of a stone fireplace or a stepped back, built-in bookcase, proceed as follows:

Stand the panel as near to the fireplace or other irregular surface as possible, plumb it and tack it in place. Measure from the edge of the panel horizontally to find the maximum distance from the panel. This is the length of the scribe. You may use a regular scriber or a block of wood cut to a sharp point on one end and marked in the center on the other end.

The scribed line must be made carefully. The wood block, or scriber, must be held exactly level at all times as it is run up and down. Don't allow it to describe an arc from one point. It is often better to locate a series of points than to scribe a continuous line (Fig. C).

Very often two panels don't butt exactly right and the wall or stud will show through the joint. Also, paneling expands and contracts somewhat with the weather. To avoid this eyesore use a can of black spray paint to spray the wall where the panels join before you install them.

The above are tips on how to get a better paneling job, both on new work and over old walls. But before you begin think the whole job through. With very few exceptions all the trim should be removed. Exception: steel bucks (steel door frames). These can't be removed without replacing the whole door jamb because jamb is part of frame. Also, you can leave all 3/4 inch flat molding (1 inch by 6 inch baseboard; 1 inch by 4 inch casing) if you plan to fur the whole wall. In this case, remove only those moldings that extend more than 3/4 inch from the wall, such as backband, or any moldings that interfere with the furring.

If you have to fit around steel bucks, choose a 1/4 inch thick panel and install plastic cap molding against the casing part of the

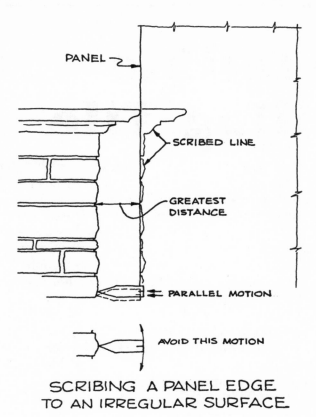

PANEL

SCRIBED LINE

GREATEST
DISTANCE

PARALLEL MOTION

AVOID THIS MOTION

SCRIBING A PANEL EDGE
TO AN IRREGULAR SURFACE

FIG. C.

buck so that you can avoid having to fit the paneling perfectly around the entire perimeter of the door.

The next step is to find all studs; you need to know this even for furring. Then proceed to install the panels in sequence around the room. If you don't intend to panel the doors, put your last piece in over the door. This way you can fill in with a small piece, rather than end up where you have to fit a wall-length strip in between panels, a difficult cutting job. Finally, install the moldings. Information on this appears in Chapter 14.

Chapter 10

Installing
Ceiling Tile

There are many different kinds of ceiling tile available. Some are accoustical, some washable, some fireproof, many fancy, some perforated and fissured. All are basically made of the same material, however, insulation board. Relatively soft, it is easy to work with —you can cut it with a sharp utility knife guided by a straightedge.

Ceiling tiles come in cartons, and it's best to open these up twenty-four hours or so before you intend to do the job. This gives the tiles a chance to adjust to the humidity or other inside weather conditions of your house.

When using the tiles work from several different boxes. Even though tiles are supposed to be the same color they often have slight differences. If you install them "mixed" the color discrepancies won't show as glaringly as they would if large blocks of tiles of slightly different colors were set side by side.

INSTALLING THE TILES

Depending on what your current ceiling is, you will or won't have to fur it out—apply straight 1 by 2 boards to level the surface. (See Chapter 7.) If wood, no furring is necessary. The tiles can be applied directly to the wood with adhesive or staples. If Sheetrock you have an option to use furring or not. A plaster ceiling has to be furred. If there is no ceiling material (just exposed joists) also use furring.

Whether you use furring or not, the first step is to work out the layout of tiles with pencil and tracing paper. The easiest way is to first make a scale drawing of the ceiling on tracing paper. The drawing should be as exact as you can make it. Walls are commonly not straight, so you should measure in many different places using a steel tape, to reflect how much distances deviate. (For example, from wall to wall, one end of a rectangular room may be 10 feet 6 inches; but at the other end or in the middle, it may only be 10 feet 4 inches because the wall is bowed there.)

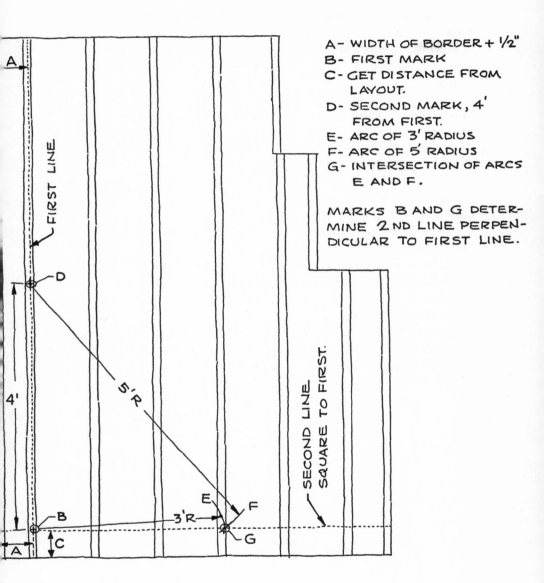

A- WIDTH OF BORDER + ½"
B- FIRST MARK
C- GET DISTANCE FROM
   LAYOUT.
D- SECOND MARK, 4'
   FROM FIRST.
E- ARC OF 3' RADIUS
F- ARC OF 5' RADIUS
G- INTERSECTION OF ARCS
   E AND F.

MARKS B AND G DETER-
MINE 2ND LINE PERPEN-
DICULAR TO FIRST LINE.

FIG. A.

When you have the ceiling plan place it on a piece of graph paper with each square representing one 12 inch square (the size tiles come in). Move the plan over the graph paper until you have achieved a layout where the border tiles are as even as possible, with no strip less than 3 inches wide. Then outline the plan on the graph paper.

Once you know the tile layout, pencil in the furring strips, if you're going to use these. Strips are placed at right angles to joists (which you can find, if not exposed, the same way as studs) one each on both sides of the room where the edges of the first tiles are, and then on 12-inch centers across the room.

The tiles must be installed squarely. To do this it's best to draw a so-called 3-4-5 triangle on the furring strips as a guide. How to do this is shown in Fig. A.

Once you get square lines start installing the tiles against them, starting in a corner. Use a stapler which the dealer will likely let you use free. Fasteners should be placed two and one half inches apart and centered on the furring strips. It's best to place three or four tiles at a time, making sure their edges are aligned, then staple them all at once (Fig. B).

As mentioned, tiles can be cut with a sharp utility knife using a straightedge as a guide. When using a knife, tiles are cut with the face up. Some are best cut from the back using an electric handsaw. Check this out for the particular tile you buy.

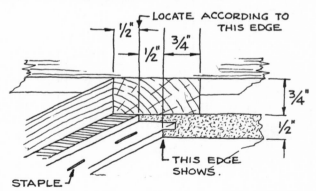

LOCATION OF FURRING STRIPS
TO SUIT CEILING TILES.

FIG. B.

Chapter 11

Installing A Suspended Ceiling

If you have the headroom in a basement, a suspended ceiling is an excellent way to hide all the wiring, junction boxes, plumbing, and valves that are usually overhead, and at the same time provide easy access to them when you need it.

INSTALLATION

The ceiling consists of a grid (a metal framework) and ceiling tiles that lay in it loose. The grid consists of main runners, 4 foot 0 inch cross tees and possibly 2 foot 0 inch secondary cross tees, and wall molding (Fig. A). The grid itself is suspended by wires as shown in Fig. B.

First, make a scale drawing of your ceiling. Lay out the main runners on it four feet apart. You will have to experiment to decide on the layout that will be best. The basics of doing this are shown in the sketches in Fig. C. Since the key to getting a good job is getting the main runners installed correctly you should try to use as few as possible since this gives fewer chances to make errors. If you can lay out the main runners so they reach from wall to wall in one piece, by all means do so. If necessary, main runners can be interlocked together.

After the main runners are located draw in the 4 foot 0 inch cross tees and the 2 foot 0 inch cross tees if you want to use them. Possible layouts are shown in Figs. D, E, and F, and show some mistakes to be avoided. Then make up your list of all the materials you need.

Next, strike a level line all around the room, a minimum of

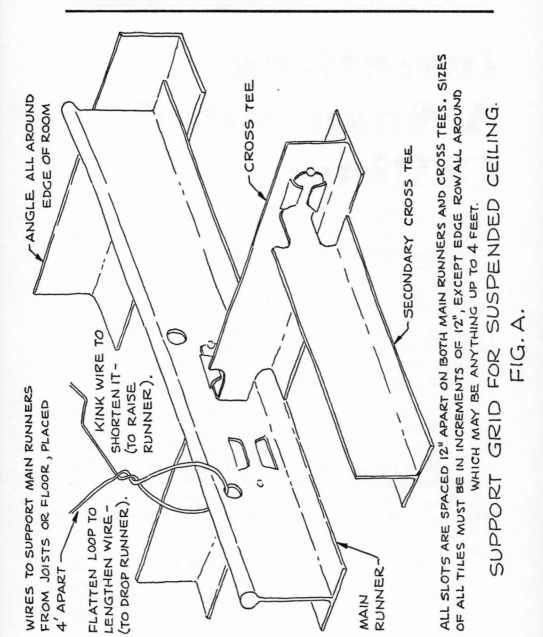

ANGLE ALL AROUND EDGE OF ROOM

CROSS TEE

SECONDARY CROSS TEE

WIRES TO SUPPORT MAIN RUNNERS FROM JOISTS OR FLOOR, PLACED 4' APART

KINK WIRE TO SHORTEN IT — (TO RAISE RUNNER).

FLATTEN LOOP TO LENGTHEN WIRE — (TO DROP RUNNER).

MAIN RUNNER

ALL SLOTS ARE SPACED 12" APART ON BOTH MAIN RUNNERS AND CROSS TEES. SIZES OF ALL TILES MUST BE IN INCREMENTS OF 12", EXCEPT EDGE ROW ALL AROUND WHICH MAY BE ANYTHING UP TO 4 FEET.

SUPPORT GRID FOR SUSPENDED CEILING.

FIG. A.

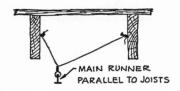

MAIN RUNNER
PARALLEL TO JOISTS

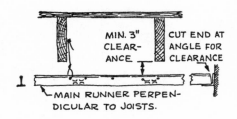

MIN. 3"
CLEAR-
ANCE

CUT END AT
ANGLE FOR
CLEARANCE

1

MAIN RUNNER PERPEN-
DICULAR TO JOISTS.

HOW TO HANG
MAIN RUNNERS
FIG. B.

NOTE: 1 INDICATES MAIN RUNNERS (4' APART); 2 INDICATES
CROSS TEES; 3 INDICATES SECONDARY CROSS TEES.

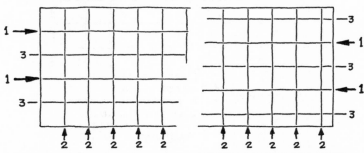

THIS LAYOUT REQUIRES ROOM
TO BE EXACT MULTIPLE OF 2 FT.

LAYOUT ALLOWS FOR IRREG-
ULARITIES IN SIZE AND SHAPE

WHEN ROOM IS OUT OF SQUARE,
SLOTS FOR CROSS TEES MUST
LINE UP SQUARELY, THE DIFFER-
ENCE BEING MADE UP BY EXTRA
LENGTH IN THE MAIN RUNNERS
(AND IN THE SECONDARY CROSS
TEES, IN THIS EXAMPLE).

LAYOUT OF SUSPENDED CEILING TILES.
FIG. C

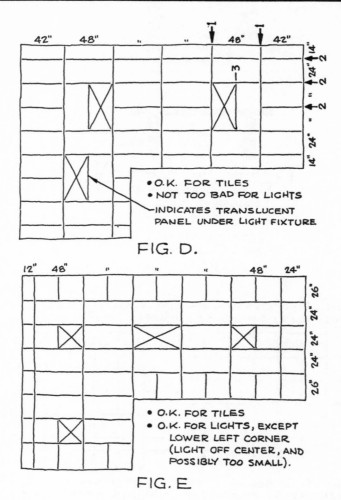

FIG. D.

• O.K. FOR TILES
• NOT TOO BAD FOR LIGHTS
—INDICATES TRANSLUCENT
PANEL UNDER LIGHT FIXTURE

• O.K. FOR TILES
• O.K. FOR LIGHTS, EXCEPT
  LOWER LEFT CORNER
  (LIGHT OFF CENTER, AND
  POSSIBLY TOO SMALL).

FIG. E

three inches below the old ceiling or the joists, allowing enough room for the grid to pass under any low-hanging obstruction.

The best way to do this is to use a level along with the chalk line. Drive a nail in the wall at one corner, attach chalk line, stretch the chalk line across the wall. Have a helper hold it tight. Then hold the level close and parallel to the line but not touching it. Direct your helper to raise or lower his end of the line and follow it with the level. When level, snap it against the wall. Extend the line around the corner and repeat the operation on the next three walls.

NO TILES CAN BE OVER 24" IN BOTH DIRECTIONS.
CORNERS ① ARE NOT POSSIBLE.

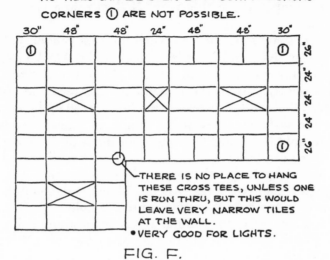

FIG. F.

The end of the fourth line should meet at the end of the first line. If there is an error, split the difference and strike the first line to meet the fourth line at a middle point. After the level line is complete, nail wall angle (also comes with system) on all around the room. Or better yet, use solid crown molding instead of wall angle.

Next, mark the walls where the ends of the main runners will fall (both ends of all main runners). Although the main runner is 12 feet long it will only span 11 feet in one piece. This is because it is designed with slots to receive the cross tees at one foot intervals, but the first slot is only six inches from the end. If the room is 12 feet, in order that the grid be symmetrical, you have to cut six inches off one end and add it on the other.

With this in mind measure for the width of the first tile from the center of one slot. Mark the runner and cut off the excess. Now measure for the overall length of the runner. Add another runner, or a piece of one, to it if necessary. Allow 1/4 inch for clearance. Use a sturdy pair of tin snips to cut the grid members. Cut the top part of the tee at a slight angle so it won't interfere with the wall.

Rest the runner on the wall molding on its marks and hang it at the center temporarily with a wire. Nail wire to a joist with large headed nails.

Use the same procedure to install the next runner on its marks four feet away. Next, install at least three 4 foot 0 inch cross tees to keep the runners spaced properly. Hang these two runners semipermanently. Install the remaining cross tees and lay in two tiles. Check the grid for square. It can be squared up by moving the ends on the wall moldings or by shims on opposite ends of the runners to hold them slightly away from the wall. Now hang these two runners permanently.

An easy way to get the runner level is to cut wires about 9 inches longer than you actually need. Then, as detailed in Fig. A, make a loop in it where it is attached to the hole in the runner and fasten the other end to the ceiling. To lower the runner all you need to do is to pull on it to stretch or lengthen the loop. To raise the runner just kink the wire with pliers. The wire used is heavy enough to hold whatever shape you make it.

Now complete the grid in the same manner. Leave the cross tees that reach the wall to last. Lay in several more tiles to check the grid for square. When you are satisfied that the grid is O.K. put in the cross tees around the walls. Cut these about an eighth of an inch short so that you don't force the grid out of square.

Now install 2 foot 0 inch cross tees if you are going to use them. Remove the large tiles if necessary, then lay in all the tiles.

You can cut the tiles with a sharp utility knife with a steel square as a guide. If you are going to use electrical fixtures that fit into the grid, you have to hang them separately—the grid will not support their weight.

Chapter 12

Installing Resilient Flooring

Resilient tile is called that because the tile gives, or yields, when you step on it. There are various types of tile available, each with advantages and disadvantages.

Linoleum tiles. These aren't very popular—most people prefer the sheet linoleum. One advantage is that they can be used anywhere in the house, even where moisture is present as in the basement. Also, they're inexpensive.

Asphalt tile. These are the least expensive tiles you can get, but they are commonly available only in dark colors. They can be installed on all types of floors including cement. On the negative side, asphalt tiles crack easily, are brittle and hard to cut. Sometimes they have to be heated so they can conform to floor bulges, and for more intricate cuts, such as around door molding. (You can hang them on the grill of an electric heater for warming—make certain they don't melt.) A shingle cutter works well for cutting. Also, they are dissolved easily by turpentine, benzine, and paint thinners.

Vinyl-asbestos tiles. These are the most popular tiles. They come in various grades and thicknesses. They are much less brittle than asphalt tiles, come in a greater variety of colors, are much more resistant to solvents, and are easier to cut. It does help to heat them before intricate cutting.

Vinyl tiles. These are divided into two groups: Regular tiles and translucent tiles. They're easier to walk on—they're softer, they can be cut with scissors, and they come in a tremendous variety of colors. Disadvantages are that they tend to scratch more readily than vinyl-asbestos and are much more expensive. Regular vinyl tiles are sold in various grades. The thicker the tile, the better.

Translucent tiles must have a uniform light color underneath. To achieve this, use clean plywood underlayment. The adhesive you use is white latex. These have a 3-D effect when you look at them. They have the same advantages and disadvantages as regular vinyl tiles.

INSTALLING RESILIENT TILE

Most people are not too concerned by the prospect of putting in floor tile. The real problem is exactly how to prepare the floor. It all depends on what is on the floor now.

Linoleum.   The tile can go on without further preparation; that is if the linoleum is sound, there are no lumps, bumps, or heavily worn spots, no places where the linoleum is cracked from the boards beneath, and no nailheads have broken through. If there are such problems, they must be corrected.

Bulges.   Bulges are commonly caused by bulging underlayment; hardboard may have expanded from humidity and plywood, another common underlayment, may have delaminated (come apart). To correct the problem, first use a sharp linoleum knife to cut away the linoleum over the bulge. Cut a rectangle that's big enough to include material over the bulge. Then cut out the underlayment with a circular saw, or if you have to, chop it out with hammer and chisel. Sometimes you don't have to take it out—it'll fall out by itself. Then replace it with a piece of plywood or hardboard in the same thickness. (Some cabinetmakers have scraps of plywood or hardboard they'll be glad to have you haul away.)

Nail the underlayment patch down with underlayment nails —small head annular ring nails. If it's hardboard place the rough side up. Space nails about two inches apart around the edges— absolutely no further—and four inches apart inside the piece (see Fig. A). Underlayment has a tendency to buckle and close nailing will keep it down tight. Next, cut a linoleum patch to fit and adhere

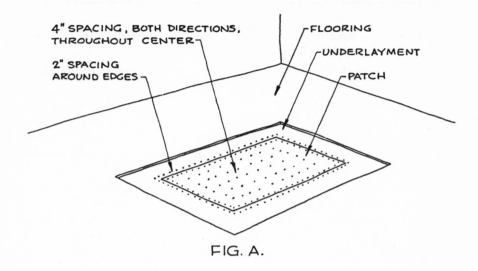

4" SPACING, BOTH DIRECTIONS, THROUGHOUT CENTER

2" SPACING AROUND EDGES

FLOORING

UNDERLAYMENT

PATCH

FIG. A.

it with linoleum paste or use cheaper tile cement. Linoleum comes in various thicknesses and you want to make certain you get the proper size. Best bet is to take a piece of the old linoleum to your tile store dealer and show it to him. He may have odd pieces of linoleum around and will give you what you need free, especially since you'll be buying your tiles from him. Incidentally, it may be that the tile you're using will be the same thickness as the patch needed.

This procedure is only for patches less than a couple of square feet in area. Making a large patch in a small floor is not worth the extra effort. On the other hand, a small patch on a large floor that will keep you from having to put underlayment all over is worth it.

Loose nails.   By this, I mean loose underlayment nails. You'll see little bulges, or nailhead-size worn spots in the linoleum. These must come out. To get each nail out, just cut out the linoleum close to the edge of the nail head. Hook the nail with a claw or tack hammer and pull it out. After pulling, fill the holes up with plaster or some other filler you have handy. If the problem is extensive—you'd spend too much time removing them—it may be best to take up the linoleum and possibly the underlayment.

Linoleum cracked from boards.   Here you'll usually see the outlines of the boards. The problem is usually caused by the boards expanding and contracting; the linoleum, which is glued to it, does not expand and contract—and you get the lines.

One other thing. The material on the floor may not be true linoleum but some other material (true linoleum is glued in place) and should be taken up. If a problem is extensive you can take up the linoleum—and the underlayment. If you try to just take off the linoleum it can cause even more problems.

To do this, you usually have to pry off the base molding to lift the linoleum and underlayment out. Just pry it off and discard it—no loving care is necessary. Removing underlayment is practical only if it is loose, as indicated by squeaking. However, if all your efforts fail to really budge it, then you have another option which is to cover the entire floor with underlayment. If you do this, and there are parts of existing underlayment that must be replaced, you don't have to make a precise patch. Just insert a piece of plywood as thick as the combined thickness of the existing underlayment and the linoleum.

If you've taken up the underlayment to the subfloor I recommend at least a half inch of plywood. But you could go thicker and it can work out well. For example, if you have 3/4 inch thick oak floors in rooms or halls adjacent to the room you're tiling, you can use 5/8 inch underlayment and 1/8 inch tile and it all adds up to 3/4 inch, and will be flush with the adjacent floors. You won't have an annoying little drop or bump between floors. The plywood sheets should run at right angles to the joists regardless of what way the subflooring runs. (Subflooring, incidentally, could be plywood, or boards, or 1 by 4 square edge, or 1 by 6 tongue and groove stock.) You can tell which way joists run by observing how the subflooring was nailed into them (see Fig. B).

Nail the underlayment through the plywood, subflooring, and into the joists with eightpenny resin coated box nails or eightpenny steel cut nails. I wouldn't use anything else (unless it was 4:30 and I had to!). The plywood should be cut and fitted so that the ends butt on a joist. (See Fig. C.) If subflooring boards are at a right angle to joists, locate edges of underlayment on board centers (Fig. D). In the case of diagonal subflooring it doesn't matter where the edge

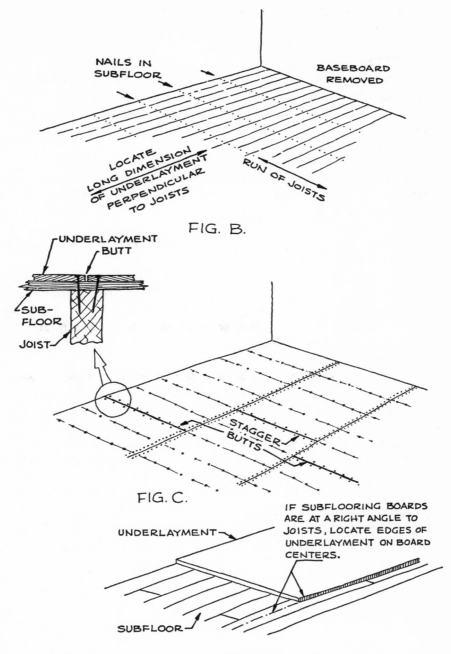

NAILS IN SUBFLOOR

BASEBOARD REMOVED

LOCATE LONG DIMENSION OF UNDERLAYMENT PERPENDICULAR TO JOISTS

RUN OF JOISTS

FIG. B.

UNDERLAYMENT
BUTT
SUB-FLOOR
JOIST

STAGGER BUTTS

FIG. C.

UNDERLAYMENT

IF SUBFLOORING BOARDS ARE AT A RIGHT ANGLE TO JOISTS, LOCATE EDGES OF UNDERLAYMENT ON BOARD CENTERS.

SUBFLOOR

FIG. D.

comes. If you don't do as suggested, the plywood can work up and down and crack the tile. If the subfloor is plywood the problem usually doesn't occur, but don't let your edge joints fall over your plywood subfloor joints.

Underlayment nailing should be on a schedule of 2 to 3 inches apart on edge seams and the ends nailed 3 to 4 inches apart where they butt and six to eight inches apart through the middle of the plywood. So installed, the underlayment is securely nailed all around the edge and there's no chance of any spring (or "whip" as the professionals say) in the middle. If there is springiness you haven't nailed properly. The idea is to get everything down nice and tight. You don't have to fit the plywood flush against walls; it can be up to one inch from them. It is also necessary when placing the plywoods, to stagger the pieces so all the ends do not fall on one joist (see Fig. C). In so doing you won't put excess stress on any particular joist and you won't need to drive so many nails into it so that it splits. When you can't get the floor up easily the underlayment can go on top. For this, use 1/4 inch untempered hardboard (this is not as hard as tempered, and is not resistant to weather). Do not use tempered because the nailheads won't sink properly—you'll have bumps all over. Hardboard is commonly available in 4 by 4 foot sheets, and 4 by 8 foot sheets.

Put hardboard rough side up. Nail it on with underlayment nails, or you can rent an underlayment staple gun, following the same nailing schedule as with the patch. When doing this on a patched floor make certain that the hardboard covers the patches completely—doesn't butt on it—to be certain there's no unevenness in the underlayment. Or, if you have one crack down in the middle you don't butt over that. When plywood or hardboard is nailed off scrape across the nails with a broad-bladed putty knife. If the knife passes over nails, fine; if not, set nails deeper using a hammer and blunt (1/8 inch) nail set. Make certain the knife will pass over the nails—pass knife in various directions. Nailheads could be cockeyed and you could miss this if you just go over them from one angle.

Existing tile.   If you can replace a few tiles, that's it. If the tiles are bad—worn, cracked—use underlayment.

Cement floor with tile, such as the asphalt tiles commonly used in Levitt homes. Here, if the tiles are in bad shape, they have to come up. You can't put underlayment on because you can't nail into the concrete. You may be able to simply scrape them up. If you can get some up and not others, take off as many as you can and level the tile-less areas with Dash Patch mixed with your tile cement (ratio is on can). Use a big square trowel, feathering it in toward the middle of the area that's tile-less. (Dry ice, incidentally, is supposed to work at taking up tile though we've never used it.) This removal method depends on your skill with a trowel; if you're not handy with it it's best to try to get all the tile up. If the cement floor is in really bad shape—cracked, deeply worn, etc.—you have a major job. It has to be leveled. It probably shouldn't be attacked by a home owner. If you have sufficient headroom you can have a two inch concrete floor put over the whole thing. If not, the only solution is to break up the old floor and cart it away and build a new floor. I won't tell how to do this because, if you're like me, you wouldn't do it anyway. If, by the way, tiles are sound, the new ones can go right over them.

LAYING OUT THE TILE

The layout for floor tile is much the same as for ceiling tile except that it is not nearly so critical for good looks to get the edges of the border tiles an even size. Furniture, rugs, and the visual uniformity of the tile pattern obscure the borders to a large extent. In a very large room it is a good idea to lay out the tiles so that they don't need to be cut (they fit in whole) along the longest wall; do this on two walls if you can. Just be sure that you don't leave the other walls of the room with a too narrow strip (less than 3 inches). The smaller the room the more important it is to get even borders. How to achieve this is explained later.

Different adhesives are used to install different types of tile. For asphalt or vinyl-asbestos tile an emulsion type paste is used. The latter can be spread on an entire floor before installing any tiles and offers two advantages: (1) You don't have to handle glue and tiles at the same time . . . it's cleaner. (2) It's faster. You lay all the whole tiles before having to cut any.

The adhesive for vinyl tile can only be spread for five or six tiles at a time. This can best be handled by having an assistant spread the adhesive while you place the tiles.

It's best to lay out the floor with squared-up guidelines before you begin laying out tiles. You want two of these lines to intersect near a door. Using the recommended adhesive means that you have to cover the whole floor at one time, so you have to start laying them near the door since you can't walk on the adhesive.

The layout shown in Fig. E is for a difficult room—one with two jogs. Most problems are illustrated in it and examining it will give you a good idea of the method involved.

Start by measuring 12-1/4 inches out from the longest wall at each end. Strike a chalk line between these two points. Measure from the line to the wall at a number of places to make sure that the 12 inch tile will cover all along the wall. The wall may be bowed in some places. The 1/4 inch will be covered by the floor molding, and will save cutting narrow strips off tiles to make them fit. If the space is too great, move the line closer to the wall until the tiles will cover.

Next, measure from this line to the opposite wall in several places to see if the border tile will turn out to be an acceptable size—at least 3 inches wide. If it does, snap a parallel line an even number of feet away from the first line that bisects a door opening. If less than 3 inches move both lines over to get even border tiles on each side. You must end up with a line that goes through a door. Next, strike another line, this one 12-1/4 inches from the wall on the door side or, as shown in Fig. E, in a jog on that side. This line must square with the first one you drew. To insure this mark off a 3-4-5 triangle. If in a jog, measure even feet into the room so you can draw another line that goes through the one that goes through the door. These bisecting lines will be obscured by adhesive later so it will be necessary to replace them. Drive a nail in the wall as close to the floor as possible (or on the floor) at the ends of the guidelines. Attach chalk lines to each nail securing the ends temporarily on a nail driven in over the doorway.

Spread the adhesive over the entire floor, except the spot in the doorway where the two lines cross. Wait as long as the directions on the can suggest, then take the lines down one at a time, draw each taut across the cross on the floor and strike.

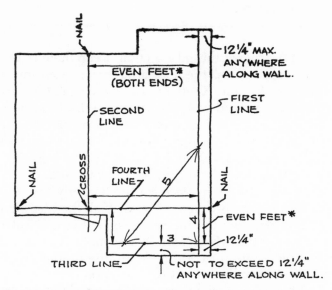

NAIL

12¼" MAX. ANYWHERE ALONG WALL.

EVEN FEET* (BOTH ENDS)

FIRST LINE

SECOND LINE

NAIL

CROSS

FOURTH LINE

5

NAIL

EVEN FEET*

12¼"

3   4

THIRD LINE

NOT TO EXCEED 12¼" ANYWHERE ALONG WALL.

* FOR 12"×12" TILE; OTHERWISE MULTIPLE OF TILE DIMENSIONS, AND CORRESPONDING EDGE DIMENSIONS WILL BE ¼" GREATER THAN TILE DIMENSIONS.

FIG. E.

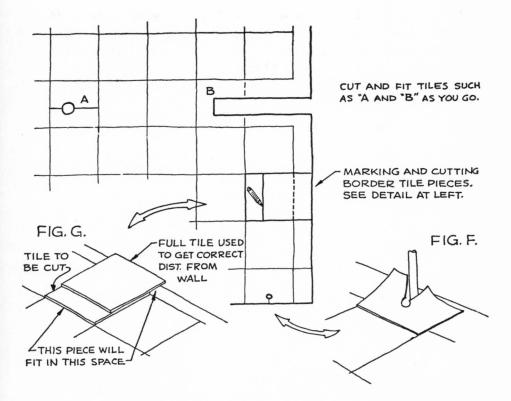

A   B

CUT AND FIT TILES SUCH AS "A" AND "B" AS YOU GO.

MARKING AND CUTTING BORDER TILE PIECES. SEE DETAIL AT LEFT.

FIG. G.

TILE TO BE CUT

FULL TILE USED TO GET CORRECT DIST. FROM WALL

FIG. F.

THIS PIECE WILL FIT IN THIS SPACE

Start laying the tiles at this intersection. Keep them right on the lines. As you proceed across the floor always start each row on the line and work away from it. Keep a sharp eye on the tile pattern if any. Some tiles are marked with arrows on the back, some have a grain to them and are turned alternately to form sort of a checkerboard pattern; some may be laid any way at all. With the exception of an obstruction, such as a Lally column, which you must fit around as you go (Fig. F), lay all whole tiles before you cut any.

After all whole tiles are in place cut the border pieces to fit. To mark a tile for cutting simply follow Fig. G. If all the tiles along one wall are the same size, use the tile piece you cut as a template and cut enough tiles for the whole wall. If the pieces are less than 6 inches cut two pieces from each tile. If one tile borders two walls, mark it from the two walls and cut out the corner.

To cut asphalt tiles straight use an asbestos shingle cutter. To cut corners out or curves first heat the tiles with an electric space heater and cut with scissors. The heater may also be used to heat tiles that won't lie flat on the floor. Asphalt tiles take several days before they lie flat.

Vinyl asbestos tile may be cut with a shingle cutter but 1/16 inch thick tiles must be cut two at a time (or one backed up with a piece of scrap). These tiles may also be cut by scoring them with a sharp utility knife and snapping them.

Vinyl tile cuts with a sharp knife or a scissors. Tin snips or good shears may also be used.

Chapter 13

Hanging A Door

There are two types of doors, interior and exterior. Both types can be further divided into flush and sash kinds (Fig. A). Picking a door that fits your needs is your first decision. Here are the different types:

FLUSH

The difference between the interior and exterior flush door is the glue—on the exterior type the glue is weatherproof. Also, the exterior doors almost always come 1-3/4 inches thick; the interior ones are normally 1-3/8 inches thick. The thicker the door the greater the resistance to warping. The exterior type, exposed to weather, would have a great tendency to warp.

Flush interior and exterior doors come solid and hollow—the door has a wooden frame around the edge with a plywood skin over this on both sides and solid blocks of wood where the hole for the lock will be drilled. The rest of the door is filled with honeycombed paper, little wood strips, cardboard, or other filler to give rigidity.

When the door is solid it is made of lumber core plywood—a solid core of wood faced on both sides by a veneer or skin of other wood.

Veneer on flush doors, either solid or hollow core is usually luan, a fairly cheap wood, but it is also commonly available in birch; you can also get ash or oak but it's not as common. Hollow doors can also be obtained with plain hardboard skins.

Veneer differs in quality. Some have excellent grain and are suitable for staining. Other veneer does not have good grain and is only good for painting. An examination of the various veneers will show you the difference. Normally, lumberyards do not carry particularly good doors in terms of veneer, just those meant for painting.

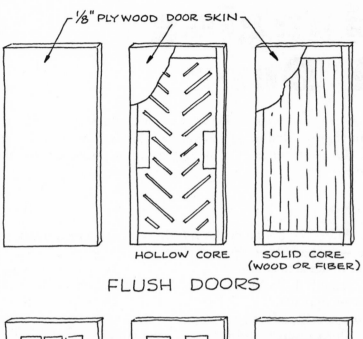

⅛" PLYWOOD DOOR SKIN

HOLLOW CORE   SOLID CORE
                  (WOOD OR FIBER)

FLUSH DOORS

SOLID WOOD "SASH DOORS"
AND ENTRANCE DOORS
FIG. A.

SASH DOORS

Sash doors are also available in interior and exterior types. A sash door is composed of parts, rather than being one solid surface like a flush door; the word sash comes from the fact that it's built like a window.

Sash doors come 1-3/8 inches and 1-3/4 inches thick, the same as flush doors. Normally, they are used as exterior doors—either for a house entrance, back door to a garage, or pantry entrance. I recommend that you get the thicker size for exterior use.

There is a much greater variety of styles in the sash type than in flush doors. Flush doors can be gotten with windows inserted (called "lights" in the trade), but the rest of the door will be flush. With a sash door, there are not only many different types of windows, but a great many designs—cross buck, panel, and so forth.

Normally, the lumberyard will have catalogues that break the doors down into "entrance doors," "flush doors," and "sash doors." All doors come unfinished.

For interior use you can use any kind of door you wish, because it doesn't have to stand up to the rigors of the weather. Generally, the plainer and simpler the door, the less you'll pay for it. But this doesn't mean that you can't get a good quality door. The more decorations or parts to the door—glass—decoration—the more you'll pay for it.

LOUVER DOORS

For closets, you can also get louver doors, or one with blinds of some type. These come 1-1/8 and 1-3/8 inches thick. While a 1-1/8 door could be used as a regular door, they are really suited to only closets, dividers, and the like. Regular doors or even large closet doors should be 1-3/8 inches thick.

Doors come without hinges. For 1-3/8 inch interior doors and all hollow-core doors you should use a pair of 3-1/2 by 3-1/2 inch butt hinges. For solid doors, 1-3/4 inch thick, you should use a pair and a half of 4 by 4 inch butt hinges. In other words, three hinges. For extremely heavy doors (we're talking 3 feet wide by 7 feet high) you can get special hinges with ball bearings and other specialized hardware. Hinges are steel plated with brass.

DOOR SIZES

Doors come in standard heights and widths, in increments of 2 inches running from 1 foot to 3 feet, 0 inches wide and standard heights of 6 feet, 6-6, 6-8, and 7 feet 0 inches; also 15 and 42 inches wide.

The commonest interior doors and exterior doors used are:

> For bathrooms: 2 feet by 6 feet 8 inches
> For bedrooms: 2 feet 6 inches by 6 feet 8 inches
> Backdoor to house: 2 feet 6 inches or 2 feet 8 inches by 6 feet 8 inches
> Front door: 3 feet by 6 feet 8 inches (on modern house and 7 feet on older house)

The very narrow doors are used in pairs as bifold doors or hinged together.

These are nominal sizes but actual sizes of sash doors can be up to 1/4 inch larger.

MEASURING FOR THE DOOR

If you're installing an entrance door, chances are that you'll have to plane or cut it down to fit in the existing framework. If you're putting in any interior door, you have a fifty-fifty chance that the door will fit into the opening without any cutting necessary. The reason for this discrepancy is the way the original interior and exterior door frameworks were installed, something we don't have to get into.

To measure for the door, first measure for height from the floor to the headpiece of the frame. Then measure for width.

In the great majority of cases (90 percent is a conservative figure) you'll need either a 6 foot 8 inch or a 7 foot high door. It will have to be cut to allow for the thickness of the saddle—the metal or wood piece on the floor beneath the door when it is closed. The door must clear this, of course. Usually, the saddle with be 3/4 inch thick, but they come thicker and thinner. The goal is to get a door that has an eighth of an inch clearance at top and bottom—that 1/8 inch is the maximum clearance. Anything more and the door will have too much space around it.

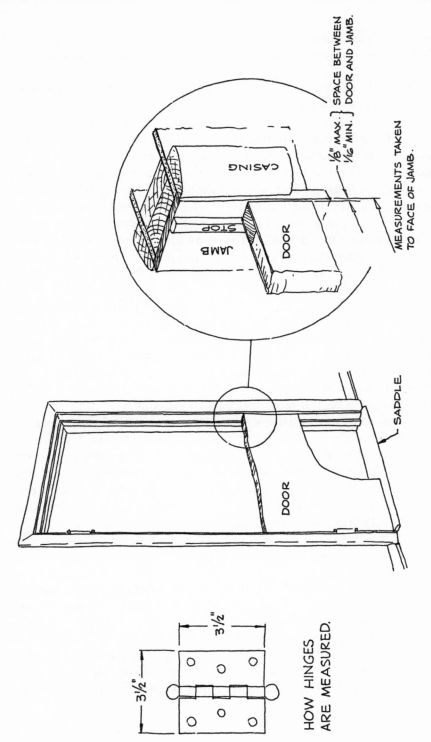

SPACE BETWEEN DOOR AND JAMB.

1/8" MAX. } 1/16" MIN. }

MEASUREMENTS TAKEN TO FACE OF JAMB.

CASING

JAMB STOP

DOOR

DOOR

SADDLE

FIG. B.

3 1/2"

3 1/2"

HOW HINGES ARE MEASURED.

On the width or sides of the door you also want clearance that doesn't exceed 1/8 inch on each side (Fig. B). Ideally, you would order a door that is perfect. But it is far more likely that you'll have to trim it. So try to get one that is close enough in width so you don't have to trim more than a total of one inch. Commonly, the width of the opening is three feet. So in this case you'd just have to order a three-foot wide door, and would only have to trim it 1/16 inch on each side. But if the opening were 3 feet 1/2 inch you'd have to order a door 3 feet 2 inches wide (based on two inch increments) and trim it down to size 3 feet 3/8 inch). There are some door designs that will not permit more than a fraction trimmed off each side.

While you can get the door delivered it's probably better —because of the rather poor way materials are handled these days—to pick it up yourself. In this way if it's damaged you can reject it on the spot. But don't be arbitrary about it. If any of the edges are dented or marred and you're going to trim them anyway, the door is okay. If you reject it and order another, you might have the same problem. It's fairly hard today to get a door that is not marred in some small way, at least on the edges. Of course if the door is marred on the face you shouldn't accept it.

Some doors are guaranteed against warping and delaminating (in the case of plywood), but the guarantee, as with anything else, is only as good as the manufacturer behind it. Read the guarantee carefully. In some cases you have to seal (paint) the bottom and top edges—something most people don't normally do—to make the guarantee good. Unsealed bottom and top edges can allow moisture to penetrate and warp the door.

HANGING AN OUTSIDE DOOR

First, let's not assume that we have a rectangular frame (jamb). Indeed, I sometimes think that frames are more commonly like parallelograms, or trapezoids!

Remove the weatherstrip, if any, and the door stop and the thin boards nailed to the inside of the door frame. A pry bar works well.

Remove the saddle if you can do so without damaging any existing floor covering, such as tile, that the saddle may be resting on or under. This makes fitting the door in the opening easier. Of course, if the saddle is in poor condition—worn, chewed-up—you should replace it. To remove the saddle, first take the screws out, then use a pry bar to lift it up, and a hammer to bang it away from the floor covering toward the outside of the house. This will minimize damage to floor covering. Make sure when removing all of the parts, to take out all the nails from the jamb. Here's a good trick for metal weatherstrip: pry the strips out gently and gradually so the nails are withdrawn with it if possible. Nails that can't be pulled will have to be driven in and set.

With the frame cleaned out, take the lock strike plate and hinges off it.

Next, cut the horns (the projections on the top of the door used to protect it in handling) off the door with a circular or cross-cut saw. Then cut enough off the bottom of the door so that if hung it would just clear the floor, not the saddle.

Try the door for fit. Just lean it in from the inside. It's likely that you won't be able to. The sides will be too wide. You'll have to plane or saw them down somewhat to be able to slide it in. Very often you'll only have to plane it in a few places. But if it requires taking off a lot of wood—more than 1/4 inch, saw an equal amount off each side.

To mark the door for cutting set it against the framework on the inside, making the sides parallel with the sides of the jamb. Many times this will mean that the door is not resting on the floor exactly because the frame is not parallel. A good way to hold it in place is to wedge a screwdriver under the high corner (Fig. C).

Then, have someone hold the door and go outside and mark it for cutting with a pencil as shown in Fig. D. When you get your marks, saw or plane as needed, just cutting next to, but not obliterating the lines. Follow the grain when planing and use a sharp plane. If you're not following the grain the plane will jam; sometimes, by the way, grain will run two different ways on the edge of the door (Fig. E). With the door planed put it back in the opening. If it doesn't fit plane it again. Take off as little as possible to make it fit.

When you can, fit the door into the opening, push it in place and use a screwdriver at the bottom edge as a wedge to jack it up so

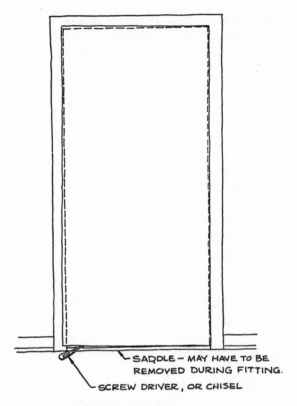

SADDLE – MAY HAVE TO BE
REMOVED DURING FITTING.

SCREW DRIVER, OR CHISEL

VIEW FROM INSIDE

FIG. C.

the top edge fits against the headpiece. It likely will not fit perfectly.
Rather, one side will be higher than the other. Anyway, jam it up
there, then follow Fig. D to scribe it with a pencil. Trim off excess
with plane and/or saw as needed.

With this done, reinsert it in the opening. If it doesn't fit plane
down again as needed. When the door fits snugly into the opening
concern yourself with the hinge side. It should be absolutely true
with the jamb. To tell, look at the joint where door meets the jamb
from top to bottom. If you see daylight all along in one unbroken
line, fine (you won't). Wherever you don't see daylight means that
the door has high spots. So mark these off with your pencil and plane
them off.

WHEN TRIMMING TO THE LINE
MARKED AS SHOWN HERE, TRIM
A LITTLE LESS SO THE LINE RE-
MAINS ON THE DOOR.

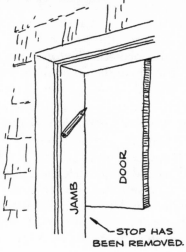

JAMB

DOOR

STOP HAS
BEEN REMOVED.

VIEW FROM OUTSIDE

FIG. D.

USE VERY SHARP PLANE, SET FINE —
OR RASP OR SAW — ON END GRAIN

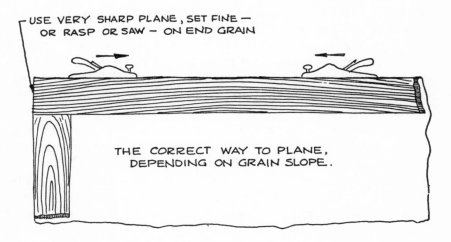

THE CORRECT WAY TO PLANE,
DEPENDING ON GRAIN SLOPE.

FIG. E.

Next step is to mount the hinges. Put the door in place, wedging it there with a shim of some sort between head and jamb, such as a fourpenny finishing nail or a couple of thicknesses of cardboard from the hinge box, or a piece of 1/16 inch plastic laminate.

Next, mark the door and the jamb mortises (recesses for hinges) where the hinges will be located. The top of the top hinge should be about 5 inches from the top of the door, the bottom hinge (its top) 12 inches off the floor. The middle hinge should be equally spaced. You should mark both the door and the jamb. The existing mortises can also be used if they're in good condition—have solid wood for driving screws and are in the proper positions.

Next, use a butt gauge (a metal pattern of a hinge) to outline the hinge patterns on door and jamb, driving it in place (it has knifelike metal edges) with a hammer. Do the same on the jamb.

Next, use a wide chisel to carefully cut out the mortises. It's best to do this in stages. First, cut out most of the wood with chisel and hammer, then finish off by hand. As you go, try the hinge in the door. It should lie flat and not wobble. If it does it means you've got a high spot.

When hinges fit neatly screw the door leaves in place, but put only one screw into each leaf on the jamb side. Put the door in place, then insert the pins and see how it swings. It may be necessary to drive one of the leaves up to make it fit properly—this is why you don't drive all the screws into the jamb. Then drive the rest of the screws in and try the door to see if it fits.

It probably won't, and it will be necessary to bevel the edge of the door on the lock side so it clears the jamb. To do this close the door against the jamb and mark it from the outside. Then take the door down and plane it to this mark on the outside edge (not off the inside edge).

Try the door to see how it fits. From the inside it should have 1/16 inch clearance to the jamb—at least 1/16 inch but no more than 1/8 inch. Here again you can check for an even line of light at the door edge. If necessary take the door down and trim again. Don't be dismayed if you have to do this a number of times. A well-fitting door will pay for itself in terms of ease of operation and lack of frustration. If the door fits on the three sides check it for fit on the bottom between door and floor. It has to clear anything you plan to put there—rugs or the like—and clear the saddle.

There are a couple of ways you can handle the saddle. You can buy an ordinary 3/4 inch or 5/8 inch thick saddle, and shim it up high enough to make the door clear the rug or buy a high saddle.

To mark the door to clear the saddle, place the saddle on the floor with the end against the door and mark each edge of the door. Don't scribe all along the door. Then use a straightedge to connect both lines. Following this, trim off the bottom of the door with a circular saw. Then install saddle and rehang the door. Check the bottom of the door for fit. If necessary remove the door again and plane where needed. To make this easier you can use a straightedge as a guide for the saw.

The lock is installed next. There are many types of locks and they come with detailed instructions, including a template for marking off the hole on the door.

Chapter 14

Molding

No matter how straight the walls, or level the floor, no matter what grade of lumber is used, or how expensive the paneling, the one thing that shows off a good job or exposes a bad one is the trim—the molding.

TRIMMING WINDOWS AND DOORS

When you trim a normal double-hung window, start out by fitting the stool, usually mistakenly called the sill. It's the molding that completes the window sill inside and is nailed to it. The big idea is to cut notches in the stool so it fits neatly around the mullions and other projecting parts of the window frame.

First, cut the stool (get stool in same thickness and width as used on other windows in room) to extend 3/4 inch beyond where the casing will be on each end. If you are using 2-1/4 inch casing, for example, the stool would extend 3 inches past the window jamb on each end; that is, be a total of 6 inches longer than the sash opening.

Cut the stool to length and mark it 3 inches in from each end. Hold one mark at the edge of one window jamb, the other mark at the edge of the other one. Mark on the stool where the mullion (wood stripping that covers spaces between jambs) edges fall.

Installed, the square edge of the stool (it has molded edge also) should be 1/16 inch from the window sash, with ends fitting tightly against the wall.

To do this, measure the distance from the face of the sash to the edge of the stool and use this measurement to scribe the ends of the stool (Fig. A). Measure each end separately because there may be a slight variation, although measurements should be the same. While you are at it, mark the mullion in the same way. Notch the stool with a fine-tooth handsaw and coping saw, leaving your pencil marks visible.

106

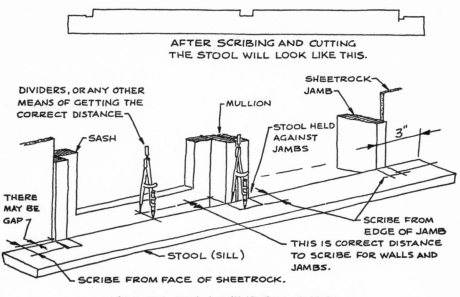

AFTER SCRIBING AND CUTTING
THE STOOL WILL LOOK LIKE THIS.

HOW TO FIT A WINDOW STOOL
FIG. A.

There are other kinds of windows that take slightly different kinds of stools but the general layout is the same. For example, the sash of a picture window may be installed in either the track for where the inside or outside sash of a double-hung window would be. Use 1 by 6 stool if the sash is in the outside position. Scribe stool to fit with the square edge tight against the sash, then scribe the entire length of the flankers (side windows). Shim the stool using scrap wood or perhaps floor molding at the outside edge next to the picture sash to hold it level. Sometimes it helps to chamfer (bevel) off the high edge of the sill to help get the stool to stay level.

FINISHING STOOL

A good clean cut on the ends of the stool is as good a way as any to finish it off, though many carpenters use a small block plane to round

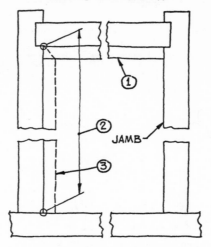

① INSTALL UPPER PIECE OF STOP
   SQUARE AGAINST JAMB ON
   BOTH ENDS.
② MEASURE SIDE PIECES OF STOP
   FULL HEIGHT.
③ CUT SIDE PIECES OF STOP, MITERED
   ON TOP, SQUARE ON BOTTOM.
④ COPE TOP END ALONG CORNER OF
   MITER, AS DESCRIBED FOR CROWN
   MOLDING.

WINDOW OR DOOR STOP

FIG. B.

the edges. To attach stool nail it to the sill right through the face, using sixpenny or eightpenny finishing nails, length depending on stool thickness.

STOP MOLDING

Next install the window stop (Fig. B). Cut all the pieces of stop that you need (each window has two side pieces and one head piece) to approximate length, making one end of each square.

Hold the head piece in place at top of window, mark other end at edge of jamb, and cut to length. Nail stop on with threepenny finishing nails.

On most modern windows the stop is the same width as the distance from the face of the lower sash to the inside edge of the jamb, so you should buy it this wide. On older windows this space is much wider than the stop, but it needn't be more than 1-3/8 inches wide. (Interior door usually uses 1-3/8 inch wide stop molding.) Nails should be countersunk but do this after you have trimmed the whole window; then sink them in order carefully so that you don't miss any.

Hold one side piece up to the jamb, square end resting on the stool and mark it at the jamb head. Do the same with the other side piece, being careful to mark each piece from the side of the window that it will be installed on. Mark both side pieces, making sure to have both a right and a left. Cut each piece on a 45 degree angle and cope to fit the head piece. (I will explain how to do this in the cove molding section of this chapter.)

The window stop either forms the inside member of the track of the lower sash or it is the covering piece for the weatherstrip track. In any case, take care to nail the stop with just enough clearance to allow the sash to move up and down freely. Try the window after the stop is nailed in place and again after nails are set. If you find that it binds, use an old wide chisel to carefully pry it away from the sash to get enough clearance. If this fails remove the molding and nail again. This time try placing a matchbook cover between the stop and sash as a clearance guide.

If you have a picture window installed with a wide stool you should use 1-1/8 inch stop around the sash instead of the parting strip that comes with the window; parting strip will not hold it tight.

DOOR STOP

Door stop is cut and fitted in the same manner as window stop, but when you nail it in place observe the following procedure:

Install the head piece with the door closed and latched, taking care not to force the stop against the door. Nail the stop with 1/16 inch clearance between it and the door. After the stop is in place try the door to make sure that it doesn't bind.

Next, install the stop piece on the hinge side. Don't force, keep your clearance, try the door after each piece is nailed in place. That way if it binds you'll know immediately which piece of stop is at fault. If necessary use a hammer and a block of soft wood to move the stop over, then nail it in its new location.

CASING

Installing the casing—the flat molding that goes around a door and windows—is mainly a matter of cutting good miter joints. Even if you have a very good miter box that cuts perfectly nine times out of ten, the casing probably won't fit simply because walls and windows are seldom perfectly square.

Before finally cutting the casing, test cut some scraps. Hold the pieces together tightly on a flat table and line the pieces up square and check the fit at the joint. Is there space at the outside or inside end of the joint? Raise the outside corner of the miter off the table about 1/4 inch; if it was open at the outside it will close; if it was tight the inside will open. The idea is to simulate a very uneven wall. If your miter box leaves the joint open at the outside of the corner, measure all your moldings at the long end. If it leaves the joint open at the inside, measure at the short end.

INSTALLING CASING

First step is to cut all the pieces you need for all windows and doors to approximate length. (Cutting to approximate length first is a good practice for any molding.) Doing this has a few benefits. You can stand it up against the wall, keeping it out of the way; it will mean less waste and you'll find out immediately if you have enough for the job before the lumberyard closes.

Let's start with the door casing. It is composed of two legs and a head piece.

Stand the leg that fits against the hinges in place. Note that it is a hinge thickness away from the edge of the jamb. As you install the casing, try to maintain this distance all around the door.

Mark the leg at the jamb head as shown in Detail A, Fig. C. Cut the miter in the leg, put in place and tack it there temporarily. Cut a matching miter on the head. Tack in place also. If the joint doesn't fit perfectly, make as many passes as necessary with a sharp, fine-tooth saw (10 point) until it does. To do this you'll have to tap the head closer each time before you cut (Detail B). If the miter is badly off use a sharp block plane to take off most of the wood before you use the saw. Mark wall at Detail C (end of head). Stand leg in place and

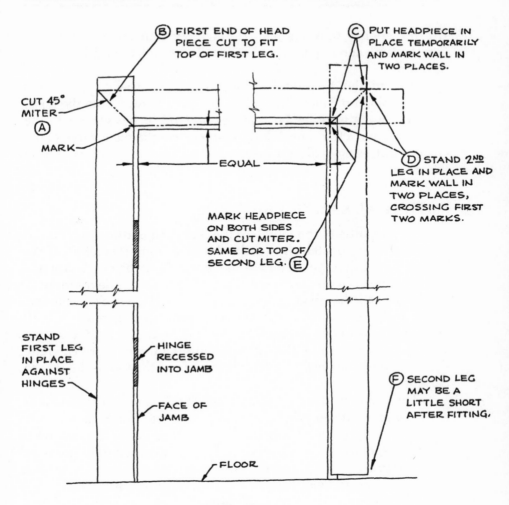

FIG. C.

mark as in Detail D, forming a cross. Also make mark at corner of jamb. Then put head in place and transfer wall marks to it (Detail E). Remove and put the leg in place, also using wall marks to mark it.

Cut the miters, using the marks that will make the pieces longest; this will insure that you don't cut the miters short. Tack both pieces in place, fit the joint, then nail all three pieces solidly.

Use threepenny finishing nails through the thin side of the casing into the jamb and sixpenny finishing nails through the thick side into the studs.

A word about casing: Clamshell casing is usually 2-1/4 inches wide and about 5/8 inch thick on the part that is away from the door. Colonial casing is either 2-1/4 inches or 2-1/2 inches wide with the face molded in a traditional design rather than the plain curve of the clamshell. Casing is always installed with the wide part away from the door.

POTENTIAL CASING PROBLEMS

If you lose a little of the length of the leg when cutting, just raise it off the floor up to 1/8 inch to make the miter tight (Detail F). If the head is a little short you can raise the legs to close the miter. Keep in mind that you can use incorrectly cut pieces in the inside of closets.

When all the casing is nailed and nails set, check the miters again. If either is open at the outside use the claw hammer to pull the corner away from the wall slightly to close the joint. If it is open at the inside run a saw through the joint, and very, very carefully drive a threepenny nail through the joint from the top or the side to close it.

The window casing is fitted like door casing except that no part of the jamb is left showing. Use a piece of casing, square cut on each end, the same length as the head for the apron under the stool. Toenail sixpenny finishing nails through the apron up into the sill to hold it tight.

For an overall view of a trimmed window see Fig. D.

Note: These instructions presume that you are using either a wooden miter box or an inexpensive manufactured one. There are several excellent miter boxes on the market that are quite expensive. These make the job easier, but for just one job the expense is not justified.

COVE AND CROWN

The smaller sizes of these two moldings have solid backs; the larger, recessed ones. Very similar to the small cove in that they are installed the same way, are toe (shoe) molding and quarter round.

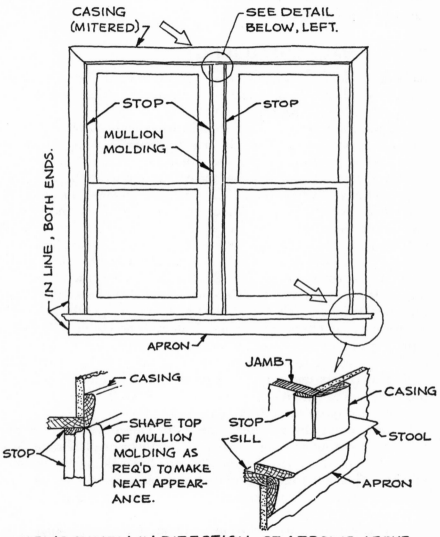

CASING
(MITERED)

SEE DETAIL
BELOW, LEFT.

STOP

STOP

MULLION
MOLDING

IN LINE, BOTH ENDS.

APRON

CASING

STOP

SHAPE TOP
OF MULLION
MOLDING AS
REQ'D TO MAKE
NEAT APPEAR-
ANCE.

JAMB

STOP

SILL

CASING

STOOL

APRON

VIEWS TAKEN IN DIRECTION OF ARROWS ABOVE
WINDOW TRIM
FIG. D.

The most common use for the larger cove and crown molding is at the intersection between the wall and ceiling. Although it is becoming more and more common to finish this joint off with tape and joint cement, moldings are more decorative and are necessary in the case of a paneled wall.

HOW TO MAKE COPED JOINTS

Baseboard, door, or window stop, crown, cove, half- or quarter-round, toe, shoe, and plywood cap moldings should all be fitted at the inside corners with coped joints.

If the room has just four straight walls with no obstructions, follow this procedure to install cove or crown molding; this will illustrate the procedure for all the moldings.

Measure each wall length at the ceiling and write the measurement on the wall where the molding will go. Arrange four pieces of 1-5/8 inch cove molding, each long enough to span one wall in one piece on the floor so that they are in order and face the same way. All the left ends should be cut square and free of cracks. Mark each piece on the edge that will go against the wall (the right end). Examine the cove to make sure that all pieces are turned the same way. If there is any visible difference in the size of the edges, use this to determine which side will be up. Arbitrarily put the side with the widest edge against the ceiling. If there is no visible difference, hold a piece of the cove molding in place in the corner of a carpenter's square to measure the distance that it will cover on each wall. If it covers the same amount on each side then there is no problem; you can use it either way. If there is a difference be careful to keep each piece turned the same way.

Next, miter the molding. There are four ways that you can miter the molding for a corner angle, but only one will be right for a particular corner. To visualize this imagine the molding horizontally in space. Then add to the end of it another piece at right angles. You can form a right angle up, down, toward you, or away from you the four ways the molding can be cut.

What you have to do to avoid a mistake, is mark the molding on the edge that goes against the wall, but place the piece in the miter

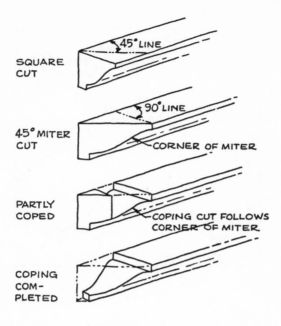

SQUARE CUT — 45° LINE

45° MITER CUT — 90° LINE — CORNER OF MITER

PARTLY COPED — COPING CUT FOLLOWS CORNER OF MITER

COPING COM-PLETED

FIG. E.

box so the marked edge is up. Follow steps in Fig. E to do the job.

Next, using sixpenny finishing nails, tack any one piece of molding temporarily in place with the square end against the wall and a little space at the coped end. For smaller moldings, use fourpenny nails. Put the coped end of the matching piece up against the first piece and nail in place. Sometimes it may be necessary to use a sharp utility knife to trim the coped end a little because walls are not exactly square or something is throwing the molding out of its proper position.

Do the same thing with the third piece as the second, then tuck the square end of the fourth piece under the coped end of the first and fit the coped end to the third piece. Nail in place.

Remove the nails from the first piece and fit the coped end to the fourth piece and nail in place, then set all the nails.

If the room has one or more corners projecting into it you will have to follow a different procedure to fit all the pieces.

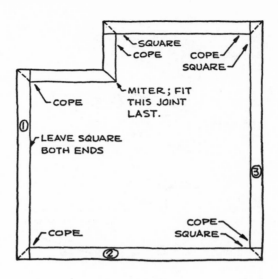

FIG. F.

Start with the longest wall and cut the molding to fit square on both ends (follow Fig. F). Then measure, cut, fit, and nail each piece in order around the room until you come to the projecting or outside corner. Fit this piece by fitting the coped end first, then hold in place and mark the end for the miter cut. Here again mark the molding on the wall edge and keep the marked edge up in the miter box when cutting. This time, however, the molding must be cut longer—angled the other way. Lay the piece aside, then work around the room in the other direction until you come to the outside corner again. Fit this piece the same way you fitted its mate, nailing the longer of the two in place first. Use a sharp block plane to refit the mitered end of the last piece if necessary. If the miter is open slightly, you can close it by using a nail set turned backwards to peen it shut. If the miter is open a lot you will have to cut a new piece.

CORNER GUARD

Corner guard is used, as the name suggests, to protect corners. It is used over paneling at any outside corner, and is commonly used

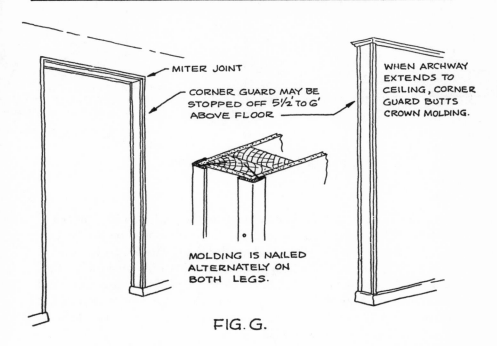

MITER JOINT

CORNER GUARD MAY BE
STOPPED OFF 5½' TO 6'
ABOVE FLOOR

WHEN ARCHWAY
EXTENDS TO
CEILING, CORNER
GUARD BUTTS
CROWN MOLDING.

MOLDING IS NAILED
ALTERNATELY ON
BOTH LEGS.

FIG. G.

around archways and to protect corners of a wallpapered wall. It may
be used in short lengths or go from the baseboard to the cove molding. It can be as long as you wish (Fig. G).

To mark the outside of the corner guard for a miter cut you
must learn to judge the thickness of the molding, and to cut it
shorter by that thickness. Use fourpenny finishing nails to secure the
guard. If there is metal corner bead in the wall drive the nails in
through the faces in pairs from both sides. Otherwise drive the nails
in diagonally from the corner.

When you miter corner guard, use a piece of scrap wood (such
as 3/4 inch by 3/4 inch baluster or 1 inch by 2 inches) to hold the face
up and square. Because of the shape the molding has, it must rest on
a block so you can cut from the face. Cut through this scrap block
along with the corner guard. If you have many cuts to make, tack the
piece of scrap in the miter box with three small finishing nails.

Baseboard molding is handled about the same as cove as far as
sequence and coped joints are concerned. However, it must be done

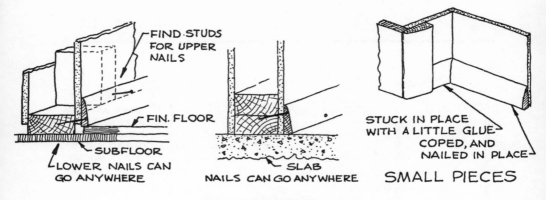

FIND·STUDS
FOR UPPER
NAILS

FIN. FLOOR

SUBFLOOR

LOWER NAILS CAN
GO ANYWHERE

SLAB

NAILS CAN GO ANYWHERE

STUCK IN PLACE
WITH A LITTLE GLUE
COPED, AND
NAILED IN PLACE

SMALL PIECES

INSTALLING BASEBOARD
FIG. H.

after the casing is installed since it butts the casing. Long pieces of baseboard that do not fit tight to the floor may be forced down by first nailing them where they rest on the floor. Then, rest the end of a short (24 inches to 30 inches) piece of wood (1 inch by 4 inches or 2 inches by 3 inches or thereabouts) on the top of the baseboard and the other end of the floor. Push it down with your foot, put your full weight on it if necessary, and nail the baseboard home. Fig. H shows details on installing baseboard.

FLOOR MOLDING

Floor molding, sometimes called shoe or toe molding, is used at the junction between the baseboard and the floor (Fig. I). It should be put down after the finishing flooring and nailed to the floor, not the baseboard. When the floor settles the molding will still cover the space between the baseboard and floor. (Over a concrete floor you will have to nail it to the baseboard, but then the concrete is not likely to pull away from the baseboard.) If wall to wall carpet is to be used, floor molding is not installed.

FLOOR MOLDING
NAILED INTO FLOOR-
ING , NOT INTO
BASEBOARD.

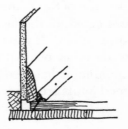

FIG. I

MULLION

To fit mullion, cut it square on both ends to reach from the stool to the casing. At the casing, round it slightly to make it blend into the casing, then nail in place with threepenny finishing nails.

Attic molding is a special molding to be used to cover the obtuse angle between walls and sloping ceiling or between the sloping ceiling and the flat ceiling of an attic room. It is nailed to the rafters with sixpenny finishing nails.

OTHER MOLDING TIPS

Butt joints tend to be hard to align. Therefore, instead of cutting an out-and-out butt when you have to join moldings, cut the ends on matching 45-degree angles. This will allow one piece to bear against the other and help keep them in alignment.

When fitting two pieces of any kind of molding along one wall, cut the longest piece first, miter both ends, cope the end to fit in the corner and nail it in place. Cut the other oversize miter, cope and fit the end in the other corner. Hold it up in place and mark the length and observe the direction of the miter, then cut it and nail in place.

While I am on the subject of moldings there are three plastic moldings made with simulated wood grains in several colors. They are made to fit 1/4 inch thick paneling only, but are very good if the color is suitable for your job.

The three shapes are inside corner, outside corner, and plywood cap. They must be installed as you install the paneling—the panels slip into it. However, it makes a very neat job. Outside corners are particularly good—neat and inconspicuous.

Chapter 15

How to Build A Porch

A very good project for the handy craftsman to embark on is building a porch. This can be built in stages as time and money permit. First, a raised patio slab is built, then a shingled roof put over it. Finally, it is closed in with screens for the summer and aluminum storm windows for the winter.

LOCATION

Your first consideration is location. A hundred years ago the porch was almost always located in the front of the house where the people watched the world go by. Today, with varying legal restrictions such as minimum setback from the road, you usually have to put it on the back.

Remember that, wherever you put the porch, some part of the house will be in shadow that wasn't before. This could be a benefit to a room that is too hot and sunny but be a drawback for one that is short of sun.

Usually, if you can arrange it it's good to have the porch near the kitchen. A screened-in porch is a great place for kids (or anyone, really) to congregate and eat during the summer. You want to keep to a minimum the steps needed to get the food there.

Consider, too, what the new porch will do to your plot and garden. Is your lot small? Will the porch elbow out any activities?

Another consideration is access. In part this depends on what you intend to use the porch for. If it's only to be an occasional gathering spot you can use a regular door which is narrow and might be slightly inconvenient in another situation.

If you intend to use the porch as an extension of an interior living area you can install a three-door unit: two are hinged together, the other is for regular use. When party time rolls around, all you need to do is push the hinged ones back and you've got a three-door opening.

Another option: A sliding glass door. It's larger than a regular door, and it invites people to spend more time on the porch. It also lets in more light than other types. If you want elegance, a pair of big French doors will do the trick. But these are difficult to install tightly.

BUILDING THE RAISED PATIO

Woodwork framing and the like should begin at least a foot above grade (ground) to help discourage termites. One step down from the house is fine. Of course you can't always get an ideal arrangement. If the house is on a slab, for example, woodwork a foot above grade is impractical from a construction standpoint. You may have to extend the slab, have no step down from the house and no foot above grade.

PLAN FOR A 10 FOOT BY 12 FOOT PORCH

First step in building the patio is to mark it out with stakes and string (Fig. A).

TRENCH IS FORM
FOR FOOTING.

STRINGS TO MARK SIZE
OF SLAB.

FIG. A.

Next, dig the trenches for the concrete footing. You can do this with a narrow blade spade. Make each trench 8 inches wide and go below frost line in your area. (8 inches is a minimum but dig it as narrow as is practical.) Check with your local building code department. If the ground slopes you can get the required depth throughout by digging a series of steps in each trench.

As you dig the trenches throw the soil in the center of the slab area. You needn't get trench sides exactly straight. Irregular lines are acceptable.

POUR CONCRETE IN TRENCH

Next, pour concrete until it reaches within a couple of inches of the lowest point of grade. When cured, lay cement (not cinder) blocks. The top of the highest course should be at least 4 inches from the top of the finished level of the existing floor and not more than 8 inches. The top course of block may have to be made of 4 inch blocks. In our figure we show two-block rows. But lay as many blocks as high as necessary to bring it within the 8 inch to 4 inch distance.

Next, build a form of 2 by 6's around the top course of blocks to contain the concrete for the slab. (If the house slab is close to ground, you don't need blocks; secure forms to ground.) The 2 by 6's should be nailed securely to stakes driven into the ground. Brace all form boards; they should be tight against the blocks and secure; wet concrete exerts great pressure. For a series of drawings on footing construction, see Fig. B.

If you are not going to enclose the patio immediately it must be pitched for drainage, one inch of pitch for every 10 feet. A simple way to determine pitch is to nail a 1 inch thick wood block on one end of a straight 10 foot board. Place the board on the top of the form, place level on board with block at outer end, and hammer down the form until you get a level reading.

When form is completed clean all dirt off the tops of the blocks with a stiff brush. You want a clean surface for the concrete. Then, to save on concrete, stuff the voids, or holes in the blocks with tarpaper, old beer cans, anything you wish except wood which rots and feeds termites.

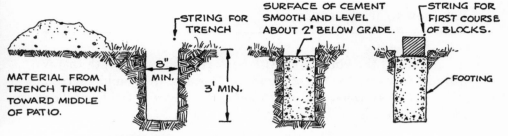

STRING FOR TRENCH

SURFACE OF CEMENT SMOOTH AND LEVEL ABOUT 2" BELOW GRADE.

STRING FOR FIRST COURSE OF BLOCKS.

8" MIN.

3' MIN.

MATERIAL FROM TRENCH THROWN TOWARD MIDDLE OF PATIO.

FOOTING

UNDISTURBED EARTH. BACK-FILL WITH CONCRETE. MAY BE FILLED WITH ANYTHING THAT WONT ROT

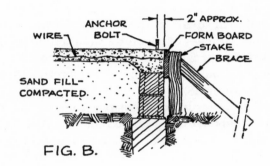

ANCHOR BOLT

WIRE

2" APPROX.

FORM BOARD
STAKE
BRACE

SAND FILL-COMPACTED.

FIG. B.

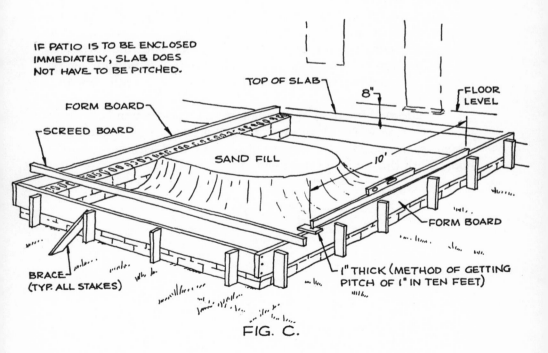

IF PATIO IS TO BE ENCLOSED IMMEDIATELY, SLAB DOES NOT HAVE TO BE PITCHED.

TOP OF SLAB

8"

FLOOR LEVEL

FORM BOARD

SCREED BOARD

SAND FILL

10'

FORM BOARD

BRACE (TYP. ALL STAKES)

1" THICK (METHOD OF GETTING PITCH OF 1" IN TEN FEET)

FIG. C.

Next, fill the porch area with bank run sand to a depth that is within 4 inches of the top of the form. To gauge this, build a screed as for driveway work, and run it along the edges of the form. See Fig. C for details.

POURING CONCRETE

Concrete can be the ready-mixed variety. As in a driveway, prop up 1/8 inch diameter 6-inch square wire mesh with bricks and blocks 2 inches off sand. Pour 4 inches of concrete, then screed it off with the tops of the forms. Or pour 2 inches of concrete, screed it off, place wire mesh, then pour another 2 inches of concrete and level with form boards (see Chapter 28).

Wait until all the water has disappeared from the concrete, then trowel it off with a steel float using semicircular strokes. Try to get it as smooth as possible. Your finish flooring will go on top of it so it should be smooth. If you don't feel capable you can hire a professional for this aspect of the job.

The last step in this part of the job is to install foundation bolts that will secure the posts to the foundation. Stick them down through the cement into the holes in the block until the threaded portion protrudes through about 4 inches. Use one bolt for every post. After placing, trowel around them and leave until concrete dries.

An alternate method of foundation wall construction is the row lock method (Fig. D). Here, the anchor bolts are set between bricks which are mortared to the cement blocks and level with the concrete floor. With this no forms are needed.

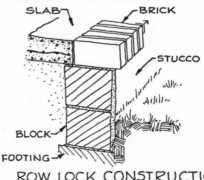

ROW LOCK CONSTRUCTION
ANCHOR BOLTS SET BETWEEN BRICKS

FIG. D.

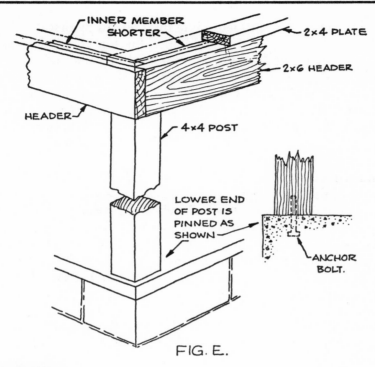

INNER MEMBER
SHORTER
2×4 PLATE
2×6 HEADER
HEADER
4×4 POST
LOWER END
OF POST IS
PINNED AS
SHOWN
ANCHOR
BOLT.

FIG. E.

HEADERS

Headers are made next (Fig. E). They will be of continuous length based on porch dimensions. Each header (there are three, one for front and one each for sides of porch) is composed of 2 by 6 boards. Cut the one for the front first. The outer member of header should be the same length as the width of the slab (10 feet). Make the inner member 3-1/4 inches shorter than this. The outside member of each header is 1-5/8 inches less than overall slab length. Cut the inside member of each 1-5/8 inches shorter than the first piece. When erected the header members form half lab joints.

(These dimensions are based on the thickness of 2 inch dressed stock. The law now allows this to be 1-9/16 inches but both sizes are still around. Always check actual dimensions of lumber before using.)

POSTS

Your vertical supports are 4 by 4 posts. Five are needed: two at the house wall, one at each outside corner of the porch, and one in the center of the outside wall. Determine their length by first deciding where the ceiling will be. It should clear the top of any door and window trim by about 2 inches. Draw a level line across the house siding there, then measure down to the top of the slab. From this dimension deduct the widths of the header and plate. This should be 5-1/2 inches (actual size of nominal 2 by 6) plus width of 2 by 4 plate, 1-1/2 inches. That should be 7 inches but with cutbacks in material the way they are today it's best to hold the pieces together and actually measure to be sure.

This will give the length of the posts at the house wall. To get the length of the corner posts use a straightedge and level to measure the difference between the wall and corner posts. (Corner posts will be longer because the slab slopes—should be 1 inch.)

Now you can start installing posts. Toenail the two posts to the house, making sure they're plumb (check wtih level). Drill a hole in the center of the end of the remaining posts for the bolts to slip into. If the placement of the bolts is not exactly right allow for it when you drill these holes.

Install your first corner post as follows: Slip it over the bolt; have someone hold it in place. Nail on outside member of header; this budges between the post on the house and the corner post. Make a brace to hold post in place.

Slip the other corner post in place and nail on the outside member of the front header. Brace this post, then nail on the outside member on the last header. With your level check to make sure outside posts are plumb in two directions; first hold level on one side, then other side of post. If either is out of plumb you may have to shim out (slip shingle behind the header at the wall or cut them a little shorter). When everything is plumb nail on the inside header members. Drive a nail every 15 inches, first from one side, then the other and so on; putting all nails in from one side could twist the header.

The fifth post should be the same length as the other posts under the outside header even if the header is crowned up slightly. Slide the end over the bolts and plumb it and toenail it to the header. If the post appears short now, it won't be when the weight of the roof is on it.

For details on framing discussed above, see Fig. F.

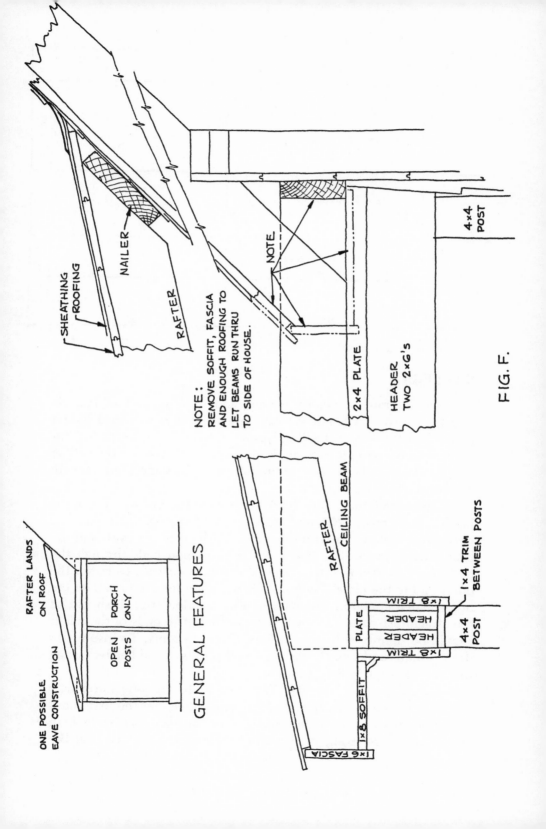

SHEATHING
ROOFING
NAILER
RAFTER

NOTE:
REMOVE SOFFIT, FASCIA
AND ENOUGH ROOFING TO
LET BEAMS RUN THRU
TO SIDE OF HOUSE.

NOTE.

2×4 PLATE

HEADER
TWO 2×6's

4×4
POST

FIG. F.

ONE POSSIBLE
EAVE CONSTRUCTION

RAFTER LANDS
ON ROOF

OPEN PORCH ONLY
POSTS

GENERAL FEATURES

RAFTER
CEILING BEAM

PLATE

1×8 TRIM
HEADER
HEADER
1×8 TRIM

1×4 TRIM
BETWEEN POSTS

4×4
POST

1×8 SOFFIT

1×6 FASCIA

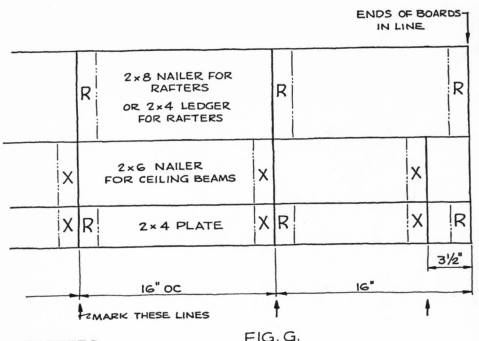

R | 2×8 NAILER FOR RAFTERS OR 2×4 LEDGER FOR RAFTERS | R | | R

X | 2×6 NAILER FOR CEILING BEAMS | X | | X

X R | 2×4 PLATE | X R | | X R

3½"

16" OC | 16"

MARK THESE LINES

FIG. G.

RAFTERS

Lay out the rafters, ceiling beams, and their respective bearing members next. Each rafter rests on a plate and a 2 by 4 ledger secured to the house. Ceiling beams rest on the same plate. For accuracy it is a good idea to mark the plate, the nailer for the ceiling beams, and also the ledger for the rafters at the same time. How to do this is shown in Fig. G.

Then install the plates on top of the headers. Make sure that the headers are straight. Nail on bracing boards to straighten them out if necessary. Follow this with the nailer for the ceiling beams and the beams themselves. Toe five tenpenny common nails through the end of each beam into the nailer and use three nails to fasten the outer end to the plate. Then install the ledger for the rafters on the house wall a minimum of 4 inches below window trim. It should be the straightest piece of 2 by 4 you can find. The ends of the nailer should be plumb with the outsides of side headers. To insure this draw plumb marks on the siding up from outsides of headers using the lines as a guide to placement.

Rafters are all 2 by 6's. The ideal is to use one rafter as a template so you can mark and cut them all alike. Set the first board so one end rests on the nailer, the other on the plate. Scribe the high end to the house wall, then trim off excess (see Fig. H). Set the

128

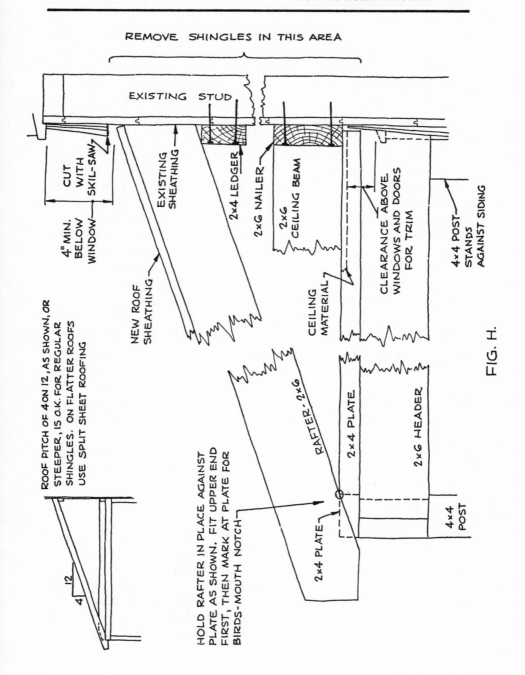

REMOVE SHINGLES IN THIS AREA

EXISTING STUD

CUT WITH SKIL-SAW

4" MIN. BELOW WINDOW

EXISTING SHEATHING

2×4 LEDGER

2×6 NAILER

2×6 CEILING BEAM

CLEARANCE ABOVE WINDOWS AND DOORS FOR TRIM

4×4 POST STANDS AGAINST SIDING

NEW ROOF SHEATHING

CEILING MATERIAL

ROOF PITCH OF 4 ON 12, AS SHOWN, OR STEEPER, IS O.K. FOR REGULAR SHINGLES. ON FLATTER ROOFS USE SPLIT SHEET ROOFING

12

4

HOLD RAFTER IN PLACE AGAINST PLATE AS SHOWN. FIT UPPER END FIRST, THEN MARK AT PLATE FOR BIRDS-MOUTH NOTCH

RAFTER-2×6

2×4 PLATE

2×6 HEADER

2×4 PLATE

4×4 POST

FIG. H.

trimmed end flush against the siding and hold the other end against the end of the plate, then mark it to give it a "bird's mouth" notch.

Try this rafter at the other end; fit it in place. Try it in other places. If it fits you can use it as a template (pattern) for cutting the other rafters. If there is a variation in the length of the rafters as shown by trying the pattern for fit, cut each rafter to length as necessary.

If both the ledger on the house wall and the porch header are straight and level but not parallel, the rafters will have a common difference in length. In this case cut a rafter to fit each end—the one you already cut and one other. Then, on two saw horses, lay all other rafter boards between the two templates, crowns up. (Sight down the length of each rafter to see if it has a curve—the curve should be turned up in the middle.) Draw two lines connecting the ends of the two patterns across the stack. Then use these marks as the lengths of the rafters and mark the ends for cutting from the pattern. See Fig I. Number them so you're sure to keep them in order.

Next step is to sheath the roof. You have a variety of materials to choose for this. You can use 1/2 inch (CD sheathing grade) plywood. In this case, use sixpenny nails every 6 to 8 inches across the face of the plywood. If you use 1 by 6 tongue and groove boards, use eightpenny nails, two per board to every rafter. If you use 1 by 8 boards, use eightpenny nails, three nails per rafter. The best sheathing is plywood. It's fast and easy to install and has good diagonal strength.

Next, trim the porch. There are various ways to do this. In addition to way shown in the main drawings, also see Fig. J.

SHINGLES

Installing shingles is next. Under the shingles goes 15-pound felt. It is best to cover part of the roof with felt and shingles first so you will have an area to work off. Felt alone is too slippery.

First, unroll a piece of felt along the left edge of the roof. Then trim it so it is flush. Secure it with large-head roofing nails. Unroll another piece along the bottom edge overlapping the first pieces about three inches. This second piece and all succeeding pieces should be cut flush with roof edges.

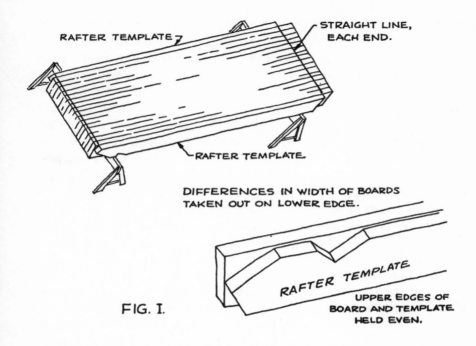

RAFTER TEMPLATE

STRAIGHT LINE, EACH END.

RAFTER TEMPLATE.

DIFFERENCES IN WIDTH OF BOARDS TAKEN OUT ON LOWER EDGE.

RAFTER TEMPLATE

FIG. I.

UPPER EDGES OF BOARD AND TEMPLATE HELD EVEN.

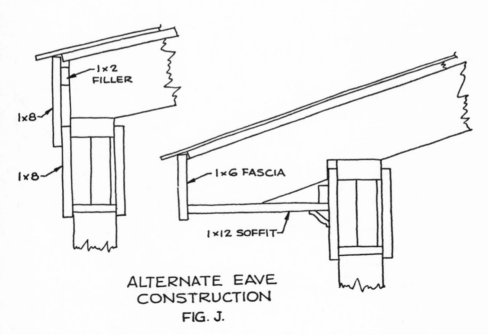

1 x 2 FILLER

1 x 8

1 x 8

1 x 6 FASCIA

1 x 12 SOFFIT

ALTERNATE EAVE CONSTRUCTION
FIG. J.

Strike two chalk lines along the side of the roof, one 5-1/4 inches from the edge, the other 11-1/4 inches. These lines will serve as guides to shingle placement, and permit the shingles, and parts of shingles, to overhang the edge of the roof 3/4 inch. Next, hammer nails in the roof 10 inches from the bottom edge at each end. Snap chalk lines horizontally across the roof from these nails. You will now have a guide for placing the first shingle which, since it is 12 inches deep (or wide) will overhang 2 inches. For other course snap lines 10 inches apart (Fig. J).

Now you are ready to start placing shingles (Fig. K). First, place a starter course upside down, slots facing upward, along the first chalk line. Then, following details in sketch, place your shingles (also Fig. L.). Shingles should be overlapped 7 inches ("5 inches to the weather," as the saying goes.)

The first regular course is placed directly over the starter course aligned with the same chalk line. The second regular course and every alternate course above is placed by aligning the lower edge of the shingle wtih the top of the vent in the shingle below. The third regular and alternate courses are placed along the chalk lines.

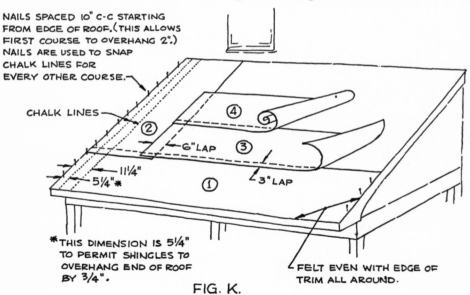

NAILS SPACED 10" C-C STARTING FROM EDGE OF ROOF.(THIS ALLOWS FIRST COURSE TO OVERHANG 2".) NAILS ARE USED TO SNAP CHALK LINES FOR EVERY OTHER COURSE.

CHALK LINES

④

②

6" LAP ③

11¼"

5¼"*

① 3" LAP

*THIS DIMENSION IS 5¼" TO PERMIT SHINGLES TO OVERHANG END OF ROOF BY 3/4".

FELT EVEN WITH EDGE OF TRIM ALL AROUND.

FIG. K.

In this manner you can keep the lines of all the courses straight. If you rely only on the vents for spacing you certainly will wind up with crooked courses.

Follow the pattern across the roof. After a goodly number of courses are installed nail on roof brackets and boards to serve as a scaffolding to work off. When you get to the siding at the top you will have to cut shingles to fit. To cut, score the shingle deeply on the back, then break it off.

On the end (right side) of the roof, tack a 3/4 inch furring strip against trim to use as a guide for cutting the last shingle in each course. Lay each shingle in place in turn and make a cut in the top and bottom edges to mark where they will be cut off. Then turn the shingle over and lay a straightedge on these cuts and cut as usual. Nail the piece in place. Here you may come to a situation in which the last tab is cut very narrow (1-1/2 inches or less). I have often seen roofs finished this way, but after a short time the small tabs blow off and the edge of the roof has a ragged appearance.

This can be avoided in the following manner. Every other course will have to be cut back. Cut away the tab that would have been small and the whole tab next to it. Then cut a piece of shingle with two tabs. Cut the right tab 3-1/2 inches wide and cut the left tab to fit the space at the end of the course. Use this piece as a template to cut enough pieces like it for the whole end of the roof. Some of these pieces can be cut from leftover pieces. This is detailed in Fig. L.

FLASHING

For flashing I recommend 3 by 8 sheets of .032 aluminum cut into 12 inch strips bent on a break. You should have about 4 inches on the roof, the rest on the siding or under it. A good building supply store can cut it for you to your specifications; failing that, you can get it done at a sheet metal shop. Or any aluminum installer can do it. If these options aren't enough you can use cold rolled coil stock. This can be bent easily over a board. How you install it depends on the siding. Your goal is to make the gap between the roofing and siding as watertight as possible.

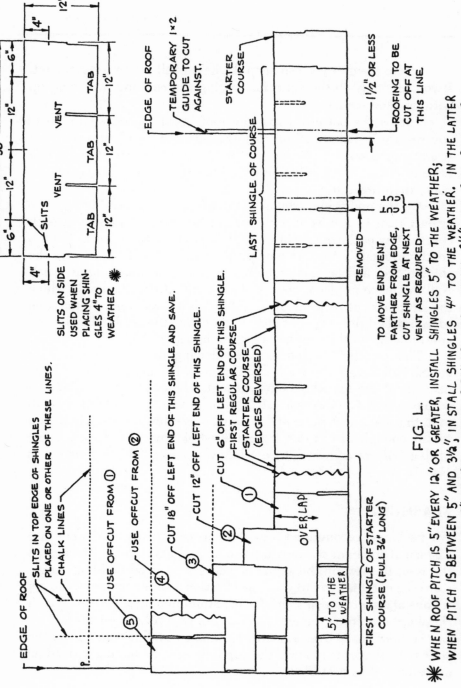

FIG. L.

* WHEN ROOF PITCH IS 5" OR GREATER, INSTALL SHINGLES 5" TO THE WEATHER; WHEN PITCH IS BETWEEN 5" AND 3½", INSTALL SHINGLES 4" TO THE WEATHER. IN THE LATTER CASE GUIDE LINES ARE 8" APART. WHEN PITCH IS LESS THAN 3½" USE ROLL ROOFING.

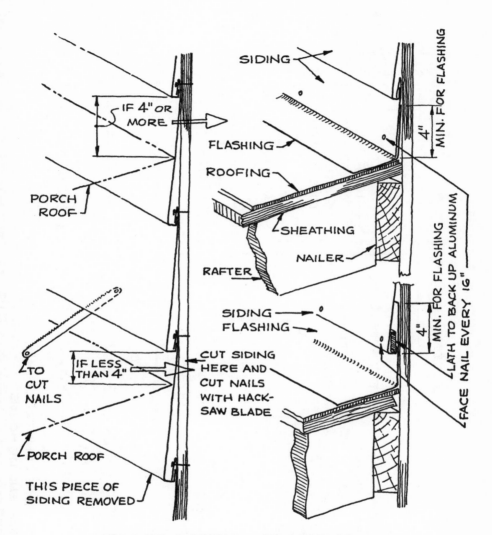

HOW TO INSTALL FLASHING
WITH ALUMINUM SIDING.
FIG. M.

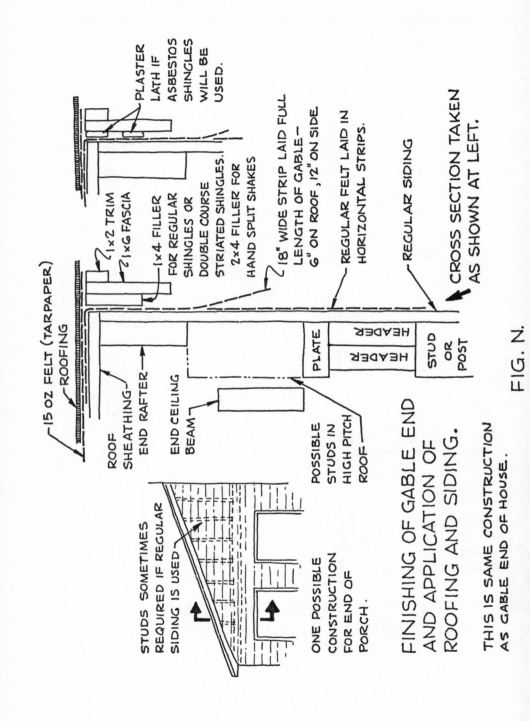

PLASTER LATH IF ASBESTOS SHINGLES WILL BE USED.

15 OZ FELT (TARPAPER) ROOFING

1x2 TRIM
1x6 FASCIA

1x4 FILLER FOR REGULAR SHINGLES OR DOUBLE COURSE STRIATED SHINGLES.

2x4 FILLER FOR HAND SPLIT SHAKES

18" WIDE STRIP LAID FULL LENGTH OF GABLE— 6" ON ROOF, 12" ON SIDE

REGULAR FELT LAID IN HORIZONTAL STRIPS.

REGULAR SIDING

CROSS SECTION TAKEN AS SHOWN AT LEFT.

ROOF SHEATHING

END RAFTER

END CEILING BEAM

PLATE

HEADER

HEADER

STUD OR POST

POSSIBLE STUDS IN HIGH PITCH ROOF

STUDS SOMETIMES REQUIRED IF REGULAR SIDING IS USED

ONE POSSIBLE CONSTRUCTION FOR END OF PORCH.

FINISHING OF GABLE END AND APPLICATION OF ROOFING AND SIDING.

THIS IS SAME CONSTRUCTION AS GABLE END OF HOUSE.

FIG. N.

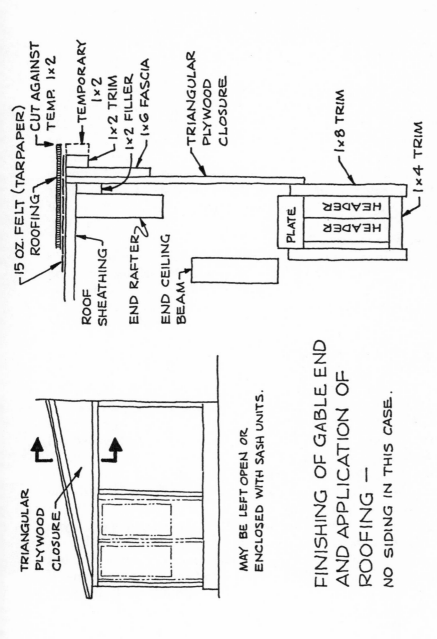

15 OZ. FELT (TARPAPER)
ROOFING
CUT AGAINST
TEMP. 1×2
TEMPORARY 1×2
1×2 TRIM
1×2 FILLER
1×6 FASCIA
ROOF SHEATHING
END RAFTER
END CEILING BEAM
TRIANGULAR PLYWOOD CLOSURE
1×8 TRIM
1×4 TRIM
HEADER
HEADER
PLATE

CROSS SECTION TAKEN AS SHOWN

FIG. O.

TRIANGULAR PLYWOOD CLOSURE

MAY BE LEFT OPEN OR ENCLOSED WITH SASH UNITS.

FINISHING OF GABLE END AND APPLICATION OF ROOFING —

NO SIDING IN THIS CASE.

If you have stucco the only practical thing is to simply apply a very healthy bead of caulking under each course of shingles at the intersection of roof and wall (apply caulk to sheathing also) as you go. You'll have to recaulk from time to time but there is no other practical way with stucco.

In the case of cedar shingles you can cover across the shingles that are adjacent to the roof, and fit the flashing up under the butts of the next course of shingles. To prevent a lot of flashing being exposed you could have adjusted the height of your roof when laying out the rafters. For asbestos shingles, remove them first. Nail the flashing to the sheathing on the house side and reinstall shingles over it. No matter what way you decide to install flashing, don't drive nails through flashing any closer than 3 inches from the roof; if the nail gets loose you'll have a potentially leaky spot in the flashing. If snow gets on the roof it will melt and drip nicely here.

Aluminum siding is a little problem. I suppose the best way is to remove the siding from the area where the rafters are to be installed beforehand. To do this, score it with a utility knife using a block of wood of a width that fits from the bottom edge of the course of siding above the cut to the exact height of the cut. Hold block against the siding and score the siding deeply all the way across a few times. Then bend the siding back and forth a couple of times and it will break neatly. Put an aluminum channel to cover raw edge of aluminum, then slide the flashing up under the channel and siding. If it works out that the edge of a course of siding is very near the top of the roof, cut the siding right at that edge and then slip in a bar to loosen the nails. Use a hacksaw blade to cut nails. Remove nail shank with pliers. See Fig. M.

To get flashing under clapboard pry the edge of the board closest to the roof out and use a hacksaw to cut the nails. Slide the flashing up under it and then renail.

The porch here, as mentioned, is 10 by 12 feet and open. If you want to screen it in, you can install additional posts (just install bolts in concrete, toenail at top to header). These won't be supportive but will form a handy and handsome place for attaching the screening. If you want to enclose the porch into a room you can do it in the normal way as described in various parts of the book. Two different ways are shown in Figs. N and O.

Chapter 16

Opening Up (Extending) A Levitt

The house we have in mind for extending is a Levitt house that was designed with a very small living room and kitchen, divided only by a fireplace. The back wall of the living room is formed by two large 8-foot windows and a door—in effect, the entire wall is glass. Above the window is a nailed-up 4 by 12 (two nailed together 2 by 12's) header so you have no other support except posts between the two windows and a post between the window and door (Figs. A and B).

House layout is such that it lends itself easily to an extension to the rear that becomes the living room. However, to keep the dining area well lighted, it's not practical to put a wall at that point. The system used allows it to be left open to the new living room with the only divider being a new header that goes between living and dining

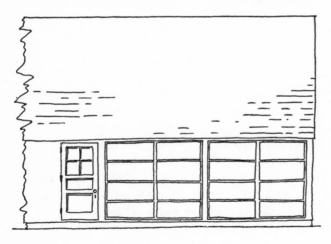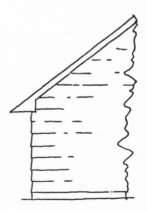

EXISTING EXTERIOR
FIG. A.

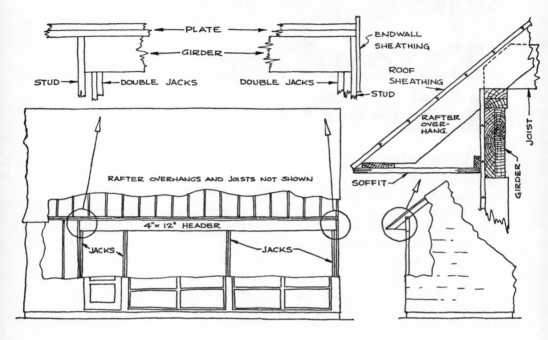

EXISTING STRUCTURE
FIG. B.

room. In other words, you take out the wall and all you leave is the header.

The existing 4 by 12 header is not enough, though, to support the twenty foot span so the problem that makes this particular extension different from any other is the supports for this bearing wall.

The system described here has been worked out and used successfully on many houses on Long Island, New York. It involves building an A-frame assembly above the header. Each leg of the A-frame is three 2 by 6's nailed together. These members are the same shape as the rafters in the rest of the room. They rest on the same ridgepole as all the other rafters and on the existing header, which is itself supported by jack studs. That is, not directly on it, but on blocking which is fitted around the existing joists and rafters. Added to the header is another 2 by 12 member to beef it up to a 6 by 12. In addition, there is a turnbuckle arrangement made of 7/8 inch steel rod that runs from the two ends of the A and down from the center of the ridgepole down through the center of the 6 by 12. The nut on the bottom can be let into the bottom of the 6 by 12 so it will not protrude. This turnbuckle is installed before the jack studs or posts are removed. Indeed, the entire construction is made before the posts are removed. Then, when the framing is in, you set up on the turnbuckle until the rod is taut, applying pressure on the ridgepole and lifting the center of the header (Fig. C).

What this configuration does, essentially, is to provide needed support at the middle of a long header. The pressure from the nut on the center rod pulls up on the center of the header and down on the top of the A, but the turnbuckle keeps the feet of the A from spreading. Normally, this twenty-foot span would require a large steel I-beam. Installing an I-beam would require building a temporary wall to hold up the house while the work progressed. This method is a very clever bit of engineering and makes the job of opening up a Levitt practical. All the other carpentry and/or mechanical work in this extension is basically simple and the same as for any other extension.

CONSTRUCTION

First step is to get a building permit. To do this you will need plans. In most localities there is a cost limit above which you will need an architect's seal on the plans.

On Long Island there are several drafting services that will obtain the permit for a nominal fee. There is one in particular that has plans for this extension on file. In some rural localities permits are still not necessary. The best thing is to call or visit the local building department and inquire about a service that supplies plans and obtains permits in your area.

The Levitt house was built on a slab; the only practical foundation for the extension is to continue the slab. How far out you can go depends upon property size, building code, zoning laws, and so forth. This will have to be determined in the process of getting your permit. It depends also, of course, on just how far you want to go.

The extension is built in three stages. Refer to art detailing these as you read the text.

First, stake out the sides of your extension (usual extension is twelve feet), dig footing so it is level with the slab inside. There is one possible problem—getting the whole slab even if the house has settled and the slab is a little off level.

To get it level, remove the saddle of the door exposing the original slab. Use this as the height of the new floor. Build a form out of 2 by 8's (or 12's if necessary) making the top of the form level with the existing slab. Use the dirt from where the footings were dug to raise the grade inside the extension to 4 inches below the existing slab. Depending on the grade you may need more or less fill than what's on hand.

At this point you should have your heating installed. You should use baseboard heating on both ends of the extension. Have the main line under the floor installed before the slab is poured. The 3/4 inch copper pipe used should be wrapped in 15-pound felt. Let ends stick up about 6 inches above the slab. Because you have radiant heat in the floor, breaking up the original slab could be dangerous to the pipes. Therefore run a section of the baseboard heating right from the foot of the stairs into the extension.

Pour the footing and slab in one piece. Install foundation bolts on each side of the door, one on each side of the corners according to the new layout of the windows.

Make the slab level as close to even with the existing slab as possible, then use Dash patch to blend it into one smooth, level-looking area. The use of a transit to check the height of the floor in several places would also tend to insure that the job was going to come out right.

After the slab is down, lay out the shoes. On slab construction, the shoe is always doubled, and bolted down. Make up the plate in the conventional manner (see Chapter 1). Then cut away the part of the existing roof overhang that is directly above the newly installed shoe.

Next, cut the studs to length (the same length as the studs in the existing wall, unless the slab came out too high or low), make up the walls and hold them in place, holding them plumb with temporary braces.

Install the header in the outside wall, then install wind braces in the new walls if you intend to use tongue and groove sheathing or "Gyplap." If you use 1/2 inch plywood sheathing wind braces are not necessary; 1/2 inch is the same thickness as "Gyplap" (gypsum sheathing).

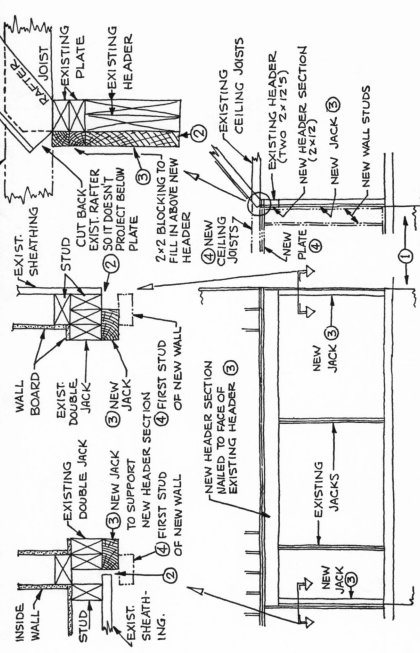

NEW CEILING JOIST ④

RAFTER JOIST

EXISTING PLATE

EXISTING HEADER

② CUT BACK EXIST. RAFTER SO IT DOESN'T PROJECT BELOW PLATE

③

EXISTING CEILING JOISTS

EXISTING HEADER (TWO 2×12's)

NEW HEADER SECTION (2×12) ③

NEW JACK ③

NEW WALL STUDS

④ NEW CEILING JOISTS

NEW PLATE ④

2×2 BLOCKING TO FILL IN ABOVE NEW HEADER

EXIST. SHEATHING

STUD

WALL BOARD

EXIST. DOUBLE JACK

③ NEW JACK

④ FIRST STUD OF NEW WALL

INSIDE WALL

STUD

EXIST. SHEATH-ING.

EXISTING DOUBLE JACK

③ NEW JACK TO SUPPORT NEW HEADER SECTION

④ FIRST STUD OF NEW WALL

②

NEW HEADER SECTION NAILED TO FACE OF EXISTING HEADER ③

EXISTING JACKS

NEW JACK ③

NEW JACK ③

①

① FOOTING OR FOUNDATION ; ② REMOVE OLD SIDING AND SHEATHING IN WAY OF JACKS AND HEADER.
③ INSTALL NEW JACKS AND HEADER ; ④ BUILD NEW WALLS AND CEILING JOISTS.

FIRST STAGE OF NEW ADDITION
FIG. C.

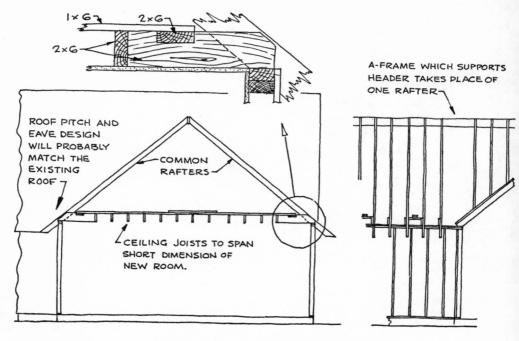

1×6

2×6

2×6

A-FRAME WHICH SUPPORTS HEADER TAKES PLACE OF ONE RAFTER

ROOF PITCH AND EAVE DESIGN WILL PROBABLY MATCH THE EXISTING ROOF

COMMON RAFTERS

CEILING JOISTS TO SPAN SHORT DIMENSION OF NEW ROOM.

SECOND STAGE OF NEW ADDITION.
FIG. D.

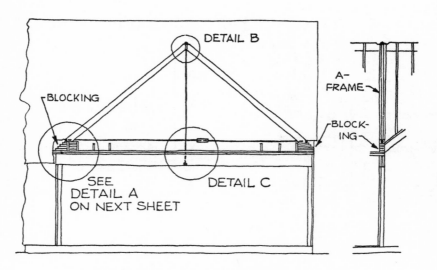

DETAIL B

BLOCKING

A-FRAME

BLOCK-ING

SEE DETAIL A ON NEXT SHEET

DETAIL C

THIRD STAGE OF NEW ADDITION—
BUILDING OF A-FRAME
FIG. E.

At this point cut away the existing roof somewhat (overhang of the roof) to make room for the A-frame. Save the boards from the soffit for reuse.

Next, install ceiling beams. These are a continuation of the existing beams and rest on the new plate. The reason you install beams now is so you can put some plywood sheathing on top of them and give yourself a place to work. Next, establish the common rafters and ridge rafter. In a hip extension, which we recommend, the rafter that comes off the end of the ridge on the hip side is the same as the common rafters and in this case serves as a pattern for the A-frame legs.

Once the ridge rafter is in place and set by four common rafters you can begin work on the A-frame. You have to nail solid wood blocking (Detail A) between the ceiling beams or floor joists according to what's in the particular house for the end of the A to rest on. When this is done you can determine the bottom cut on the A-rafter and cut all six pieces needed. Notch them for the end of the turnbuckle, and install. Then, install the turnbuckle (Details B and C), the other member of the header, and the other bolt. It is not necessary at this time to install all this. Building sequence would be better if you left windows in the original wall as long as possible to keep the house clean.

After the A-frame is in place install two boards for the valley rafters to hang on. These are laid right on the existing roof in this case. You wouldn't use a valley rafter as such but these two members could be 1 by 6's and give you a nailer for the ends of the short valley rafters.

Next, install the rest of the common rafters, followed by the hip rafters and jack rafters. To cut any rafter you should first have a good Stanley framing square. It comes with a pamphlet on the use of the tool. It is theoretically possible to mark and cut all the pieces on the ground exactly right. But to be on the safe side cut one rafter and make sure it fits before you cut up the whole lumber pile.

Tip: When you make the double angle cuts for the tips of the jack rafters or the bottom of the cripples remember the offcut is symetrical and will fit the other side of the roof. Therefore keep

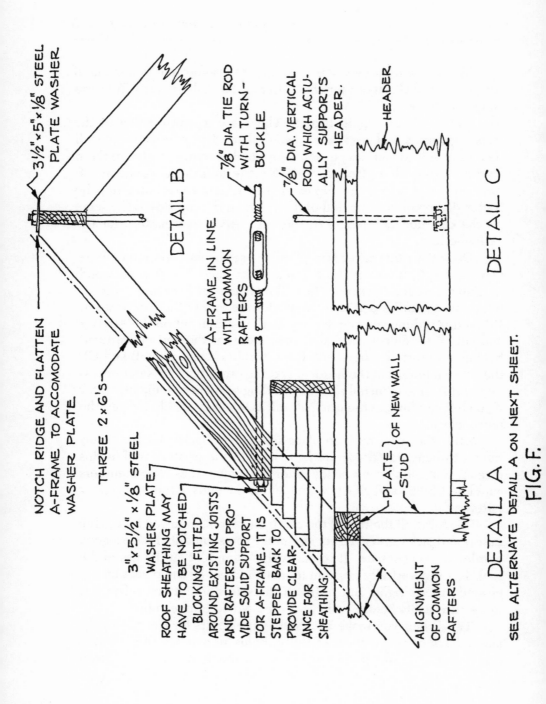

NOTCH RIDGE AND FLATTEN A-FRAME TO ACCOMODATE WASHER PLATE

3½" × 5 × ⅛" STEEL PLATE WASHER

THREE 2×6's

DETAIL B

7/8" DIA. TIE ROD WITH TURN-BUCKLE

A-FRAME IN LINE WITH COMMON RAFTERS

7/8" DIA. VERTICAL ROD WHICH ACTU-ALLY SUPPORTS HEADER.

HEADER

DETAIL C

3" × 5½" × ⅛" STEEL WASHER PLATE

ROOF SHEATHING MAY HAVE TO BE NOTCHED AROUND EXISTING JOISTS AND RAFTERS TO PRO-VIDE SOLID SUPPORT FOR A-FRAME. IT IS STEPPED BACK TO PROVIDE CLEAR-ANCE FOR SHEATHING.

PLATE } OF NEW WALL
STUD }

ALIGNMENT OF COMMON RAFTERS

DETAIL A
SEE ALTERNATE DETAIL A ON NEXT SHEET.

FIG. F.

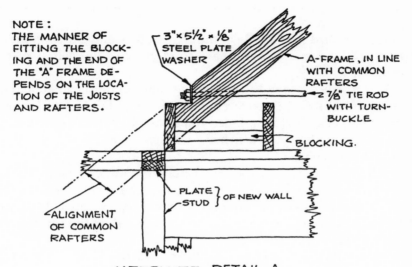

NOTE :
THE MANNER OF
FITTING THE BLOCK-
ING AND THE END OF
THE "A" FRAME DE-
PENDS ON THE LOCA-
TION OF THE JOISTS
AND RAFTERS.

3" × 5½" × ⅛"
STEEL PLATE
WASHER

A-FRAME , IN LINE
WITH COMMON
RAFTERS

2 ⅞" TIE ROD
WITH TURN-
BUCKLE

BLOCKING.

PLATE } OF NEW WALL
STUD }

ALIGNMENT
OF COMMON
RAFTERS

ALTERNATE DETAIL A
FIG. G.

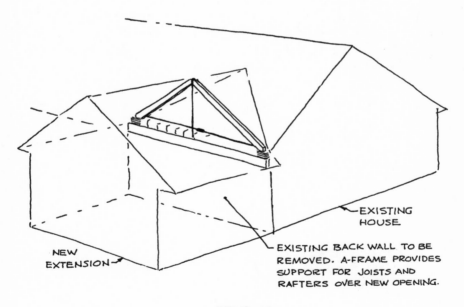

NEW
EXTENSION

EXISTING
HOUSE

EXISTING BACK WALL TO BE
REMOVED. A-FRAME PROVIDES
SUPPORT FOR JOISTS AND
RAFTERS OVER NEW OPENING.

FIG. H.

these cuts toward the middle of the 2 by 6 stock and cut two rafters from one 2 by 6 and you will have to make only one half as many difficult cuts.

When rafters are in the rest of the roof can be sheathed and at least papered in; that is, covered with 15-pound felt to give temporary protection against rain. Since you have the roof cut open there's a good chance that you will have leakage so finish it quickly to minimize the damage.

Start the roof shingles so they extend the same distance off the edge of the roof as the existing shingles. The whole roof can be completed at this time with the exception of the one area at the top of the A-frame where the nut for the vertical rod on the turnbuckle has to be placed.

Next take out windows and doors and install in a new wall immediately so you won't have to worry about their getting broken while waiting for installation. Install the vertical rod in the A-frame and tighten the nut on the bottom of the header until the post stands loose. When you can lift it out of the way you know that the header is carrying the whole load of the roof and not sagging. From this point on finish the outside of the house, the soffit, shingles, roofing, and the inside—wiring, insulation, Sheetrock, and so forth. These operations are covered in various other parts of the book.

Chapter 17

A New Kitchen

Remodeling a kitchen is a popular home improvement, probably the most popular of all, and that's not surprising. It's where the lady of the house spends most of her time. A good-looking efficiently designed kitchen can make her job a lot easier.

The key to an efficient kitchen is good layout of cabinets, appliances, and sink. They should be selected and arranged based on the individual needs of the homemaker.

I'll first discuss what's available and some other considerations and then get into the layout and installation.

KITCHEN CABINETS

The kitchen requires both base (floor) and hanging cabinets, also called hangers. Each is essentially a box with shelves and doors. You can purchase them in ready-made stock sizes, or have them custom made; you give the cabinetmaker dimensions and he will make the cabinets to suit. I usually install custom cabinets simply because stock sizes often do not fit without wasting a lot of space. That is, to make a row of cabinets fit in a given space, you have to use fillers (boards between which is nothing) to take up the extra space that the stock sizes can't fill, or use smaller cabinets and leave large spaces next to doors or windows. Builders often use stock sizes successfully on model homes because they are able to predesign the kitchen so the cabinets fit without any waste space.

Stock sizes vary according to the manufacturer, but they are commonly available in 6 inch increments (12 inches, 18 inches, etc.) up to 42 inches or 48 inches wide. Standard depth of base cabinets is 24 inches, hanging cabinets 12 inches. Base cabinets are 34-1/2 inches to 35 inches high. Hangers are 30 inches to 34 inches high, but shorter ones for use over the range or refrigerator are 15 inches, 18 inches, 20 inches, and 24 inches high. These dimensions are also

149

about what you will find in custom-made cabinets, except the custom cabinetmaker will make the lengths to suit and can vary any dimension. The usual overall height of cabinets from the floor to the top of the hanger is 84 inches.

There are three basic kinds of cabinets: wood, plastic-laminate covered, and metal. Wood and plastic-laminate covered are available in both stock and custom sizes, but I know of no custom metal cabinets.

Wood.   There are various ways to check quality. The front frame should be made with either doweled or mortise-and-tenon joints. The bottom of the hangers should be thick enough (not 1/4 inch hardboard) so that you can screw gadgets to them. The bottoms of the base cabinets, if not made of heavy wood, should be reinforced enough to take the weight of the pots and pans that will be stored in them. Long hangers or bases over 60 inches should have partitions in them to prevent sagging in the middle. (Adjustable shelves, by the way, make the cabinet more useful since you can get big platters to stand on edge in the cabinet.) The sides of base cabinets or extra deep hangers should be made of 1/2 inch plywood; thinner plywood must be reinforced. Wide boards often check (split down the middle) therefore they are not suitable for finished sides.

The backs of cabinets are not structurally important; 1/8 inch plywood or hardboard is sufficient, but they add to the practicality of the cabinets. They keep dirt from falling down behind the cabinets and provide a permanent covering for the wall. This will make it unnecessary to paint the inside.

Doors can be whatever you wish, plywood or solid wood. This doesn't affect the quality of the cabinet, but the fancier the doors the more they will cost. Also, consider the finish. The stain may be sprayed or hand rubbed; this doesn't affect the utility of the cabinet but depending on the type of wood can make considerable difference in the overall appearance. Of course hand work costs more. The stain, you will find, may be covered with clear lacquer or urethane. This must be heavy enough to afford protection. Other finishes are also used and it is impossible to tell, with any certainty, what was used by looking at the finished cabinet. The main thing to look for is that the stain is well covered. I've seen cabinets delivered as "finished" with nothing but stain for a finish. Compare cabinets and finishes and you'll immediately see which are better.

Plastic-Laminate Covered Cabinets.   On this type quality varies from poorer than basic wood cabinets to much better. A big advantage of this type of cabinet is easy cleaning.

Poorer cabinets are made by covering sheets of flakeboard with plastic laminate, cutting it into cabinet components and then assembling (Fig. A). You can tell this type of construction by face joints

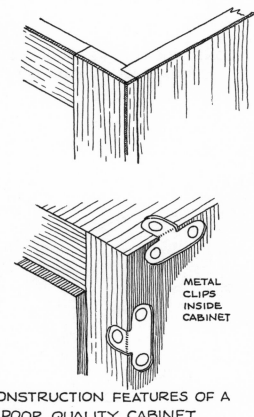

METAL
CLIPS
INSIDE
CABINET

CONSTRUCTION FEATURES OF A
POOR QUALITY CABINET
FIG. A.

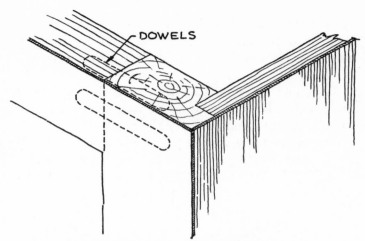

DOWELS

CONSTRUCTION FEATURES OF A
GOOD QUALITY CABINET
FIG. B.

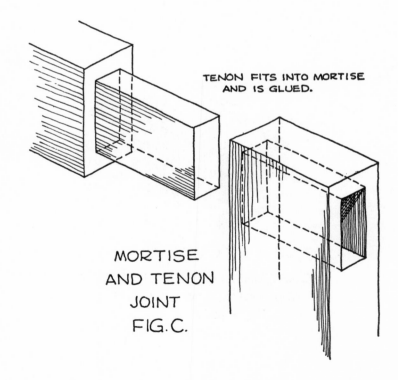

TENON FITS INTO MORTISE
AND IS GLUED.

MORTISE
AND TENON
JOINT
FIG. C.

in the laminate and the flakeboard, a double seam in the laminate at the front corner of the cabinet, and little metal clips on the inside that hold the cabinet together. Good plastic-laminate covered cabinets are constructed first, then covered (Fig. B). All the things I said about wood cabinets apply, except flakeboard is included as a good material for the cabinet body (sides, back, bottom), but not the front frame. This should be made of solid wood with doweled or mortise-and-tenon joints (Fig. C). The only way flakeboard is acceptable as a cabinet front is when the whole front is composed of it with no joints. However, in this case, the stiles and rails should be at least 2-1/2 inches wide. I mention this here because this method is not commercially practical, but works well if you want to make a cabinet yourself and do not have the facility to make proper joints.

There is a material used for the inside of cabinets that is manufactured for this purpose. It is flakeboard with a plastic covering. It is just a thin plastic sheet, not high pressure plastic laminate as is used on the outside of the cabinets. The main advantage is to the cabinetmaker because the inside of the cabinet is, in effect, prefinished and eliminates the necessity of spraying a finish on. This covering is of no particular advantage to the user. It is no better than a good lacquer finish.

You will find that stock plastic-laminate covered cabinets come in a limited selection of colors and patterns. Custom cabinets, however, can be made up with any pattern or combination of colors or patterns you wish. Although wood grains are still the most popular patterns in use in kitchens, bright solid colors also make very attractive units.

Metal Cabinets.   I don't recommend these. Generally they warp and bend easily. The finish is just sprayed enamel, usually white, and when it chips, the metal shows through. Of course you can get good ones but availability is limited.

ACCESSORIES TO LOOK FOR ON BETTER CABINETS

Drawer slides come in different designs, from the old fashioned wooden runners that fit into dadoes in the drawer sides (these are bad) to metal tracks with nylon rollers and ball bearings. The main thing to look for is good rollers with ball bearings. These will give you many years of trouble-free service.

Bread boxes can be obtained in plated steel or stainless steel. They can either be mounted on wooden slides or good drawer hardware. They come in standard height and depth and to fit drawer openings of even inches in width from about 7 inches to 24 inches.

Adjustable shelves, whether on metal pilasters or the little brackets that fit in holes in the cabinet sides, allow you flexibility in fitting in large items such as platters.

Magnetic catches are generally better than roller catches, but get the kind in plastic housings rather than those in metal housings.

CABINET COST

You won't automatically pay more for custom cabinets than for stock ones. It really depends on where you buy the cabinets. Markup can be great—as much as 50 percent. The smaller the cabinet the more you'll pay per foot. Probably the best place for custom cabinets is a large cabinetmaking shop. They'll likely be glad to sell cabinets they don't have to install. For stock cabinets, there are companies who make all the various sizes and kinds and you can go directly to one of their distributors. If you can use stock sizes, it's a quick way to get cabinets (six weeks is normal waiting time to get custom units). Check the Yellow Pages.

It's usually a good idea to buy cabinets from a local company. If something is wrong with them (for example, wrong size, missing doors, rough spot on finish, transit damage) you can wait an inordinate amount of time to get the problem corrected if the cabinetmaker is three states away. If something is wrong a reliable cabinetmaker will send a serviceman to make the correction.

DON'T BEGIN BEFORE YOU HAVE CABINETS

It's wise not to start ripping out anything in the kitchen until the cabinets have arrived and you've checked them to make sure they're complete and that nothing that has to be done can't be done on the job (minor touch-ups, for example). The wife of an electrician friend of mine once ripped out cabinets wtihout even ordering new ones. They were incomplete, and by the time the job was started the family had spent four months without a kitchen, and going to restaurants had wrecked their food budget.

COUNTER TOP

This should also be made by the cabinetmaker to your dimensions. It is installed directly on top of base cabinets to fit into a prescribed area.

Check counter top for flaws. Also make sure that the sink cutout is in the right place. Counter tops are commonly made of plywood or other sheet material and then covered with plastic laminate. There are three basic styles.

The first type is the Formica counter, so-called from days when Formica was the only brand on the market, with stainless steel edging. This has passed out of the picture pretty much; the edging is a dirt collector.

The next is self-edge or edge-glued. This type has a strip of plastic laminate glued to the edge. It's big advantages is that it does not collect dirt. A disadvantage is that it has nothing at the edge to prevent spills from slopping right off the top.

The newest is the post-formed top (Fig. D). The flakeboard base of this top is covered with one continuous piece of laminate. The

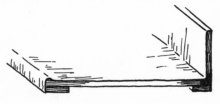

POST-FORMED COUNTER
FIG. D.

laminate starts from the top edge of the back down around the corner across the deck. At the front there is a small ridge to form a retainer to prevent small spills from slopping off the edge. The laminate continues to the bottom of the front edge. The advantages are self-evident. The disadvantages are that an L-shaped top has to be mitered at the corner to be made to fit and extra high back splashes must be made in two pieces. Also, configurations like peninsulas are not possible. Regular 1/6 inch laminate is harder than the post-forming material. Lastly, you are limited to twelve feet in length. Color choice is also limited.

SINK AND APPLIANCES

If you are putting in new cabinets it makes sense to put in new appliances and a sink for a totally new look. More important, though, you want to avoid the necessity of having to alter your new kitchen cabinets a few months after they are installed because the old stove or refrigerator wears out. Of course you could use the old appliances to save money, but if you do first go out and select the model and size of new appliances that eventually will replace the old, then plan the cabinets to accommodate these sizes. Compromise is often the solution. For instance, buy a new range and use the old dishwasher and refrigerator.

Sinks may be stainless steel, porcelain on steel, or porcelain on cast iron. The cast iron is better and more expensive than steel. The stainless steel comes in a wide range of quality and price. Buy a good quality sink. Porcelain or stainless steel is a matter of personal preference. The most common sink size is 21 inches by 24 inches in sinks that require a mounting rim, and 22 inches by 25 inches in self-rimmed sinks. There is a whole range of larger sizes and models, but unless you have the room for a larger one don't even bother to look. In terms of the overall cost of a kitchen a new sink is so inexpensive that it really doesn't pay to use the old one.

The size of dishwashers has been standardized in the industry. They are 24 inches wide by 24 inches deep by an adjustable height to fit under a 36 inch high counter top. Dishwashers are shipped without outside panels; panels come in several colors and are packaged separately. When the dishwasher is installed under the counter, it usually needs only front panels. If, in your layout, the side of the dishwasher is exposed you can buy a side panel to match the front. This is especially useful if you are adding a dishwasher at the end of an existing counter top, where the side will be exposed. You can also buy a chopping block top that mounts on the machine.

RANGES, WALL OVENS, AND SURFACE UNITS

The standard sizes of freestanding ranges are 20, 24, 30, 36 and 40 inches. Built-in or slip-in units come in about the same widths but the other dimensions vary all over the lot. When they wear out or break, they are replaceable only with another unit like the one you are discarding. The 30 inch freestanding range has the largest oven of all sizes and comes in the greatest variety of styles. For these reasons I strongly recommend it. Larger ranges have storage compartments next to the oven. The overall result of using these larger sizes is to take space from both the oven and the adjacent cabinets. If you have a spacious kitchen, this, of course, matters less than it would in a small one.

Wall ovens have the same drawback as slip-in ranges. That is, they often have to be replaced with the same oven that you are replacing. However, in the case of the wall oven you can design the front of the oven cabinet so that, in the future, it could be cut out to take a larger oven.

Freestanding ranges can be replaced size for size regardless of who made them. That is, if something goes wrong with the range, you can buy any company's model of the same width and it will fit the available space easily. (I once had an odd size 39 inch wide stove to replace, and since nobody makes that size anymore, installation was a problem. I had to make room for a 40 inch stove.)

WALL FANS AND RANGE HOODS.

Venting is another consideration in a new kitchen. You need a means to remove smoke and cooking odors. This is done with an exhaust fan of some kind. The simplest is a wall fan mounted in an outside wall. The housing of the fan is the entire ductwork. It can be mounted separately or in a blank range hood. This is a metal box, open on the bottom, that is mounted on the wall over the stove, usually under a cabinet. The hood is 6 inches to 8 inches high and extends about 20 inches out from the wall.

Range hoods also come with fans mounted in them, or as components to be mounted in them when installed. The hoods are available both ducted and ductless. The ducted hood is an improvement over the ordinary wall fan. It places the fan as near the source of the steam, odors, and smoke as possible and the hood helps contain them.

Whatever kind of fan you have it must be large enough to do the job. The average kitchen requires a fan rated at 250-300 CFM (cubic feet per minute). A very important thing to remember is that any fan only moves air, it cannot draw from a vacuum. That is, it must have a source of air, an open window or a door standing ajar. Then it will do a good job of removing heat, moist air, odors, and smoke. This heat loss is bad in winter but good in summer. The ductless hood draws the air in the room through a filter. It removes smoke and odors and then blows the air back into the room. This is good in the winter because you don't lose heat. This type hood was invented to solve the problem of installing a hood where ducting is impossible—the landlord won't allow it or it is impractical because the duct would be too long and collect grease which could become a fire hazard. An added disadvantage is that the filter requires changing which is a periodic expense. I have come to the conclusion that, except for the cases mentioned, the ducted hood is the better of the two.

In addition to the systems mentioned there are others. For example, there are very large and ornate hoods with extra large fans. Also, there are remote roof-mounted and wall-mounted fans. These are less noisy because the fan is outside the house. Most fans have propellers but there is a turbine type fan that is usually very good. It is rated at 800-1000 CFM, and is easy to install.

LAYING OUT A KITCHEN

Since there are so many possible layouts, it would be impractical to present them here. There are all kinds of pamphlets available (from the government, for example) and it would be a good idea to familiarize yourself with them. Unless you have unlimited space you'll have to make some compromises. However, here are some desirable arrangements you should try to work into your plan:

The stove, sink, and refrigerator should be at the corners of a triangle, preferably equilateral, and the total walking distance of the triangle not more than 21 feet or less than 17 feet. You may not be able to achieve this distance but it's something to strive for.

The stove and refrigerator should not be next to one another. The stove creates heat. The refrigerator, therefore, operates in the hottest part of the kitchen. However, you could live with this situation if you had to.

The range should be located against an outside wall. This makes ducting short and simple. If you can't work this out you still have the option of putting the range on an inside wall and using a ductless hood.

The stove should not be under a window. Curtains could catch fire. Of course, you could cover the windows with shutters or some non-flammable material.

The dishwasher should be next to the sink. You can rinse the dishes and put them right into the dishwasher. If you have a dishwasher a double sink is not necessary in a minimal kitchen.

There should be adequate counter space on both sides of the sink, especially between the range and the sink.

There should be counter space on both sides of the stove or surface unit.

A sink is usually best located under a window.

Open appliance doors should not obstruct doorways.

Work out the layout of the kitchen with pencil and paper, based on the above, at this time. Measure all parts of the room and then make a drawing to scale.

Next, you can proceed to lay out your kitchen. First find out if the room is square. (This is especially important if you plan to install an L-shaped or U-shaped counter top.) This determines the measurements of your counter top and cabinets, and insures that you'll get them installed squarely.

To determine squareness build a 3-4-5 triangle out of straight 1 by 2 boards. Make the triangle as large a multiple of 3-4-5 as you can; 6-8-10 for example. Hold this in the corner where the counter top will go, with the short leg of the triangle corresponding to the short leg of the counter top. It would be good if the short leg of the triangle could be worked out so it is the exact length of the counter top.

The gap between triangle and wall, or walls, will tell you how much out of square it is. If the angle formed by the two walls is slightly obtuse—say up to an inch in the length of the short leg of the counter top, you can have the counter top cut square and installed as is. The gap will be so slight that it is easy to camouflage it with molding so that it won't be noticeable. To get the cabinets squared up when you install them, just nail a board the thickness of the gap (or gaps) to the studs to shim out the wall.

If the gap is more than an inch, have the counter top cut to fit exactly. The cabinets will be able to be installed to fit if you have the corner ones built with an extra wide stile, sometimes called a scribe. You can cut this at an angle so it mates with adjacent cabinet.

If the angle formed by the two walls is acute you can achieve squareness of counter top and cabinets by cutting a section of Sheetrock out of the wall, "letting" them into it.

Sometimes, if there is an existing L-shaped counter top, you needn't use a 3-4-5 triangle. You can tell how much the walls are out of square by measuring the gap between an existing L-shape counter top and the walls (Fig. E).

Now knowing what modifications you will have to make draw the outline of the room. Next, proceed to draw parallel lines to represent the faces of the hanger and base cabinets. Then pencil in the dimensions of the sink and major appliances. Allow 26 inches for a 24 inch sink. Try to incorporate the tips previously given. Your overall objective in the layout is to fit in as much usable cabinet space as possible, and a convenient working arrangement. The cabinet section under the sink, by the way, should have an opening large enough to allow installation and repair of the pipes. This requires that you have a pair of doors without a stile between (Fig. F).

The biggest problem in laying out an L-shaped kitchen is the corner cabinets. You can simply butt straight cabinets at the corner, but this makes the space there tough to use. You can use diagonal-

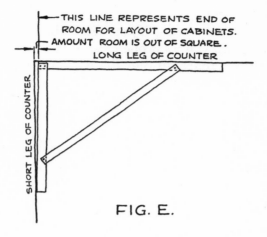

THIS LINE REPRESENTS END OF
ROOM FOR LAYOUT OF CABINETS.
AMOUNT ROOM IS OUT OF SQUARE.
LONG LEG OF COUNTER

SHORT LEG OF COUNTER

FIG. E.

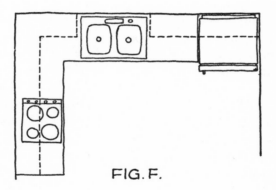

FIG. F.

front corner cabinets. The base corner cabinet uses 36 inches of wall space on each wall. the hanger 24 inches. These cabinet sizes are commonly used because they have proved to be practical; if you made the cabinets smaller, the doors would be too small to make the cabinets easily accessible. If they were much larger you couldn't reach the back of the hanging cabinet. There's another way to use L-shaped corner cabinets. They may have a door that folds in half in the corner or be built around a lazy Susan with the doors as part of the Susan. Base cabinets here use 36 inches or 42 inches on each wall. The hangers in this case are conventional.

While you are making the layout remember to consider the window treatment. Do you want open shelves to flank the window or do you want the cabinets to butt the window casing? Also, remember that each cabinetmaker has his own idea of what standard dimensions are and they may vary from what I have given.

Take your layout to the cabinetmaker. He is experienced and will notice any glaring errors; he may also have suggestions on better ways you can use the space. Of course the human element enters into this. If you wish you can also get a salesman from the cabinetmaker to lay out your kitchen for you. While this will cost, it may be worth it.

RIPPING OUT EXISTING KITCHEN

I'll say again, don't rip out anything until you have the new cabinets on hand. Before you start removing anything it's necessary to turn off water, gas, and electricity. If you have shutoff valves beneath the sink, fine. Just turn them off. If you have to turn off water from the main valve, now's the time to install valves under the sink so that you can turn the water back on in the rest of the house. The method of doing this is shown in Chapter 25. Turn off electric power at the fuse box or circuit breaker panel; using a wrench, turn off gas at the nearest gas cock. To find this trace the pipe back from the stove or at the meter. Note: when turning the gas back on at the meter, turn the cock very slowly so that a sudden boost in gas pressure doesn't rupture the diaphragm in the pressure control system. If you do break the diaphragm call the gas company immediately.

When moving the appliances out you can protect floors (assuming you're not putting in a new one) by sliding the units out on a piece of rug, scatter rugs, or rent a dolly.

Take out the sink and counter top, then proceed to remove the cabinets. I think it is good practice to screw cabinets in place, and if the man who installed your old cabinets agrees with me it will make removing yours easier. Just remove the screws. Otherwise if they're nailed use a pry bar to remove the base cabinets first, then the hangers. Where cabinets are nailed together, you can use a hacksaw to sever connections. When the end of a cabinet abuts a wall, it is likely to be nailed through the end as well as the back.

Move the cabinets out as soon as you take them down. One last thing, don't promise the old cabinets to your friends until they are off the wall. You may find that the easiest way to remove them is to demolish them in place.

INSTALLING CABINETS

Install base cabinets first. Each should be level with the ones adjacent. This insures that the counter top will be level. Floors are generally no more than 3/8 to 1/2 inch out of level, but our examples cover any eventuality.

Put a corner base cabinet in place and lay your level on it. If it's out of level, hammer temporary shims under the low corners to raise it. Best shims to use are Number 2 undercourse shingles. Buy a bundle. Sooner or later you will use them if you're an active, handy person.

Put in adjacent cabinet and level this with the first. If it is higher, raise the first up to it. Continue with the rest of the base cabinets in the same manner.

When all are temporarily shimmed measure the distance between the bottom of the cabinets and the floor and see how much out of level they are. If it's less than 3/4 inch the cabinets are ready for final fitting and fastening. If the space under the cabinets is more than 3/4 inch it's better to trim them off than leave them shimmed higher than 3/4 inch. To do this scribe a line on the kick plates and cabinet ends parallel to the floor, the line being one half the maximum shim thickness. Remove the cabinets, trim, then replace them and reshim them level.

Draw a level line on the wall where the tops of the cabinets fall. Remove the cabinets, then secure a nailer (usually 1-1/4 by 2 inches but of the proper size to fit your cabinets to the wall.) Replace cabinets, relevel (the shims may be knocked out of position) and secure to the nailer with 2 inch Number 10 flat head wood screws spaced every 16 to 18 inches. Make sure that the cabinets fit snugly together, using a sharp plane to scribe edges if necessary.

Finally, screw the cabinets together at the stiles. Use Number

10 wood screws, length depending on how wide the stile is. If you're screwing into pine, drill a shank hole through the stile of the first cabinet only, then drive the screw. If you're going through a hardwood such as birch, ash or oak, also drill a pilot hole that goes into the second stile. Fastening cabinets together can be done with nails, but screws are more secure, and if you make a mistake during installation it's an easy matter to separate the cabinets. Prying out nails could mess things up.

INSTALLING THE COUNTER TOP

Once the base cabinets are in place, install the counter top. Assuming you have one with a high back splash, you will first have to cut openings in it for wall receptacles. This must be done very carefully.

To do it, follow Fig. G and draw plumb lines, using a level, on the walls indicating where the edges of the outlet box are. Then draw a level line on the wall an inch or two above where the top edge of the back splash will be. Measure from this line to the bottom and the top of the outlet and mark the dimensions on the wall where they'll be readable after the back splash is in place.

Set the counter top in place tight against the wall(s), getting it as close to its final position as possible. Then transfer the plumb lines

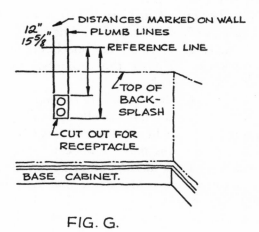

FIG. G.

from the wall to the face of the counter top to get sides of outlet and measure down from the horizontal reference line to mark the top and bottom. Move the top away from the wall. Drill a starting hole large enough to receive a jigsaw blade in two ·diagonally opposite corners of the outline. Cut the section out using the jigsaw and going from the back of the back splash. Sawing this way will reduce the chance of chipping the laminate. Once the outlet holes are cut out, you can no longer adjust its position. So get the top as close to final position as possible before marking. If necessary cut away the Sheetrock or plaster so the top fits well against walls. In the unlikely event that the counter does not fit on the base cabinets as it should, it may be necessary to unfasten and relocate some of these. Before you do this, make certain that the error is not in the top itself.

SECURING COUNTER TOP

The counter top only needs to be fastened enough to keep it from sliding around. Drive a screw up through the frame in the top of the base cabinet at each corner into the counter top. Use screws that are the right length. The point should not be closer than 1/8 inch to the laminate. To get proper size measure the combined thickness of the frame of the base cabinet and the counter top. Make sure, above all, you don't penetrate the laminate.

If you have base cabinets on both sides of a stove their tops must be exactly level with each other, especially if you also have a high back splash and a "U" hanger. The latter is a hanging cabinet that is full height on each end with a shorter section in the middle. It is designed so you can mount a range hood in it. The long sides rest on the top of the back splash flanking the range. Incidentally, it is a better idea to cover the wall behind the range with the same plastic laminate as used on the counter top, than to let the back splash run through; the latter will interfere with the mounting of the hood.

SECURING HANGING CABINETS

The hanging cabinets must be fastened to the wall studs. In kitchens studs are likely to be arranged to accommodate the plumbing pipes and will be in random locations rather than on 16 inch centers.

Therefore you must locate them before you start cabinet installation. And make the marks where you can see them while you are holding the cabinet in place. Depending on your situation, this could be on the wall below the cabinets, on the top of a high back splash, on the wall over the cabinets if you are able to see that high, or on the face of a drop ceiling.

If you have a high back splash start installation by resting the first cabinet—the corner cabinet if you have one—on the back splash and against the wall. Hold the cabinet up with one hand and drive a tenpenny finishing nail through the top rail in the cabinet back into a stud to hold it in position. Make sure that the nail gets a good bite.

When driving nails be sure that you don't hit a water pipe; a nail will penetrate copper water pipe. It's unlikely that pipes will be above the sink level unless there is a bathroom above the kitchen. If the plumber did his job carefully the water pipes will be installed through the middle of the studs, or between studs in a double wall.

Check the cabinet for plumb with your level. If it isn't plumb drive shims behind it to make it so. It should be plumb in two directions; on the face and sides. If the cabinet is secured permanently to a warped wall it can make the doors difficult or impossible to operate. After it is plumbed properly screw it in place with Number 10 wood screws which are long enough to penetrate the studs about one inch. Hold up the next cabinet to check the scribe edge for fit. If necessary, secure it temporarily for marking the edge for trimming or have someone hold it in position while you mark it. After marking, trim with a plane. It's best to plane the edge at a slight angle. This makes it easier to make the cabinets fit together well.

Continue around the room as described above. After all are in place screw them together through the stiles as you did with the base cabinets. If the first cabinet to be installed abuts a wall it must also be scribed and fitted.

If the cabinets don't have a high back splash the procedure is slightly different. For one thing you could install them before the base cabinets. You'd be able to get closer to the cabinets for easier nailing.

These cabinets rest on a nailer temporarily secured to the wall. The top edge of the nailer (a 1 by 2 or 2 by 4, or whatever) should be even with the bottom edge of the cabinets. When this is in hang the cabinets as you would the ones that rested on a high back splash.

SOFFIT

When the hanging cabinets are in there'll be a space above them. You enclose these with fascia. It's purpose is to prevent dirt from collecting on the tops of the cabinets.

First, tack a nailer (1 by 2) to each cabinet top, recessed 3/8 inch from the face. When cabinets are in, tack a corresponding nailer (2 by 4 inches or 1 by 12 inches if the only beam is back in the corner of the ceiling) to the ceiling, also set back 3/8 inch from cabinet face. Cut a piece of 3/8 inch Sheetrock to fit in place between cabinet top and ceiling, tacking it on with a few small nails. Later, cover the joints with molding. There are a number of possibilities for finishing off the walls, floor, and ceiling. Various treatments are covered in detail in other chapters.

Chapter 18

Installing A Counter Saver

A common kitchen occurrence when food is being cooked is for the water to boil away with the result that the food begins to burn. The housewife rushes into the kitchen and instinctively grabs the pot and looks for some place to put it. So she puts it right on the plastic-laminate counter top—and creates a beautiful brown ring.

Sometimes the insurance company will pay for a new counter. But more often these days, they won't. To make sure you never have to ask them, put in a counter saver.

A counter saver is a piece of ceramic/glass that is 3/16 inches thick and comes in 11 by 15, 16 by 20, 16-3/8 by 21-3/8 and 18 by 24-7/8 inch sizes. It won't burn, cut, absorb stains, or break under normal use (one I installed did break—a woman slammed frozen beef patties on it). If it does, the manufacturer, Corning, guarantees replacement up to one year. It comes only in one color, white. There are similar products to the one Corning makes but I have never installed them so I can't guarantee their invulnerability. I know that they do have the year's guarantee.

LOCATION

The number one place to put the saver is near the stove. Another place might be halfway between the breadbox and the refrigerator, where it's good for sandwich making. Or put it in the spot on the cabinet where the homemaker does most of her work—mixing batter, mashing potatoes, and such. These activities wear the pattern off regular plastic laminate. The counter saver won't wear—I hope—we haven't had any complaints.

INSTALLATION

This is easy. Full instructions are included with the counter saver, but I'll tell you how to do it anyway to give you an idea of what's involved, and to pass along some tricks I've learned.

A cardboard template (pattern) of the counter saver is provided. First step is to mark where the unit will go by outlining the template on the counter top with a soft pencil. If you can, locate the outline so that you can do the cutting of the counter saver's corners with a saber saw. In other words don't have these corners fall near any obstructions, such as the back splash, which would not leave room for the saw to pass. Also you should have clearance below the saver for the clips that secure it. (Most base cabinets don't have tops so this isn't usually a problem.) And provide at least a half-inch clearance between your cut and the back of the base cabinet facing piece. This is also to provide room for clips.

If you're doing the job without a template (you may be using an existing counter saver from a kitchen that is being remodeled, or you're installing a stainless steel one, or a brand without a template), use the steel rim as your pattern. Set it on the counter top right side up, then pencil it in the outline going around the outside. You might find that it is a little wiggly on all sides because the rim is slightly distorted. So after you've made the outline join the corners with straight lines as shown in Fig. A.

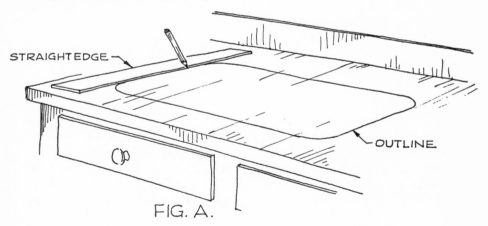

STRAIGHT EDGE

OUTLINE

FIG. A.

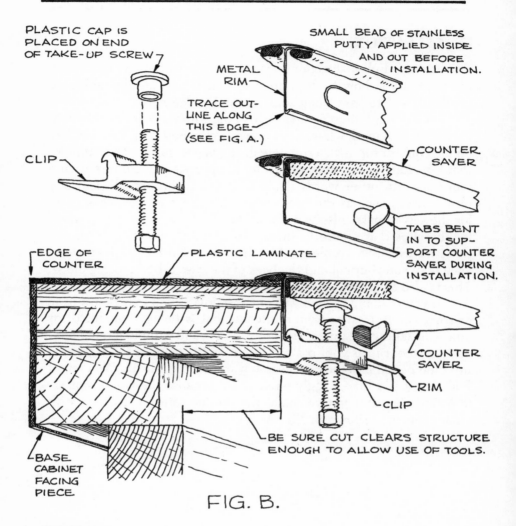

PLASTIC CAP IS
PLACED ON END
OF TAKE-UP SCREW

METAL
RIM

TRACE OUT-
LINE ALONG
THIS EDGE
(SEE FIG. A.)

SMALL BEAD OF STAINLESS
PUTTY APPLIED INSIDE
AND OUT BEFORE
INSTALLATION.

CLIP

COUNTER
SAVER

TABS BENT
IN TO SUP-
PORT COUNTER
SAVER DURING
INSTALLATION.

EDGE OF
COUNTER

PLASTIC LAMINATE

COUNTER
SAVER

RIM

CLIP

BE SURE CUT CLEARS STRUCTURE
ENOUGH TO ALLOW USE OF TOOLS.

BASE
CABINET
FACING
PIECE

FIG. B.

CUTTING

Next, cut the straight lines of the cutout using a very sharp, fine-tooth crosscut blade in a circular saw, cutting each side of the outline up to the point where it starts to curve. To cut, hold the guard back on the saw, place the toe on the surface and gradually let the blade cut into the line. Wear safety goggles and watch the saw blade.

Guides of circular saws are usually inaccurate, especially if you've dropped the saw at some time in the past. Cut so the lines disappear as you go. Cut all four sides; then cut the corners with a jigsaw equipped with fine-toothed wood-cutting blade.

Now try the rim to see how it fits. It should go in without any force at all but shouldn't flop around. If necessary, you can use a half-oval wood rasp to enlarge the cutout. Make downward strokes against the plastic laminate edge so you don't chip it. Tip: Never use the largest counter saver—if you make a mistake you can always make a new cutout and install a bigger one.

Next, pack a fairly soft putty, such as plumber's stainless putty or a good grade of house caulk, on both the inside and outside flanges of the rim: a 3/16 inch thick bead is good. (For this and additional details see Fig. B.)

Drop the counter saver into the rim, then bend in the tabs on the rim to hold the saver in place. Then place the assembly (counter saver and rim) into the hole. If the joint or weld in the rim is noticeable it should be situated in the rear.

Finally, install the clips provided to lock the unit in place.

If you are installing a counter saver in a new kitchen it's a good idea to position it in the counter top before that is installed.

Chapter 19

Installing A Dishwasher

The job of installing a dishwasher has three aspects—plumbing, electrical connections, and carpentry. If there are existing cabinets you have to work around them or in them. If you are installing new cabinets, no problem—just allow space for the dishwasher. If you are laying out a brand new kitchen provide future space for a dishwasher if you're not going to install one now. A false cabinet front can be installed over the dishwasher space and can be removed easily to install the machine.

DISHWASHER IN EXISTING CABINETS

In old cabinets finding space for the dishwasher can be a challenge. If possible the machine should be installed next to the sink. Other locations are acceptable, though, such as under the wall oven or through a wall into a closet or garage.

Dishwashers have standard dimensions. They're 24 inches wide by 24 inches deep by 34 to 35-1/2 inches high (legs are adjustable). When installing one, minimum space width allowed should be 24-1/8 inches. The machine rests on the floor and is set flush against the back wall.

To make a place for the dishwasher under a counter top the cabinet front and everything behind it must be cut away—shelves, partitions, cabinet flooring, even the cleats, if any, on the wall.

First, measure the distance from the floor to the underside of the counter top and the depth to the wall. If you have an old counter covered with ceramic tile the chances are the dishwasher will be too big to fit under it.

But if it does, check the plumbing. If the sink is under a window chances are that the waste pipe comes across in front of the wall and will obstruct things. In this case pipes will have to be rerouted.

When you have determined that the counter height and the

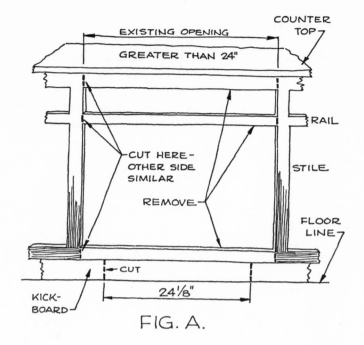

EXISTING OPENING
GREATER THAN 24"
COUNTER TOP
RAIL
STILE
FLOOR LINE
CUT HERE-OTHER SIDE SIMILAR
REMOVE
CUT
KICK-BOARD
24⅛"

FIG. A.

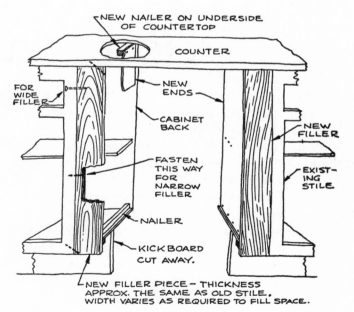

NEW NAILER ON UNDERSIDE OF COUNTERTOP
COUNTER
FOR WIDE FILLER
NEW ENDS
CABINET BACK
NEW FILLER
EXIST-ING STILE
FASTEN THIS WAY FOR NARROW FILLER
NAILER
KICKBOARD CUT AWAY.
NEW FILLER PIECE — THICKNESS APPROX. THE SAME AS OLD STILE. WIDTH VARIES AS REQUIRED TO FILL SPACE.

FIG. B.

plumbing will accommodate the dishwasher the next thing is to decide where to cut the cabinet. If you find that the door opening next to the sink is 24 inches wide all you have to do is cut out the rails flush with stiles (vertical pieces) and count your blessings. It may be, though, that the opening is too small or too large. If the opening is too large but not large enough for the extra space to be used as a slim cabinet, 32 inches or less, then the space will require filler boards on each side. See Figs. A and B on how to do this.

If the opening is too small but only by about an inch or so, it may be possible to cut a small section off each side to make an opening 24-1/8 inches. See Fig. C. If the opening is much too large or small, see Fig. D. As indicated, cut cabinet rails off 2 inches shorter (opening 26-1/8 inches) on one side than finished opening. Make a new 2 inch wide stile and screw or nail it to the cut ends of the rail. Make sure stile is plumb (Fig. E).

As mentioned, everything behind this opening must go —shelves, cabinet flooring, partitions, even cleats on the wall. If in doing so you cut away one or both ends, you must build new ones. You can use 3/8 inch or 1/2 inch playwood, cutting each, or both, to fit behind the cabinet face (stiles) and under the counter. Mark on this end all the parts of the cabinet that need to be supported. Use 3/4 inch by 3/4 inch or 1 by 2 strips, securing them as nailers to the underside of the counter and bottom shelf.

If the cabinet has a stepped back front there is an additional problem. The end of a stepped back cabinet will not cover the sides of the dishwasher completely (see Fig. F).

To rectify this a facing piece must be used (Figs. G and H). It can be of almost any thickness depending on the space available, but the opening for the dishwasher must be made wider to accommodate the piece. I recommend using 5/4 inch material if there is room. If so, make the opening 26-3/8 inches. If you have an available opening that is 25-3/4 inches use nominal 1 inch stock on each side. (It used to measure 13/16 inch but now it measures 3/4 inch.)

The face piece should be flush with the upper face of the cabinet and continue straight to the bottom of the dishwasher. Cut a kick space in it to match the dishwasher front.

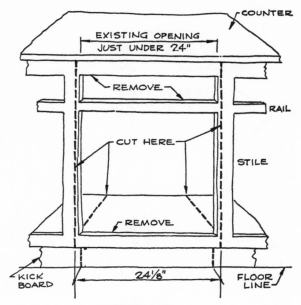

COUNTER

EXISTING OPENING
JUST UNDER 24"

REMOVE

RAIL

CUT HERE

STILE

REMOVE

KICK
BOARD

24⅛"

FLOOR
LINE

FIG. C.

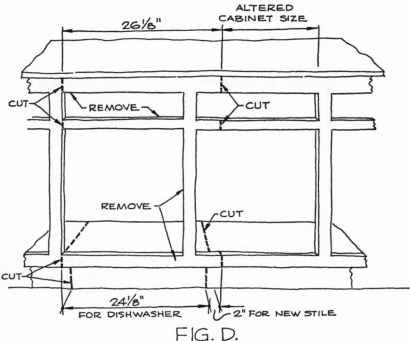

26⅛"

ALTERED
CABINET SIZE

CUT

REMOVE

CUT

REMOVE

CUT

CUT

24⅛"

FOR DISHWASHER

2" FOR NEW STILE

FIG. D.

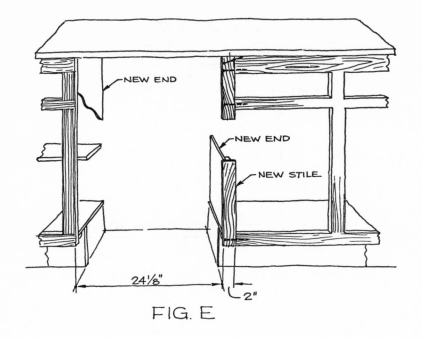

NEW END

NEW END

NEW STILE

24⅛"

2"

FIG. E

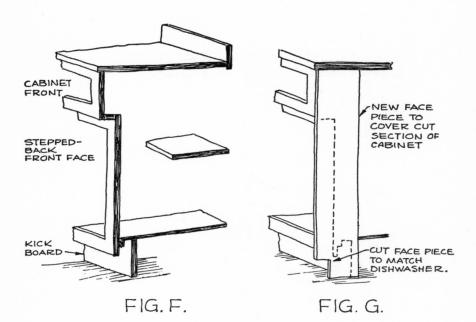

CABINET FRONT

STEPPED-BACK FRONT FACE

KICK BOARD

FIG. F.

NEW FACE PIECE TO COVER CUT SECTION OF CABINET

CUT FACE PIECE TO MATCH DISHWASHER.

FIG. G.

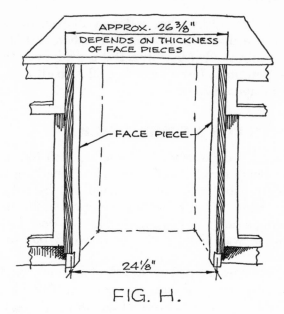

APPROX. 26⅜"
DEPENDS ON THICKNESS
OF FACE PIECES

FACE PIECE

24⅛"

FIG. H.

MODIFYING DOORS AND DRAWERS

Doors and drawers will have to be cut down to fit the new opening size. If the opening is very small and adjacent to a larger opening you may want to use dummy doors or drawer fronts. To cut down a drawer see the chapter on how to make a drawer. To do it properly you first take the drawer apart carefully, cut parts to correct size, then reassemble.

To cut down a door, first remove the hardware. You have to use a little judgment because there are many different styles. To modify a standard lip door which is 1/2 inch larger in height and width than its opening proceed as follows.

Measure the opening and cut the door off 1/2 inch wider. Use a very sharp block plane to round the edge to match the other edges, then sandpaper smooth. If you have the power tools this can be done on the table saw with a molding head or with a shaper or router.

Next, rabbet the edge at the back to form the lip. This may be done with a skill saw with a guide, or better still, on a table saw. If you want to install the dishwasher under a wall oven you will have to raise the oven to make room for the dishwasher; if it is an electric oven the job requires only carpentry. If it is a gas oven the gas pipe will have to be rerouted. I won't give specifics on either job because there are too many variables.

OTHER SPOTS FOR A DISHWASHER

Another place for a dishwasher is through a wall into a garage or closet. If it is a bearing wall it will have to be framed out the same as for a window or door, and you will need a 4 by 4 header. See Chapter 3 for doing this. Frame out the opening 26 inches by 37 inches, installing a jamb and casing similar to a door jamb. On the other side of the wall build a simple plywood box to cover the dishwasher.

When connecting the dishwasher the job should be done so the dishwasher can be removed easily for service. This means that all pipes must pass behind the dishwasher legs or up through the floor.

Normally, the dishwasher is hooked to the hot water and waste line under the sink. However, if you choose a location away from the sink you can bring the pipes up from the cellar. Just make sure the supply line has a valve and the waste a trap. There is a special tail piece for the sink with a tee for the dishwasher waste with the waste line usually 1/2 I.D. (inside diameter) copper pipe. Use soft copper (it comes in a coil) and route it in gentle curves up and back from the tail piece starting in line with the angle of the tee, then down to the back of the cabinet. Go through the cabinet next to the wall about 6 inches to 8 inches off the floor, then go down to the floor and curve around on the floor to the connection on the dishwasher. Don't kink the tube. I can't give you more specific instructions because each company makes its machine a little differently. The water supply is cut into the hot water line with a tee and is usually 3/8 inch O.D. tubing. Use a valve right where you cut into the water line so that the water can be shut off for servicing. Follow the same general line as the waste pipe. The chapter on plumbing goes into specifics which you can adapt for this installation. The electrical connection should have its own circuit and is really a job for an electrician, particularly the installation of a new fuse or circuit breaker in the panel. Running the wire from the dishwasher to the panel may be done by the home handyman. This can save you some money. The wires at the dishwasher should be long enough to let the machine be pulled out for service. For more details see Chapter 27.

Chapter 20

Storage

One of the prime needs that homeowners have, I've discovered, is more storage space. There are a variety of ways to achieve it.

BUILT-INS

In this type of storage you use the house structure and build the storage unit into it. Some good places are behind attic knee walls, along the wall in a stairwell, in the attic or cellar.

Figure A shows how to build an unfinished dresser into an attic knee wall. First cut the knee wall studs, then frame the area out with 2 by 4's. You may have to provide additional flooring pieces on the attic joists where the dresser will rest, or build up the subfloor even with the finished floor. You could just push the dresser in place and leave it at that, but for good looks it should be trimmed, as shown in the details. Remove drawers so that you can nail through the dresser into the studs with eightpenny finishing nails to hold it in place. Trim as you would a door jamb. Use threepenny finishing nails through casing into nailer and sixpenny finishing nails into studs.

FIXED WALL-TO-WALL SHELVES

Another useful type of storage unit is wall-to-wall shelves. These may be out in the open in a room or inside a closet. You will displace some clothing but you'll gain a lot of shelf space.

You can use 3/4 inch stock pine up to 16 inches wide for the job. If the shelves are to be no longer than three feet, as in a narrow closet, all you need to do is nail cleats to the wall for the shelves to rest on, using a nail at each end of the cleat. Often, however, there is nothing (studs, paneling, or sheathing) to provide nailing for the front end of the cleat. In such cases use the method illustrated in Fig. B. Cut a piece of shelving stock to the distance from the floor to where you plan the bottom shelf. Stand one piece at each wall and place a shelf cut to length across them, then check for level. Use a piece of shingle to shim up the low side of the shelf (shove shim on

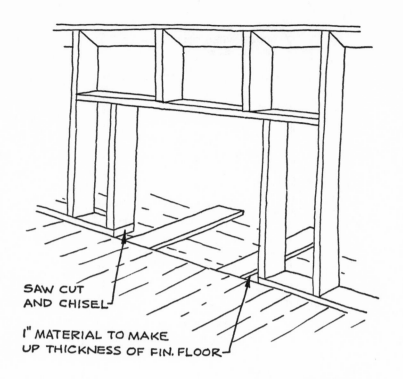

SAW CUT
AND CHISEL

1" MATERIAL TO MAKE
UP THICKNESS OF FIN. FLOOR

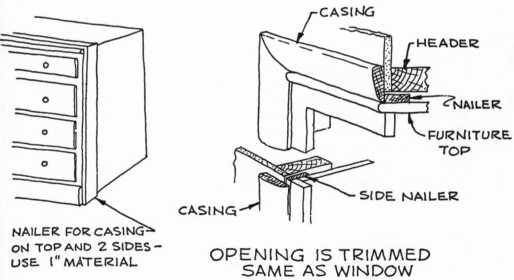

CASING

HEADER

NAILER

FURNITURE
TOP

SIDE NAILER

CASING

NAILER FOR CASING
ON TOP AND 2 SIDES —
USE 1" MATERIAL

OPENING IS TRIMMED
SAME AS WINDOW

BUILDING-IN UNFINISHED FURNITURE

FIG. A.

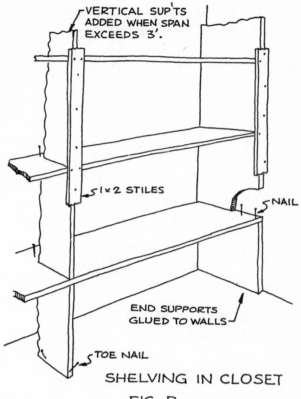

VERTICAL SUP'TS ADDED WHEN SPAN EXCEEDS 3'.

1 x 2 STILES

NAIL

END SUPPORTS GLUED TO WALLS

TOE NAIL

SHELVING IN CLOSET

FIG. B.

bottom of support). When level, you can measure the thickness of the shim to see how much to shorten the high side.

After the first shelf is leveled use panel adhesive to glue the shelf supports to the walls. Then cut two more supports the length of the distance between the bottom shelf and the next shelf; make certain that these pieces are exactly the same length and square. Glue them in place and put the next shelf on top of them. Nail the ends of the shelves into the supports as you go up. Continue with as many shelves as necessary.

If the shelves are longer than 4 feet and you are going to store heavy things on them, use a center support the same length as the end supports. If the shelves are very long, use vertical supports every 30 inches if you plan to store heavy things.

A More Finished Appearance. If the shelves are in a finished room you can trim up the face after all the shelves are in place. You can also make them a little differently.

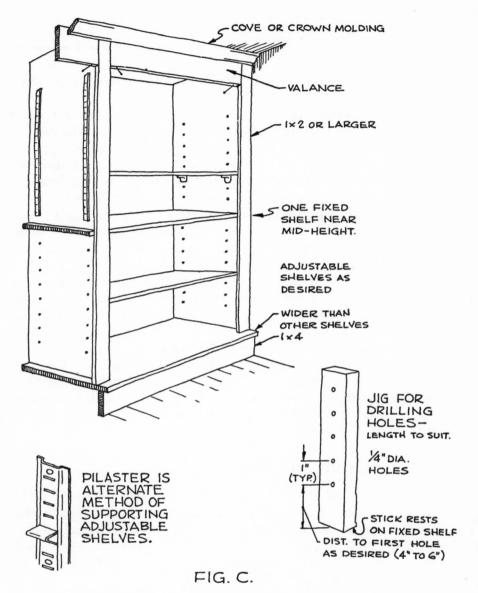

COVE OR CROWN MOLDING

VALANCE

1×2 OR LARGER

ONE FIXED SHELF NEAR MID-HEIGHT.

ADJUSTABLE SHELVES AS DESIRED

WIDER THAN OTHER SHELVES

1×4

PILASTER IS ALTERNATE METHOD OF SUPPORTING ADJUSTABLE SHELVES.

JIG FOR DRILLING HOLES— LENGTH TO SUIT.

¼" DIA. HOLES

1" (TYP.)

STICK RESTS ON FIXED SHELF

DIST. TO FIRST HOLE AS DESIRED (4" TO 6")

FIG. C.

Make the first shelf about four inches off the floor and two inches wider than the other shelves. Use 1 inch by 4 inches for supports and make a face piece to close in the front (see Fig. C). Make the rest of the shelves narrower and place another piece of shelf support material over the top shelf to the ceiling. Use a good clean 1 by 2 or larger for stiles and 1 by 6 or larger for a valance across the top. The valance should be fitted between the stiles and glued and toenailed in place. Trim off the top with cove or crown molding.

If shelves are to be adjustable the principle is about the same as for fixed ones, except the shelf supports are one piece. If the space is long and you are using one or more continuous center supports, make one fixed shelf in the above manner about halfway up the wall. Use pilasters and clips to support the shelves or use shelf brackets that push into 1/4 inch holes that you drill. To ease drilling, make a drilling jig out of a piece of 1 by 2 or lattice (see detail, Fig. C). You can drill holes about 1 inch apart or just to support the shelves at the height you want them. Either way you can always drill more holes if you want to move the shelves later.

Freestanding shelf units are built about the same way. But they have to hold themselves together with no walls to help. For this the back and sides must have diagonal braces. The easiest way is to use solid backing and sides.

The basic way to make a freestanding cabinet is to use 3/4 inch material: lumber, plywood, or flakeboard for the sides and the same for top, bottom, and shelves. Use 1/8 inch or 1/4 inch hardboard or plywood for the back and simply nail and glue it together. The face can be made of 3/4 inch pine of appropriate width for stiles and rails. Add doors if desired.

HANGING UNIT IN GARAGE

I have often made a storage area in a garage with a high ceiling by hanging a 4 foot wide shelf across the back, just high enough for the hood of the car to be pulled under it. The unit is basically a floor framed with 2 by 4's and covered with 5/8 inch sheathing plywood, that is attached to the garage walls on three sides and is hung from the joists or rafters at the front side (Fig. D).

TO BUILD THIS UNIT

To build this unit, strike a level chalk line across the back wall of the garage about 3 feet 8 inches off the floor and continue this on both side walls 4 feet out. Cut two 2 by 4's as long as the width of the

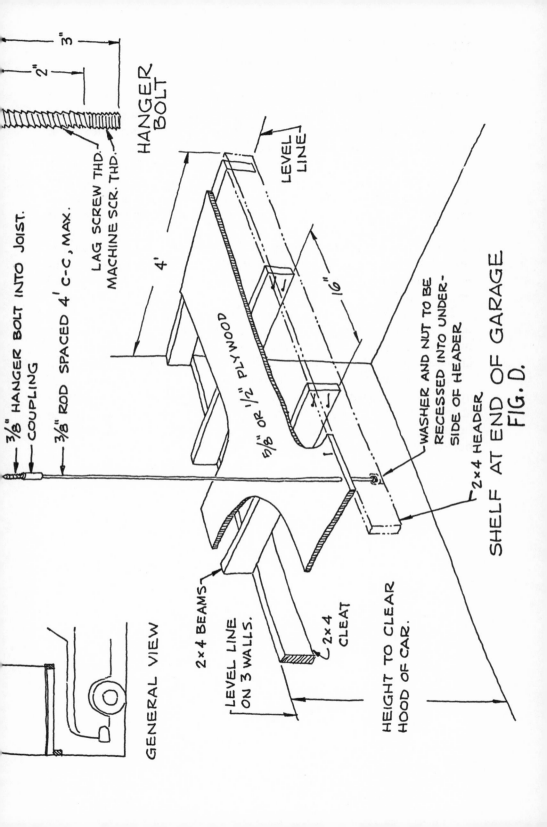

HANGER BOLT

3" / 2"

LAG SCREW THD.
MACHINE SCR. THD.

3/8" HANGER BOLT INTO JOIST.
COUPLING
3/8" ROD SPACED 4' C-C, MAX.

LEVEL LINE

4'

1'6"

5/8" OR 1/2" PLYWOOD

WASHER AND NUT TO BE
RECESSED INTO UNDER-
SIDE OF HEADER

2×4 HEADER

GENERAL VIEW

2×4 BEAMS
LEVEL LINE
ON 3 WALLS.

2×4 CLEAT

HEIGHT TO CLEAR
HOOD OF CAR.

SHELF AT END OF GARAGE
FIG. D.

garage. Place these on the floor side by side with their ends even and mark 16 inch centers on both. Make sure that centers are laid out so that the end of the plywood will fall on the center of a 2 by 4. Nail one of these marked 2 by 4's below the chalk line on the back wall with sixteenpenny common nails, two per stud. For each mark on this stringer cut a 2 by 4, 46 inches long. Nail one of these above the line on each side wall, one end resting on the stringer. Nail the other stringer to the ends of these pieces. Use a temporary support in the middle of this long 2 by 4. Then nail the remaining 2 by 4's in place. At the wall, one end rests on the stringer, the front end butts the other stringer. It is better to toenail with three tenpenny common nails than to nail through the stringer with two sixteenpenny common nails.

The front edge will be supported by a number of hangers. Each hanger consists of one 3/8 inch by 2-1/2 inch hanger bolt, one 3/8 inch coupling and a length of 3/8 inch threaded rod, and two nuts and washers available at a hardware store. Locate the top end of the hanger in a joist or rafter. The hangers should be no more than 4 feet apart or from a wall. The lower ends must go through the outside stringer. Use a plumb bob or a straightedge and a level to help locate both ends of the hanging rods. Use a nut and washer on top and bottom of the shelf. Counterbore for the bottom nut and washer and cut the rod flush with the bottom edge of the stringer.

Chapter 21

Making Drawers

A variety of projects around the home such as kitchen cabinets, storage units, and workbench require making drawers. Often, if you are dissatisfied with a cabinet or a piece of furniture it is mainly because the drawers no longer work. You need new ones.

There are many ways to make drawers, probably as many as there are cabinetmakers. The most sophisticated have dovetail corners. To make these by hand is impractical. And to buy machinery for the purpose would not be justified for only a few drawers. What I am going to describe here is a good, practical way to make drawers that can be done with a minimum amount of machinery—with either table saw, router, or radial arm saw and molding head.

A drawer is really nothing more than a well-made box. But the use of good quality drawer hardware such as that made by Knape & Vogt, or Standard Keil, or Grant Pulling Hardware Co. makes the drawers a pleasure to use.

There will be a difference in the construction of the drawer depending on the type of front used.

Listed in order of their construction difficulty, easiest first, are:

No. 1 overlaid slab drawers
No. 2 lip drawers
No. 3 flush drawers

To make any of the types mentioned (see Fig. A), start by measuring the opening—width, height, and depth—in the cabinet. Your drawer should be a minimum of 1/8 inch less in width and height than the opening, and unless there is some special reason such as large objects to be stored, it need not be more than 18 inches to 20 inches in overall depth even if the cabinet is deeper.

Next make a list of the exact sizes of all the parts needed.

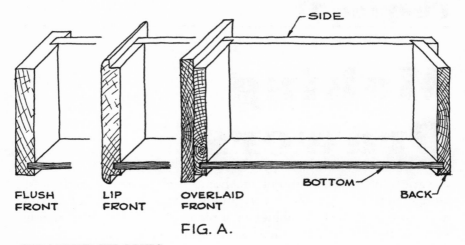

FLUSH FRONT   LIP FRONT   OVERLAID FRONT   BOTTOM   BACK

FIG. A.

DRAWER FRONTS

Overlaid drawer fronts should be 1-1/4 inches wider and higher than the opening.

Lip drawer fronts are 1/2 inch or 5/8 inch wider and higher than the opening.

Flush drawer fronts are the exact size of opening. The edges on flush drawers must be beveled and trimmed for clearance at the time that the finished drawer is installed in the cabinet, but having the front the exact size makes it easier to establish the rabbet sizes and dado locations.

Material for drawer fronts must match or complement cabinet doors. The drawings show 3/4 inch stock but this depends on design.

SIDES FOR ALL DRAWERS

Sides should be 1/2 inch by 1/4 inch less than the height of the opening by depth you have decided on. (See Fig. B.)

(Use 1/2 inch Number 2 pine stock for sides, cutting pieces to avoid the knots. Often you can wind up with entirely clear pieces at less cost than clear pine, which is very expensive.)

BACKS AND BOTTOMS

The back and the inside member of the overlaid drawer front should be 1/2 inch by height of sides by 1-1/2 inches narrower than opening (to allow for hardware).

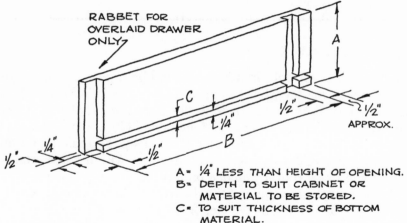

RABBET FOR
OVERLAID DRAWER
ONLY

A = 1/4" LESS THAN HEIGHT OF OPENING.
B = DEPTH TO SUIT CABINET OR
    MATERIAL TO BE STORED.
C = TO SUIT THICKNESS OF BOTTOM
    MATERIAL.

NOTE:
OVERLAID FRONT IS MADE IN TWO PIECES. INNER PIECE OF FRONT
IS IDENTICAL WITH DRAWER BACK.

DRAWER SIDES
OTHER ONE IS MIRROR IMAGE
FIG. B.

To get the size of the bottom, measure the finished box pieces. For very small drawers use 1/8 inch plywood or Masonite. On large drawers, or drawers designed for heavy contents, use 3/8 inch plywood. On all others use 1/4 inch plywood or Masonite. But do make the bottoms of all drawers in any one unit the same, for convenience in making the parts.

A Typical List (For Lip Drawer):

16 inches W by 3-3/4 inches H by 22-1/2 inches (depth of
    drawer to be 20 inches)
Lip Front: 3/4 by 16-1/2 by 4-1/4 inches
Sides: 1/2 by 3-1/2 by 20 inches
Back: 1/2 by 3-1/2 by 14-1/2 inches
Bottom: 1/4 by 14-1/2 by 20 inches approx.

With all your mathematics figured out, cut out pieces: fronts to exact size, sides to exact size, back to exact height and approximate width. You must verify the width after you cut dadoes in side. This work may be done either on a table saw or radial arm saw or, if you have them, both.

CUTTING DADOES

Next, cut dadoes for bottom in the side and back pieces. Procedure is the same no matter what the drawer style. Examine each piece before you cut it. Make the dado in the best face keeping the best edge away from the saw fence. The fence should be 1/4 inch from the dado blade and the blade set to cut 1/4 inch deep. You can do this on a table saw or radial arm saw or with a router with a fence attachment. If you use a router practice on a piece of scrap wood first.

Next reset the saw and cut the dado in the drawer front. For lip drawers the dado should be 5/8 inch from the lower edge. For a flush front the dado should be. 5/16 inch above the lower edge.

For the sides, reset dado head to cut 1/2 inch wide (the thickness of the back), 1/4 inch deep, and cut dado in the back end of each piece. Be sure to make a right side and a left side by cutting the dado in opposite ends of the side pieces; cut dado into the same face as the previous one 1/2 inch from the end.

In case of flush drawers dado the ends of the front with 1/2 inch setting.

For an overlaid drawer a rabbet is cut in the front end of each side the same size as the dado. This can be done by setting the fence of the saw right next to the dado head. Face the fence with wood to avoid damaging the cutting tool. This is a good standard practice anyway. Shape the edges of the drawer front to suit. For lip fronts there is a special cutter that does the whole job in one cut. However, you can use a 3/8 inch quarter round cutter either in the router or a molding head on the table saw or radial arm saw. The remainder of the cutting may be done with a plywood cutting saw blade in the table saw or the dado head in the radial arm saw.

One cutting rule: Always feed your work into the approaching cutting edge of any cutting tool. This is true for all stationary machinery. It is also true for hand held tools in that the relationship between the rotation of the cutting tool and the direction it passes the wood are the same as with stationary tools, that is, a router is exactly the same tool as a shaper except it is hand held.

If you feed the wood from the wrong direction, the machine can pull the work right out of your hand. This could ruin the work or your hand, or both.

MAKING A LIP DRAWER

The lip drawer front (Fig. C) is rabbeted 3/8 inch by 3/8 inch on the top and bottom edge. The ends are rabbeted 3/8 by about 1-1/4 inches to allow room at the sides for clearance for the hardware. All dadoes may be done, as I said above, on a table saw, radial arm saw, or a router. The router requires clamping a straightedge to the work or the use of a fence.

Assembled, the drawer box must be 1 inch to 1-1/16 inches narrower than the opening. Hold the two sides together, back to back so that you can measure the combined thickness of the remaining stock behind the dadoes. It is necessary to check this because the 1/2 inch stock may not be exactly 1/2 inch thick and the dadoes might be off a little bit too. For instance if the stock was 1/32 inch too thick, and the dado 1/32 inch too shallow, the combined error would be 1/8 inch. This is greater than our 1/16 inch tolerance and must be allowed for. For example, if the drawer opening is 16 inches, the box must be 15 inches. To check, hold your ruler with the 15 inch mark on the back of the dado and read it on the back of the other dado.

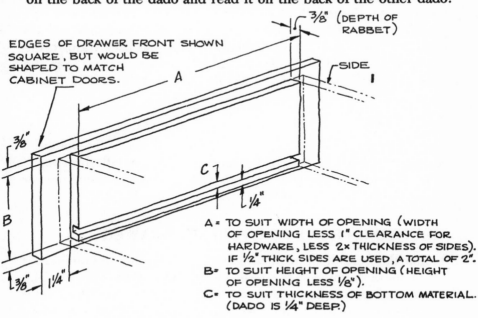

3/8" (DEPTH OF RABBET)

EDGES OF DRAWER FRONT SHOWN SQUARE, BUT WOULD BE SHAPED TO MATCH CABINET DOORS.

SIDE

A

3/8"

B

3/8" 1 1/4"

C

1/4"

A = TO SUIT WIDTH OF OPENING (WIDTH OF OPENING LESS 1" CLEARANCE FOR HARDWARE, LESS 2× THICKNESS OF SIDES). IF 1/2" THICK SIDES ARE USED, A TOTAL OF 2".
B = TO SUIT HEIGHT OF OPENING (HEIGHT OF OPENING LESS 1/8").
C = TO SUIT THICKNESS OF BOTTOM MATERIAL. (DADO IS 1/4" DEEP.)

FRONT FOR LIP DRAWER
FIG. C.

This saves doing the arithmetic. You can read the width of the back member of the box right off the ruler.

Cut the back member to length. Fit the side dadoes over the ends of it and measure the combined width of all three pieces. They should be 1 inch less than the drawer opening (as in our example no larger than 15 inches), and no smaller than 14-15/16 inches. Recut if necessary. For an overlaid drawer front, the inside front member is cut to the same length.

This measurement is also the width of the drawer bottom. Write it on your list.

For a lip drawer, hold the side pieces in place against the front piece and measure the width of the box. This should be the same as the back. If it is too large cut equal amounts off each end rabbet to make the box fit. Too small? Then a shim may be necessary.

For a flush drawer fit the side pieces into the dadoes and check the measurement. If the box is too wide or narrow you can make a small adjustment by making the rabbet wider or making a corresponding shim. For a large adjustment make a new front. For a lip front drawer the length of the bottom piece is taken from the side piece. Measure from the back dado to the front end and add 1/8 inch. For an overlaid drawer measure from the back dado to the front rabbet and add 1/2 inch. For a flush drawer measure from the back dado to the front end and add 1/4 inch. Cut the bottom piece.

ASSEMBLY

Now fit all the pieces together dry. Adjust the size of the bottom if necessary. Then glue the corners and nail together with threepenny finishing nails. Do not glue the bottom as this may cause the drawer to set up slightly out of square.

MOUNTING FRONT OF OVERLAID DRAWER

Mount the front of an overlaid drawer; drill the inside member for six or more Number 8 flat head iron wood screws (Fig. D). The number of screws depends on the size of the drawer. The screws must be in a uniform pattern over the entire area of the front, close to the top and bottom and the ends.

USE SIX OR MORE SCREWS; SELECT
LENGTH CAREFULLY SO THAT SCREWS
WON'T BREAK FACE OF OVERLAY FRONT.

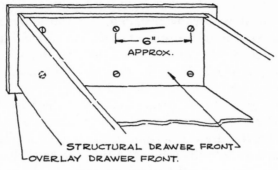

6"
APPROX.

STRUCTURAL DRAWER FRONT
OVERLAY DRAWER FRONT.

FIGURE D.

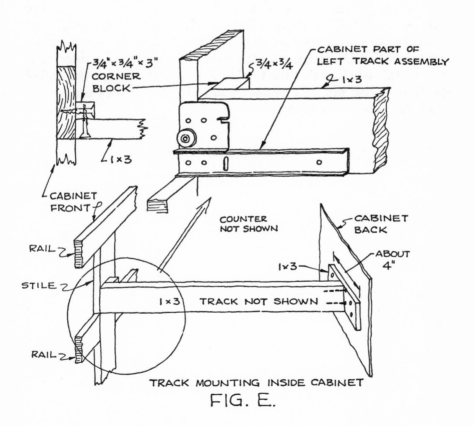

3/4" × 3/4" × 3"
CORNER
BLOCK

CABINET PART OF
LEFT TRACK ASSEMBLY

3/4 × 3/4

1 × 3

1 × 3

CABINET
FRONT

RAIL

STILE

RAIL

COUNTER
NOT SHOWN

CABINET
BACK

ABOUT
4"

1 × 3

1 × 3   TRACK NOT SHOWN

TRACK MOUNTING INSIDE CABINET

FIG. E.

Be sure to align the drawer on the front properly centered right to left and top to bottom. Next mount the hardware. You will have to provide a place in the cabinet to hold the hardware (Fig. E).

If the cabinet is already installed, cut the 1 by 3, 3/4 inch shorter than the inside measurement of the cabinet and use a 3/4 by 3/4 by 3 inch block in the front end, and a 1 by 3 by 4 inch block in the back as shown in Fig. E. If the cabinet is not installed you can nail directly through the back of the cabinet.

Mount the cabinet half of the hardware to the 1 by 3. Use only the elongated holes in the hardware with the screw in the center of the hole. Mount the drawer portion in the same manner.

Put the drawer into the cabinet. Adjust the track up or down so that the drawer works smoothly. Make sure the tracks in the cabinet are parallel.

When the drawer works smoothly, putting a screw in each end and one near the middle is sufficient. The screws must go in perfectly square so that they are flush with the track when set. Remove any screw that interferes with the free movement of the drawer. If after all this you find that the tracks are too tight, mortise the end of the cabinet half into the cabinet frame slightly. If they are too far apart shim them out slightly.

Chapter 22

How to Make a Simple Bar

A bar should be built like a good piece of furniture—carefully and solidly. The one shown here is simple to make. You can use 1 by 12 pine, or flakeboard, if you prefer; the latter is less expensive but harder to handle. If you use boards, common grade Numbers 2 or 3 will be fine. As with most projects once you figure out your lumber needs you can get the lumberyard to cut them to exact sizes needed for a nominal fee. Or do it yourself.

The bar may be "dry" or "wet"—have a sink and waste disposal. If you plan a wet one you must locate it close to plumbing. Ideally, you'd locate it in a spot where you can tie into a gravity waste line—the waste runs out by gravity. Most basements don't have this arrangement and you have to install a waste pump. This is an automatic pump with a small reservoir. Water runs in and triggers a float switch which pumps out waste automatically. At any rate this is really a job for a plumber.

BUILDING THE BAR

The bar is designed to be anchored at one end to the wall and be located in a corner of the room. There should be about 30 inches between its back side and the back wall.

First step is to build a base from 1 by 4 stock following the sketch for dimensions as shown in Fig. A. Nail the pieces together with sixpenny nails.

Next, cut the lower vertical end piece on the wall side and secure to the wall, one end resting on the floor. Either nail into the studs or, if these aren't accessible, use toggle bolts or Molly fasten-

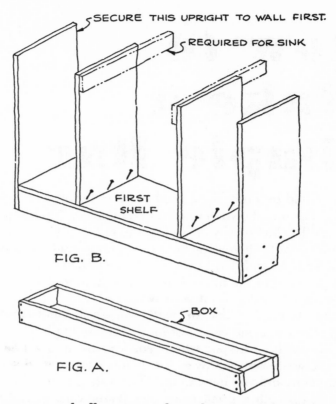

SECURE THIS UPRIGHT TO WALL FIRST.

REQUIRED FOR SINK

FIRST SHELF

FIG. B.

BOX

FIG. A.

ers. Also use panel adhesive or white glue. You want this piece nice and tight.

Set the base tight against this piece and determine if it's level. Usually, it won't be more than 1/2 inch, if at all, out of level. Use cedar shims (these are tapered and serve well), pieces of Masonite or some other hard material to build up the side that's low. Next cut the other end piece. The distance the base is off will have to be compensated for when cutting this piece. If the base is out of level near the wall cut the end piece that much shorter so, when installed, it will be the same height as the piece on the wall. If the far side is out of level cut the piece that much longer. When the base is leveled and the end cut to size, nail the base to the wall shoe, then secure the end to the base.

Next secure the first shelf to the box. It is the same length but overhangs the base slightly in back. This provides a kick space so that the bar will not be scuffed—or toes stubbed—at the bottom.

Secure vertical shelf supports to the structure (Fig. B). The end

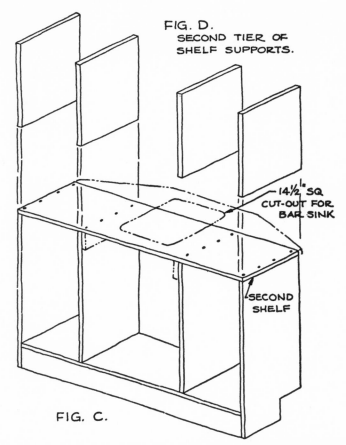

FIG. D.
SECOND TIER OF
SHELF SUPPORTS.

14½" SQ
CUT-OUT FOR
BAR SINK

SECOND
SHELF

FIG. C.

supports are notched to conform with the base and the first shelf and secured with sixpenny nails. The intermediate supports are toenailed in place. When securing use a squiggly bead of white glue wherever wood meets wood. If you are going to have a sink, also glue and nail blocks of wood to the uprights to help support the next shelf which the sink rests on.

The bar shown is 8 feet long. For this, two intermediate supports were used based on one every three feet. If your bar is longer you'll have to use additional supports.

SECOND SHELF

Nail the second shelf to the uprights, then secure the second group of uprights and structural top (Figs. C, D, and F).

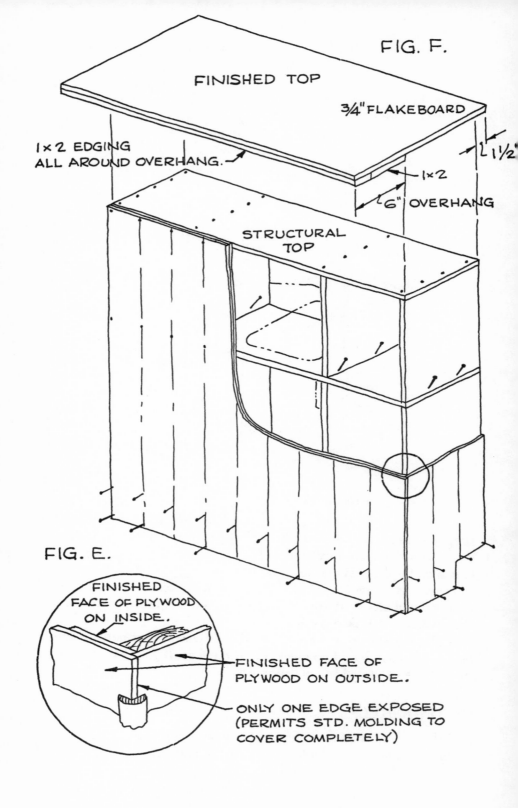

FIG. F.

FINISHED TOP

3/4" FLAKEBOARD

1×2 EDGING
ALL AROUND OVERHANG.

1½"

1×2

6" OVERHANG

STRUCTURAL
TOP

FIG. E.

FINISHED
FACE OF PLYWOOD
ON INSIDE.

FINISHED FACE OF
PLYWOOD ON OUTSIDE.

ONLY ONE EDGE EXPOSED
(PERMITS STD. MOLDING TO
COVER COMPLETELY)

NOTE 1. METHOD OF INSTALLING TRIM IF THERE IS NO SINK.
NOTE 2. SHELF AND TRIM IF THERE IS TO BE A SINK.

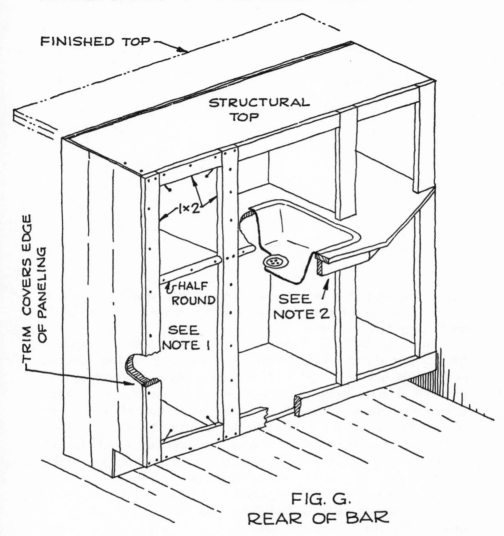

FIG. G.
REAR OF BAR

At this point you can nail the facing or skin of the bar to the structure (Fig. E). A good choice is prefinished paneling with a distressed finish. This is dotted with black marks; you can use black-headed nails, going through the black marks and the heads won't be prominent. If you use white paneling, you can sink the nails a little below the surface and cover the heads with dabs of white

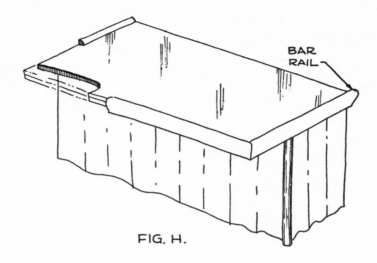

BAR
RAIL

FIG. H.

putty, but the putty doesn't exactly match the paneling, tends to yellow faster. White nails, on the other hand, easily pick up black marks from hammer blows.

Next use small nails to install corner board molding on exposed front corner of bar. Use prefinished molding to match the paneling or finish it before installing. Use threepenny nails, putting side piece on, then the facing piece. You can use regular plywood instead of paneling, and upholster it. To do this first install a layer of foam rubber, then cover it with Naugahyde, securing it with nails suited to the purpose. If you do upholster, the plywood should be 3/4 inches thick so nails don't penetrate through to the other side of the bar. One tip: round corners off before installing foam.

The finished top can be either 3/4 inch flakeboard or plywood. It should extend an inch and a half from the base in the back and six inches in the front. Before installing it double up the overhang edge in front by nailing on a 2 inch strip of flakeboard or a 1 by 2 (3/4 inch actual thickness). To secure strips use 1-1/4 inch annular ring underlayment nails. These hold securely and won't come through the top. To secure the top itself simply nail it on.

After securing, cover with plastic laminate following instructions on the can of contact cement used to adhere it. Trim off excess laminate with a router or laminate trimmer.

Trim the back of the bar with 1 by 2 pine (not furring strips) and half round molding as shown in Fig. F. There are slight variations, depending whether you have a shelf for a sink or not. The top is then trimmed (Fig. G.). Half round molding (half a circle in cross section) may be used on the back edge of the top. Bar rail may be used on the front and end. The bar rail should be mitered on the corners and secured with sixpenny nails and glue.

The back bar can simply be a shelf on the wall. There should be a minimum of 30 inches between it and the bar and its height from the floor should be about 42 inches. A shelf depth of 12 inches is good.

If you wish you can make a top with an extended bar shelf as indicated in Fig. H.

Chapter 23

How to Install Oak Flooring

Often, when making home alterations such as moving a wall, adding a closet or a small extension, you are left with a gap in the hardwood flooring. You could cover the entire floor with any number of different kinds of flooring, but it is far more economical to use regular oak flooring to fill in the gap. Of course you could do an entire floor with oak flooring. It has a durability and beauty that is all its own.

Hardwood flooring is commonly oak but maple and walnut are also used. Walnut is often seen as a contrasting color in a border of flooring around a room. Maple is often used as gym flooring. I mention this as a matter of interest and because if you try to match an existing floor you could possibly run into something other than oak.

DOING AN ENTIRE ROOM

Hardwood flooring comes in 12-piece bundles. Each bundle contains pieces of approximately the same length. I've seen bundles marked one foot, but most commonly they start out at two or three feet and go up to about nine feet. To figure the amount of flooring (Fig. A) that you need for a given area, first determine the actual area in square feet and add 33-1/3 percent for waste to this amount. Divide this number by three. Each bundle is marked with its nominal length. Buy enough bundles so that the total of their nominal lengths equal the above number. For example, if the area is 10 feet by 15 feet, or 150 square feet, adding 33-1/3 percent equals 200 square feet; divided by 3 equals approximately 67. The total lengths of the bundles you buy should equal 67, give or take a foot or two.

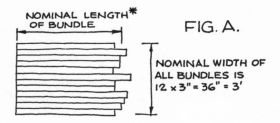

FIG. A.

NOMINAL LENGTH* OF BUNDLE

NOMINAL WIDTH OF ALL BUNDLES IS 12 x 3" = 36" = 3'

NOMINAL AREA COVERED BY ONE BUNDLE IS NOM. WIDTH × NOM. LENGTH, OR 3 × NOMINAL LENGTH.
ACTUAL AREA IS 25% LESS, OR ¾ OF ACTUAL AREA, BECAUSE ACTUAL WIDTH OF BOARDS IS 2¼" RATHER THAN 3".

*ACTUAL LENGTH OF PIECES VARIES UP TO 6" MORE OR LESS THAN NOM. LENGTH.

Of course you can give the square footage to your dealer and he will give you a varied assortment of bundles sufficient to do the job. The boards themselves have a groove on one side and a tongue on the other; they are also end matched with a tongue and groove.

Oak flooring must be installed on a subfloor, assuming you're doing a brand new room. This may be plywood, 1 inch by 6 inch tongue and groove sheathing, or 1 inch by 4 inch boards. Which you use is not terribly important; the easiest is plywood but pick the one with the best price. For information on how to install it, see Chapter 12 on installing resilient flooring.

Before you start to lay the flooring make sure that the subfloor is flat and smooth—no dirt, plaster, joint cement, or protruding nails to interfere with the flat placement of the flooring. If the subflooring is loose, cupped, or humped up in places, drive tenpenny common nails into the bad spots to flatten them. If you can't get it perfectly flat you can take down the high spots when you sand the finished floor later.

USE BUILDING PAPER

Use building paper between the subfloor and the oak flooring. This paper is made with resin in it to help prevent noise caused by the expansion and contraction of the floor. If the finished floor moves a

little, it presses against the paper instead of the subfloor, and re-
duces squeaking.

In general, oak flooring lays flatter if it is at right angles to the
subfloor boards, but it stays tighter if it is at right angles to the joists
and nailed to them. The best way, I believe, is to install the subflooring diagonally and the finished floor at right angles to the joists. This
way it can be both tight and flat. Of course you can also use plywood.
When laid, oak flooring is toenailed through the tongue into the
subfloor, and preferably into the joists below the subfloor.

Existing flooring in an adjacent area (another room, say) may
not have been installed in the best way but you will have to continue
the new floor in the same direction as the old. If the old flooring has
the grooved side facing the new area you will have to make a
"feather" (the equivalent of two tongues), and put it in the groove of
the existing flooring and put the first piece of the new flooring
groove side to that (Fig. B). When you do this you face nail the last
piece of the existing flooring with tenpenny finishing nails (you may
have to drill for them).

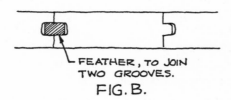

FEATHER, TO JOIN
TWO GROOVES.
FIG. B.

Start the job by installing the subflooring, if necessary. Next lay
out the building paper. Lay one strip at a time absolutely flat, with
additional strips overlapping an inch or two as needed. Before you
start nailing the flooring lay it out bundle by bundle, according to
length. In this way you can easily select the size pieces you need.
The nailing schedule is one nail into every joist. Use seven- or
eightpenny steel cut nails. As you approach the wall to finish the
floor, the last three or four pieces have to be face nailed. If you can't
nail into the joists then nail about every 8 to 12 inches all the way
across the floor. Avoid nailing too close to the ends of the pieces of
the flooring because you can split them.

Ⓐ PICK LONGEST PIECE YOU HAVE.
Ⓑ THRU Ⓒ FILL IN WITH PROGRESSIVELY SHORTER PIECES IN INCREMENTS
       GENERALLY 4 TO 6 INCHES.
Ⓓ THRU Ⓔ FILL IN WITH SMALLER PIECES, AS REQUIRED, UP TO THE
       LONGEST REMAINING PIECE.
Ⓕ THRU Ⓖ USE LONGEST AVAILABLE PIECES, IN SIZE ORDER, WITHOUT
       REGARD TO INCREMENT; SHIFTING OF BUTTS WILL BE AUTOMATIC.
Ⓗ THRU Ⓘ SAME AS Ⓑ THRU Ⓒ.
Ⓙ THRU Ⓚ SAME AS Ⓓ THRU Ⓔ.
Ⓛ THRU Ⓜ SAME AS Ⓕ THRU Ⓖ.
CONTINUE CYCLE UNTIL FLOOR IS FINISHED.
LAST THREE ROWS OF FLOORING TO BE FACE NAILED, USING PILOT HOLES.
NOTE: THE SECOND TIER, PIECE Ⓓ ETC., MAY NOT REACH THE OTHER WALL.

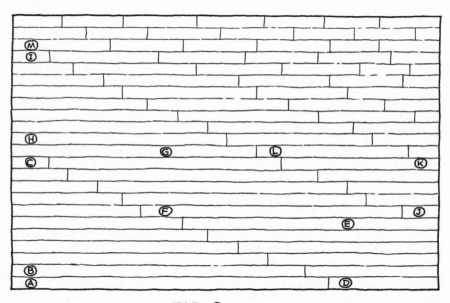

FIG. C.

Start installations with the longest piece of flooring that you have. Place the groove side toward the wall, parallel and about 1/4 inch away from it. Face nail this piece in place. Then nail in succeeding pieces each about 6 inches shorter than the one before. Use only the straightest pieces for these starters. Carry this out as far as you can until you use the shortest precut piece. Then cut pieces to continue the stagger pattern until the last piece nailed in is about 9 inches or so. Starting again at the wall use pieces that are all approximately the same length. As you lay them in place they will also stagger 6 inches automatically until you come to a piece that butts the wall. Then use successively shorter pieces—precut pieces first, then cut pieces until you get down to about a 9 inch piece. Continue this way until you get to the far side of the room and it's necessary to cut pieces to fit. Cut all pieces on a sawhorse using an 8 or 10 point crosscut saw (Fig. C).

It's not necessary to cut ends of boards terribly accurately or straight, since the Sheetrock and baseboard molding on the wall will cover the cut ends. If you come within 1/2 inch of the shoe it's okay. Indeed, you really don't want flooring to be tight against the shoe because it will expand and contract due to weather; a little space in there will eliminate problems of the floor buckling in damp weather. This little space should be allowed on all sides of the flooring.

FACE-NAIL LAST PIECES

The last three rows of boards can't be toenailed—you won't have any room to swing the hammer. Best thing to do is to cut and fit all these pieces and put them in place (staggering joints remains the same) without nailing. Then simply drop or slide the last piece (in the corner) in place. To do this you may have to cut a portion of the groove away. With all pieces in, go back and draw them up snug by driving a flat bar (see Fig. D) into the subfloor and pulling boards tight, then drive tenpenny finishing nails through the flooring, going into joists (one nail per board) if possible. If hitting joists isn't practical you'll have to take pot luck and drive into whatever there is. In any case you'll save a lot of time and muscle power by predrilling for the nails on these pieces. If you are not going to get into the joists

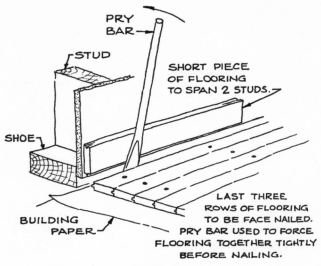

PRY BAR
STUD
SHORT PIECE OF FLOORING TO SPAN 2 STUDS.
SHOE
BUILDING PAPER
LAST THREE ROWS OF FLOORING TO BE FACE NAILED. PRY BAR USED TO FORCE FLOORING TOGETHER TIGHTLY BEFORE NAILING.

FIG. D.

make certain that you only drill through the flooring and not into the subfloor. Drill each hole of a size so that it just fits snugly on the nail shank and is smaller than the head. After these face nails are in go back and set them with a nail set.

For nailing flooring there's a special flooring hammer; it weighs 32 ounces and usually has a grid end (crosshatch) so it won't slip off the nails. If you hit your finger with this hammer it will do an exceptionally good job on it! You have to learn to use it. You ought not to attempt to nail any great amount of flooring without it because driving cut nails through hardwood flooring take a good healthy belt with a heavy hammer.

The exact angle that the nail should be driven is also important. If you drive the nail too flat it won't reach far enough into the subfloor. If you drive it too straight you'll only succeed in breaking the tongue off. I think a 45-degree angle is about right.

Also start the nail carefully. It's not necessary to drive it home as deeply as a finishing nail, but it should be tucked well down in the corner between the tongue and the face of the flooring. It takes practice to get it almost all the way down without putting a "nice" hammer mark on the edge of the flooring. After you drive use the head on the next nail as a "drift" (see Fig. E) and give it another tap to drive it flush.

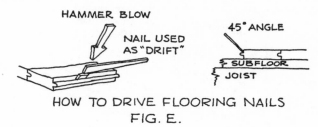

HOW TO DRIVE FLOORING NAILS
FIG. E.

If nailing doesn't sound like something you'd want to try, there is a nailing machine that can be rented. I've never used it myself, but have seen a job done with it and it did very well. The machine is used by holding it in one hand and hitting it with a mallet which automatically drives in special nails. It's probably easier to learn how to use it than to learn how to drive cut nails. I would say the choice between machine and regular nailing would depend largely on the amount of flooring you have to lay. The more flooring the more it would make sense to go out and rent the machine.

In addition to end-matched hardwood flooring there are other types of flooring that may be laid—yellow pine or fir—that are not end-matched and come in long lengths. This flooring is often used right on the joists without any subflooring and is common in the second story of houses which have regular oak flooring on the first floor. It's a little cheaper, especially since you don't need a subfloor, though it can be laid just as easily over one. The only disadvantage is that the flooring does not come with square cut ends and it has to be cut precisely so there is no space where the two ends fit together. I think it's sort of a nuisance to use, to keep moving those big long pieces around in a small room. The ideal would be to have flooring span the whole room without any joints; if joints are necessary, they have to be made carefully by hand.

Final step in installing a new floor, no matter what type and how much was put in, is to sand it off. You should do the whole floor. For this you can rent a big floor sander from rental outfits in the

Yellow Pages. It involves sanding by degrees, going from very rough sandpaper through the finer sandpapers. Two sanding machines are necessary—the edger and the big sanding machine. Dealers will give you a short course on using them.

There are many finishes available—varnish, stain, shellac—but probably the best is polyurethane varnish. You can apply this according to the directions on the can.

"PATCHING" A FLOOR WITH FLOORING

There are a variety of situations you may have to contend with when filling in a gap in existing flooring. I'll describe how to handle the situation where you have taken out a closet and partition wall between rooms to make one large room, and you can adapt the instructions for any situation you face.

The overall procedure no matter what gap you are filling is to treat it like a small room. So, for example, in taking out a closet and wall there will be short pieces of flooring inside the closet. Pry these up with a bar and discard the pieces until you have a nice clear area approximately rectangular or square in shape. If necessary to make pieces fit exactly, you can cut the flooring square, then cut pieces to fit using a miter box for perfect squareness. Once the floor is cleared what you do depends on the way the flooring runs in adjacent areas.

If it's parallel simply measure the area for flooring as you would a regular floor. For example, for an area 9 feet long by 4 feet wide, to get enough flooring to fill 36 square feet, you order 1/3 more, or 48 square feet.

Lay the flooring as you would a regular room starting with the large pieces and working down. If the existing flooring has a tongue on the last strip on one side, and a groove on the other, you can start fastening your first strip on the tongue side then work across to the groove. The last strip can be fitted by cutting the bottom lip off the groove on your last piece, and trimming it on the other side so it fits in snugly (Fig. F). Then simply drill pilot holes and face nail the last piece in.

If the last strips on the adjacent flooring areas are groove pieces, make a "feather" to start, as described earlier in this chapter.

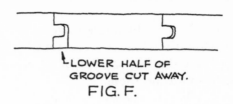

LOWER HALF OF
GROOVE CUT AWAY.
FIG. F.

If the flooring in the rooms runs in opposite directions—one parallel to where the closet was, the other at right angles, proceed as follows. Use a circular saw to trim off the ends of the strips that run at right angles in an even, straight line. Best way to insure this is to nail a 1 by 2 furring strip to the floor as a guide for cutting. Then ride the base of the saw against the edge of the strip to insure a straight cut. (Snap a chalk line on floor first.)

This cut must be as straight as it is possible to make it. There is a big chance that you will hit a nail with your saw, which will ruin the saw blade. To minimize the risk cut off as little of the ends of the flooring as possible. If you do hit a nail stop immediately. Don't try to saw through it. Try to chip the wood away from it with a chisel. Then either drive the nail right through the flooring into the sub-floor or pull it out with a nail puller or a small claw. After the nail is out of the way continue to cut with the saw. Change blades if necessary.

In this case start to lay the flooring parallel to the long side of the patch and finish at the butt ends just cut. In the case of a very small patch all the pieces are fitted and put in place, then face nailed. You will not necessarily finish with a full-width piece. You may have to cut the last to fit.

Chapter 24

Making Steps

A key consideration when making wood steps is that the steps be safe and easy to walk on. If the tread (the part you step on) is too narrow, it will be difficult; a too-shallow riser (the front of the step) can also cause problems.

You should plan steps so that the riser height will fall between 6-1/2 inches and 8-1/2 inches; the tread should be 2 inches longer than the riser.

To figure this you have to measure down from the floor, landing, porch, or the like to the ground, and then divide by various numbers until you get proper riser height. For example, if the distance from landing to ground was 19 inches, you could divide by two and you'd get 9-1/2 inches. This would be one inch too high. Divided by three, though, you'd get 6-1/3 inches which would be acceptable. You'd have three risers. Of course, it may be that things will come out very neatly. For example, if the height were 24 inches you could divide by three and get 8-inch risers.

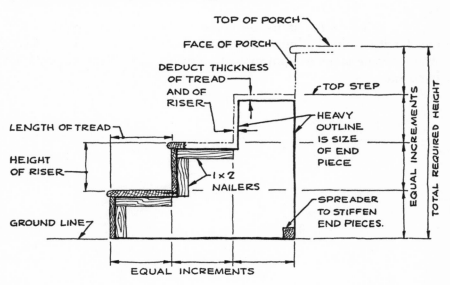

211

The steps here are built with two supporting pieces that enclose them like a box. To find the dimensions of these two side pieces, first draw the overall dimensions of the steps. Then simply subtract the thickness of the tread (1-1/8 inch yellow pine stair tread is recommended) and the thickness of each riser (see the sketch.)

Armed with the dimensions cut the two side pieces from 3/4 inch exterior fir plywood, being careful to make one for the right and one for the left side. Fasten 1 by 2 nailers to the edges of these pieces using 1-1/4 inch underlayment nails and plastic resin glue. Cut the risers (use Number 2 common pine) and treads. The latter may go up to four feet. If you go over this width you need another supporting piece in the middle. Then fasten the pieces on the sides using nails specified and plastic resin glue.

To guard against water standing on the steps, drill 3/4 inch drainage holes 6 inches apart down the length of each step.

The steps should be set on a footing. For this you can use 4 inch (4 by 8 by 16 inches) solid cement blocks set end to end and flush with ground top in a small trench under the perimeter of the steps. Finally, when you set the steps in position toenail them to the house or other structure, and paint them as you would the trim of the house.

Two tips. If the steps are going to run over 24 inches high, check with your building code to see if a railing is required. Also when cutting steps use power tools. Tread is difficult to cut with a hand saw.

Chapter 25

A New Bath And Other Plumbing Improvements

There are many plumbing improvements the do-it-yourselfer can make, from putting in a kitchen sink to installing a complete new bathroom. Here are some of them.

A NEW BATH

A new bath job may range from just taking out the fixtures (sink, tub, toilet) and installing new ones, to ripping out everything to the studs and starting from scratch. If you have a very old bathroom probably the best thing is to go down to the studs. However, if you are modernizing a bathroom that is still in fairly good condition think twice before you start ripping things out. Another caution. If you have only one bath you'll have to go slowly. Plan your work so that you don't inconvenience anyone. Take the fixtures out only when you're ready to get the new ones in immediately.

There are certain things you must do when removing fixtures. The first is to turn off the water supply. Usually, there are valves for turning off the basin and toilet. Basin valves (there are two) are under the sink; the toilet valve is under the water closet. The two tub valves can be in the cellar beneath the tub, or they may be in a panel in a wall behind the tub, or in a slab house in the utility room. If you can't find the appropriate valves you can turn off the main valve in the basement. This will shut off water—hot and cold—to the entire house.

When you disconnect any fixture it's important to pay careful attention to how it's connected. It'll make the job of putting the new one in easier.

If the sink is in a counter top, you will have to loosen clips that hold it to the counter top; the faucet has two thin supply pipes leading from it that hook up with water pipes coming out of the wall. For this a basin wrench is handy for removing nuts that are up close to the back of the sink.

The basin also is tied into the waste line. Here there is a slip nut that holds the drain pipe in place in the "trap" or pipe section where water is trapped to provide a seal against odors and vermin getting into the sink—and house. When all nuts are loose you can just lift the sink up and out of the way.

TOILET

First flush the bowl. Use a pot to remove all water from the bowl (or as much as you can). One type of bowl has a flush elbow and this is connected to the tank. Unscrew with a wrench and take the bowl and tank out separately. New type toilets have the tank and bowl in one piece; these are taken out as a unit. In either case toilets are connected to the floor with two or four bolts which must be removed before you can lift the toilet out of the way.

TUB

If yours is the old-fashioned type of tub with decorative feet the piping will be exposed and it will be a simple matter to disconnect the tub. Just use a wrench on the exposed nuts.

Another type of tub is built into the wall. To remove this you have to open the walls first to get at where the tub is connected to the water and waste lines. If Sheetrock, just rip it off with a pry bar, first removing the escutcheons (decorative pieces below faucet handles). If plaster use a sledgehammer. A hammer is useful in either case.

For removing any tub from the waste line, check downstairs in the cellar if you can to see if the waste line from the tub can be unscrewed from the waste line proper. If you can, just loosen the nut and lift straight up on the tub; the attached waste line will come up and out.

If you can't disconnect the tub waste line from the waste line proper, the only recourse is to disconnect it at the drain flange from inside the tub. This is difficult to do because it's usually corroded. At any rate, slip wrench handles into holes in the drain, then slip a screwdriver between the handles and turn. It may be necessary to cut the chain fitting out with a hammer and cold chisel.

Incidentally, if piping is ancient (lead water pipes) or very old (galvanized iron pipe) or just old (brass pipes), these should now be replaced with copper pipe. Some portion of this work will probably best be done by a plumber. Most local building codes require it. All the pipes that are going to end up covered and inaccessible must be in A-1 condition. You don't want them to develop problems requiring that the wall be opened up for repairs.

INSTALLING A TUB

In position the tub stands on the floor but the back rim also rests on a ledger strip nailed on the studs. You can make this ledger strip out of anything that is available from a 1 by 3 to a 2 by 6.

First measure the tub from the underside of lip to the floor to determine the exact height (Fig. A). It should not be too low so add an extra 1/8 inch and be certain it is level. If the floor is very far out of level you will have to take this into account.

Use your level to check the level of the floor. If the floor is more than 1/4 inch out from the back wall to the face of the tub, put the tub in place and then shim it up level temporarily with shingles or pieces of wood.

Use a straightedge board cut to length of tub to level the tub end to end at the back wall and then front to back on each end (Fig. B). Don't be surprised if you can't get both ends level. Large metal castings are often distorted. If both ends are level that's great—but if one end is out of level it should pitch toward the front the way the

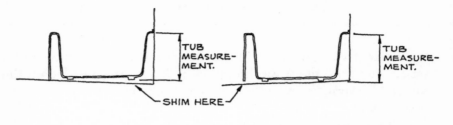

TUB MEASURE-MENT.

TUB MEASURE-MENT.

SHIM HERE

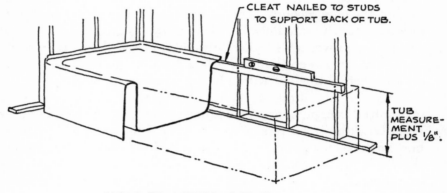

CLEAT NAILED TO STUDS TO SUPPORT BACK OF TUB.

TUB MEASURE-MENT PLUS ⅛".

HOW TO LEVEL A TUB
FIG. A.

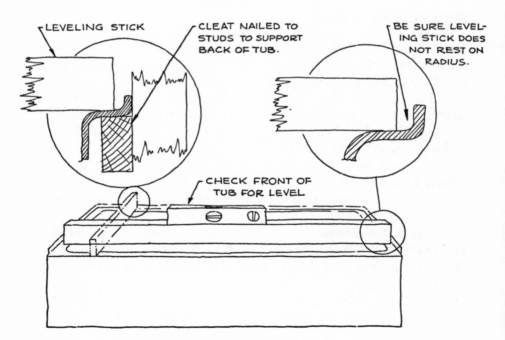

LEVELING STICK

CLEAT NAILED TO STUDS TO SUPPORT BACK OF TUB.

BE SURE LEVEL-ING STICK DOES NOT REST ON RADIUS.

CHECK FRONT OF TUB FOR LEVEL

HOW TO LEVEL A TUB
FIG. B.

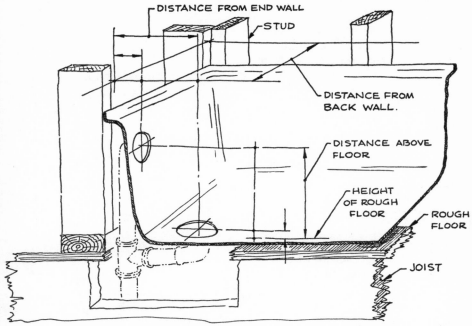

DISTANCE FROM END WALL

STUD

DISTANCE FROM BACK WALL.

DISTANCE ABOVE FLOOR

HEIGHT OF ROUGH FLOOR

ROUGH FLOOR

JOIST

THREE DIMENSIONS REQUIRED FOR EACH OPENING
TO INSURE PIPING WILL FIT TUB.

FIG. C.

water runs. Sometimes it is impossible to get the tub perfectly level, so don't expect it.

After you are satisfied that the tub is level mark the studs where the top of the tub is. Slide the tub away from the wall. Measure the thickness of the back edge of the tub. Allow this amount from the lines on the studs to the top of the ledger and nail the ledger solid. Now move the tub back in place and shim the front edge. It should now be level and rest solidly on the ledger and the floor and shims.

CONNECTING TUB

If you have easy access to the tub connections from the outside (i.e., open to an unfinished area), a tub is no more difficult to connect to plumbing than a sink or basin. But if you don't have this advantage it will be rather difficult to make the connections.

After the tub is shimmed up mark the wall where the center of the overflow and drain holes fall. You need three measurements to locate the exact center of each hole—the distance from two walls and height off the floor (Fig. C). Nail the shims in place so that the

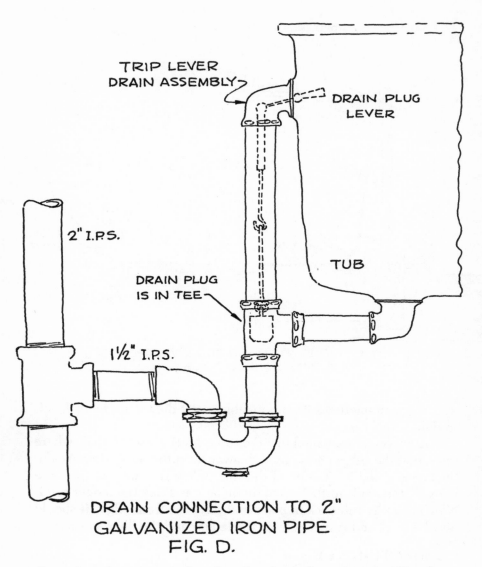

TRIP LEVER
DRAIN ASSEMBLY

DRAIN PLUG
LEVER

2" I.P.S.

DRAIN PLUG
IS IN TEE

TUB

1½" I.P.S.

DRAIN CONNECTION TO 2"
GALVANIZED IRON PIPE
FIG. D.

tub can be taken away and replaced without the necessity of leveling it all over again.

Remove the tub. Make whatever alterations are necessary to the floor framing to make room for the drain pipes. Assemble the drain pipes on the tub and screw them up tight, then remove them as an assembly. Now hold the assembly in approximate place on the

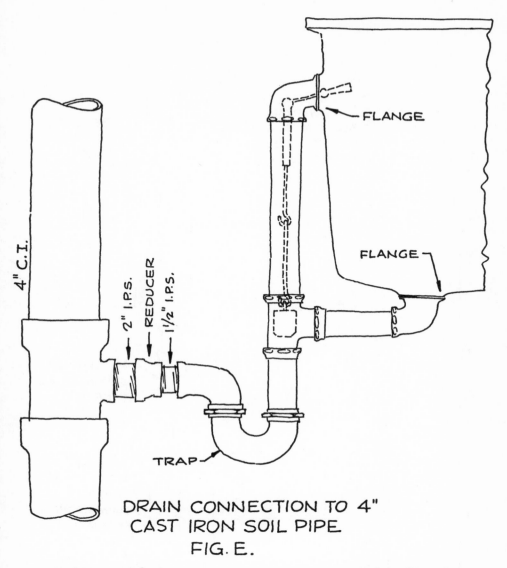

DRAIN CONNECTION TO 4"
CAST IRON SOIL PIPE
FIG. E.

waste pipe according to your measurements to get an idea where the trap has to be.

I can't tell you exactly how to hook up the trap waste because almost every case is different depending on framing set up. See Figs. D, E, F, and G for typical installation situations.

The brass tub trap has a joint in it so that the "U" part can swing

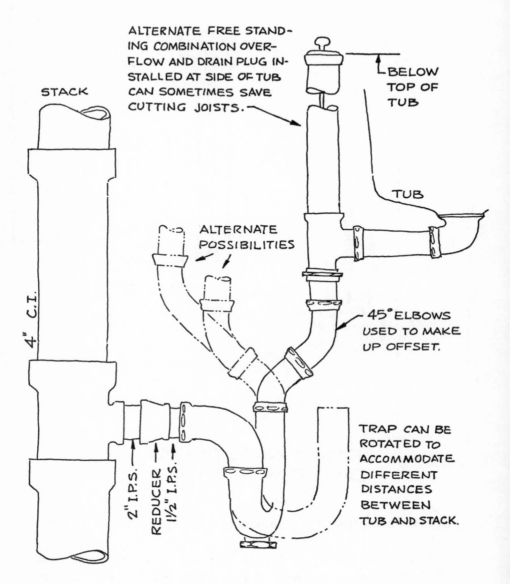

ALTERNATE FREE STAND-
ING COMBINATION OVER-
FLOW AND DRAIN PLUG IN-
STALLED AT SIDE OF TUB
CAN SOMETIMES SAVE
CUTTING JOISTS.

STACK

BELOW
TOP OF
TUB

TUB

ALTERNATE
POSSIBILITIES

45° ELBOWS
USED TO MAKE
UP OFFSET.

4" C.I.

2" I.P.S.

REDUCER
1½" I.P.S.

TRAP CAN BE
ROTATED TO
ACCOMMODATE
DIFFERENT
DISTANCES
BETWEEN
TUB AND STACK.

FIG. F.

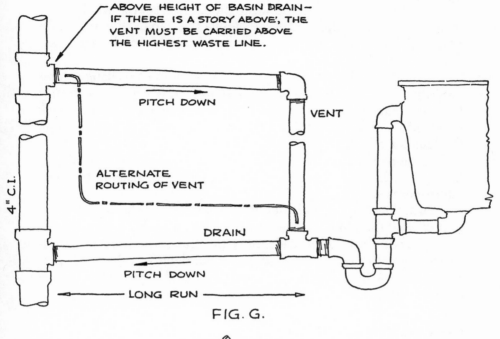

ABOVE HEIGHT OF BASIN DRAIN—
IF THERE IS A STORY ABOVE', THE
VENT MUST BE CARRIED ABOVE
THE HIGHEST WASTE LINE.

PITCH DOWN

VENT

4" C.I.

ALTERNATE
ROUTING OF VENT

DRAIN

PITCH DOWN

LONG RUN

FIG. G.

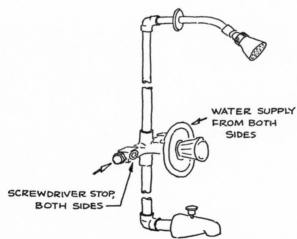

WATER SUPPLY
FROM BOTH
SIDES

SCREWDRIVER STOP,
BOTH SIDES

FIG. G1.

180 degrees or more. This gives a great flexibility for alignment. Screw the trap directly on the waste pipe. Then set the whole thing up and make up all the joints tight; adjust the trap to align the waste flange (lip) and overflow flange according to the marks and measurements you took earlier.

Use tape to hold the washers in place on the two flanges temporarily. Then put the tub in place. If you did everything properly the two flanges will line up with the two holes in the tub. Pack plenty of stainless putty around the drain fitting and screw it in using the handles of a large pair of pliers and a screwdriver to turn it.

If there is access to the back and bottom of the tub, all the fittings can be made up after the tub is in place, making the final adjustments with the trap.

Installing the hot and cold water supplies and shower body are part of what the plumber does. However, the shower body ought to be replaced, screwed, or soldered at this time. The shower body is the fitting with the hot and cold water and diverter valves (see Fig. G1). The new fittings may not have the same dimensions as the old so some adjustment must be made in the water pipes.

INSTALLING A TOILET

Here again I'll assume that the roughing—pipes installed in the wall—has been done. There'll usually be either a 3 inch copper waste pipe or a 4 inch lead pipe coming up through the floor which is 12 inches (to the center of pipe) from the finished wall (see Fig. H for toilet details). On a ceramic tile floor the brass toilet flange is installed directly on the floor, otherwise you must use a marble slab. Different toilet flanges are made for use with lead or copper pipe. You need one to match the kind of waste pipe you have. If you have copper the flange you use may be either straight or offset. The offset flange is used to get more or less clearance from the wall if the waste is not exactly right.

If a lead pipe is not exactly right for the flange to fit it may be dressed (bent) by tapping it gently with a dressing tool, or use your hammer handle to tap it gently in the direction you want it to go and to make it round (the lead is going to be out of round because it is so soft).

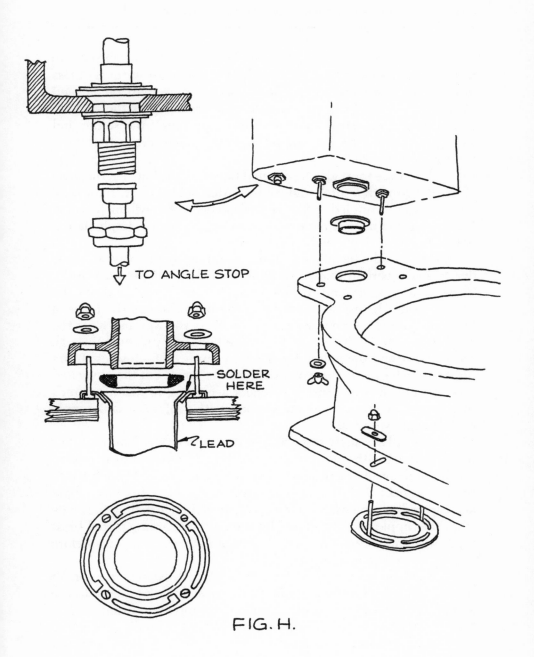

TO ANGLE STOP

SOLDER
HERE

LEAD

FIG. H.

In any case the flange must be placed so that you can put two bolts opposite each other. Then solder the flange for watertightness to the pipe. For copper pipe the flange and pipe must be cleaned with steel wool and coated wtih soldering paste. Apply the solder a section at a time. Heat an area with a torch, melt the solder and work your way all the way around the pipe. Make certain that there is no gap in the solder.

A lead pipe must also be cleaned before soldering. Tin the edge of the flange with a torch and solder. (Melt solder on it, then wipe off.) Don't use a torch directly on the lead because it will melt easily. Final soldering may be done with a soldering iron, or simply flare it out and peen it down with a hammer.

Next, put the flange bolts in place and set up the bowl and tank dry to make certain that everything fits. Then set the tank aside. Place a wax ring around the horn (toilet rests on this) and put the bowl in place, being careful to bring the bolts through the holes in the toilet. Rock the bowl gently to compress the wax and work the bowl so it rests solidly on the floor. The bolts will protrude through the wax ring and the bolt holes. Tighten gently on both sides. Don't use too much pressure or you can crack the bowl. Put the elongated washers and nuts on. Install the tank according to manufacturer's directions and hook up the water supply with a soft brass tank supply and an angle stop (valve).

To install the angle stop valve (water supply valve) there are two possibilities: It either is attached to copper pipe (sweat fitting) coming out of the wall or a threaded fitting which is likely 3/8 inch I.P.S. (iron pipe size). Before attaching anything, use a temporary nipple and cap and turn on water to test for leaks. When installing the angle stop, the nipple and cap should be replaced by chrome plated brass nipples. Remember to put the chrome escutcheons in place before installing the angle stop.

The angle stop is made for either 1/2 inch copper pipe or 3/8 inch I.P.S. (use the one according to the roughing) on the wall side and a 3/8 inch O.D. (outside diameter) compression fitting on the fixture side. The tank supply pipe must be bent carefully so as not to kink it, and cut to proper length to fit into the compression fitting. New plastic supply pipe eases this job. Also, it must be straight in the compression fitting. Put on the nut and ferrule before making it up on the tank end, making certain the nut threads properly. Make it up tight and turn on the water. Adjust the float rod to stop the water level at the proper place.

The steps detailed above will become clearer if you check other toilet installations, or pay careful attention when you remove an old one.

KINDS OF SINKS

There are three common kinds of sinks you can install. All come with a separate rim or are self-rimmed. Installation is similar.

Porcelain on Steel.   This is the least expensive sink but also the least durable. However, it is a serviceable sink and there is nothing really wrong with it.

Cast Iron.   This is more durable than steel; it has a heavier porcelain coating and won't chip as easily.

Stainless Steel.   This comes in many different qualities, and you should shop carefully. The best is made of a heavy gauge steel and is more expensive than cast iron. Stainless steel comes in a variety of finishes, including a dull, brushed effect which is preferred over a polished finish.

INSTALLATION

No matter what type of sink you are installing, the first step is to make the cutout in the counter top. Refer to Chapter 18 on installing a counter saver for this.

If the sink is steel and self-rimmed it can be dropped right into the hole after application of a healthy bead of putty. Then secure the sink from the bottom with clips as with the counter saver.

If the steel sink has a rim, it is the rim that is first fitted in the counter. Then the sink is clipped in place in the rim, and the sink and rim dropped in place.

The cast iron sink wtih a rim is also simply dropped into the

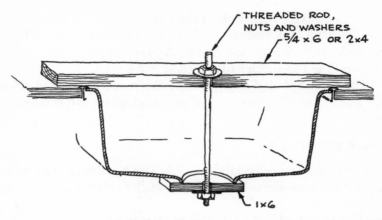

THREADED ROD,
NUTS AND WASHERS
5/4 x 6 OR 2x4

1x6

IF DOUBLE SINK USE TWO RODS.

FIG. H1.

cutout after application of a sealer to the rim area. The sealer comes with the sink.

The cast iron sink with a rim requires that a jig be made. As shown in Fig. H1, the sink is assembled with a jig, the whole thing lifted up and installed in the hole.

INSTALLING FAUCETS

If you have a choice install the faucet on the sink before the sink is in place. Sinks have three holes through which the faucet is installed; some sinks have a fourth hole for the spray or detergent dispenser (Fig. I). The center hole is used for the spray hose (Fig. J) or the pop-up drain fitting rod. There are other types of faucets that have the hot and cold water supplies both in the center hole and two screws to clamp the faucet in place in the other holes. See Fig. K for yet another type.

Some faucets come with plastic or rubber pads to seal them to the sink; others require putty around the holes in the sink. If the faucet must be installed after the sink is in place a basin wrench is

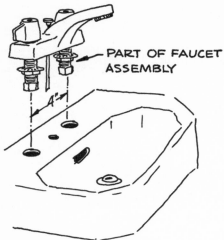

PART OF FAUCET
ASSEMBLY

4"

TYPICAL FAUCET
ON WASH BASIN
4" DECK TYPE
WITH POP-UP DRAIN
FIG. I.

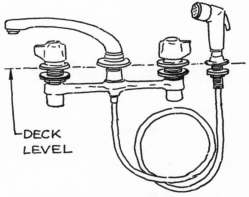

DECK
LEVEL

TYPICAL KITCHEN FAUCET
8" CONCEALED TYPE WITH SPRAY
FIG. J.

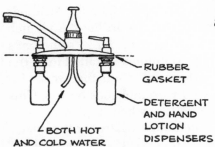

RUBBER
GASKET

DETERGENT
AND HAND
LOTION
DISPENSERS

BOTH HOT
AND COLD WATER
SUPPLIES THRU
CENTER HOLE

FIG. K.

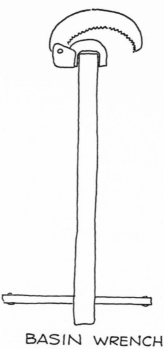

BASIN WRENCH
FIG. L.

necessary (Fig. L). You can purchase one in your local hardware store or plumbing supply house. The wrench will tighten or loosen a nut according to which way the jaws are turned. There are four positions for the jaws. Two will give extra leverage. Two work well by using one hand to close the jaw and the other to turn the wrench with the slide lever handle.

You can buy any type of faucet that goes into the drillings (holes) on your sink or basin. The most common drillings are 4 inch centers for a basin and 8 inch centers for a sink. Sinks sometimes have an extra hole for a spray. Both are commonly installed from the top with nuts underneath. However, there are others that work vice versa with fancy handles held in place by escutcheons on top. This type may also be tightened from the bottom when in place.

First put the rubber gasket on the faucet wherever it contacts the sink. Use plenty of putty if there is no gasket. Push it in place, put washers and nuts on from the underside; have a helper hold faucet in position and tighten nuts with a basin wrench.

Next attach the faucet supplies to hot and cold water. (These are

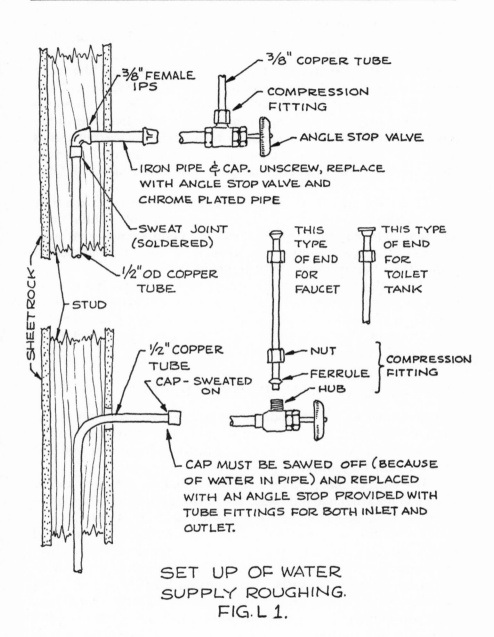

3/8" COPPER TUBE

3/8" FEMALE IPS

COMPRESSION FITTING

ANGLE STOP VALVE

IRON PIPE & CAP. UNSCREW, REPLACE WITH ANGLE STOP VALVE AND CHROME PLATED PIPE

SWEAT JOINT (SOLDERED)

THIS TYPE OF END FOR FAUCET

THIS TYPE OF END FOR TOILET TANK

1/2" OD COPPER TUBE

STUD

SHEETROCK

1/2" COPPER TUBE

CAP - SWEATED ON

NUT

FERRULE

HUB

COMPRESSION FITTING

CAP MUST BE SAWED OFF (BECAUSE OF WATER IN PIPE) AND REPLACED WITH AN ANGLE STOP PROVIDED WITH TUBE FITTINGS FOR BOTH INLET AND OUTLET.

SET UP OF WATER SUPPLY ROUGHING.
FIG. L 1.

available in chrome or brass in lengths of 12 inches, 18 inches, 24 inches, and 36 inches.) Slip the nuts over supply pipe and screw to the faucet. Once attached, bend carefully parallel to the compression fittings. At least an inch of the pipe must be straight above the point of connection for proper sealing. Mark the pipe and cut off the excess so that about 3/8 inch will slip into the fitting. Slip the nuts and ferrules over the ends of the pipes. Then slip the ends of the pipes into the fittings and carefully turn down on the nuts. It is important that the end of the pipe is aligned exactly in the fitting. Make sure the nut is threaded properly before you tighten it (Fig. L1).

Remove aerator if any from faucet. Turn on one valve at a time and check for leaks. If the connections leak at the nuts tighten them just enough to stop the drip. Use only open end wrenches on compression fittings and always use another wrench to "hold against yourself" so that you don't twist the pipe.

When the water supplies are tight turn on water full blast to check the waste connections. If they don't leak put in the plug, allow the sink to fill about 1-1/2 inches deep. Then pull the plug and watch again for leaks. If there are any leaks tighten nuts carefully. If it still leaks disassemble waste connection and do it over.

INSTALLING A STRAINER AND TAILPIECE

A strainer and its corresponding tailpiece is used on either a tub, basin, or sink (Fig. M). There are several types of strainers on the market. If you examine them before you try to install one you will soon see how they work.

The most common one is made up with a large rubber washer and a metal washer and nut under the fitting. Inside the fitting there is a chrome flange. This section is beaded in stainless putty.

To install it take the inside section of the strainer in hand and press a bead of putty about 1/2 inch thick all around the underside of the flange. Press this section down into the hole in the fixture from the inside and put the washers and nuts on from the outside. The excess putty will squeeze out. Have an assistant use the handles of a large pair of pliers inserted between the cross in the bottom of the strainer, and a large screwdriver to hold the strainer from turning

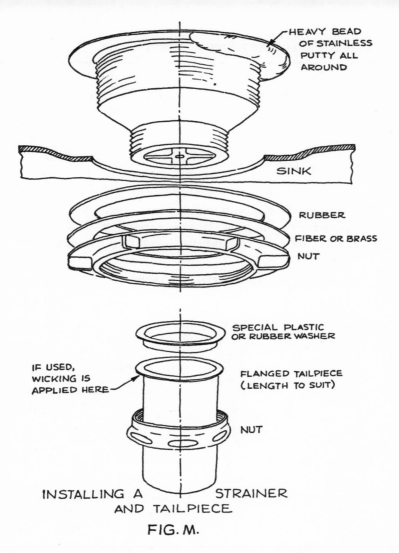

HEAVY BEAD OF STAINLESS PUTTY ALL AROUND

SINK

RUBBER

FIBER OR BRASS

NUT

SPECIAL PLASTIC OR RUBBER WASHER

IF USED, WICKING IS APPLIED HERE

FLANGED TAILPIECE (LENGTH TO SUIT)

NUT

INSTALLING A STRAINER AND TAILPIECE

FIG. M.

while you take up on the nut from below. Make certain that the rubber washer doesn't become displaced while you do this. If it does, release the pressure on the nut and replace the washer. It may be necessary to remove some putty from the underside of the fixture. Take up on the nut again just tight enough so that the strainer is snugly in place and doesn't easily turn from the pressure of the wrench.

The tailpiece is connected to the strainer with a nut and there is a special washer that fits into the end of the tailpiece.

The connection can also be made up with lamp wick as a slip joint but the wicking must be put around the tailpiece, not where the washer would have been.

ASSEMBLING PIPE

In doing plumbing work in the jobs described above and in any other jobs you may attempt you will run into a variety of situations where you will have to join pipe. Here is a roundup of various types of pipe assembly and joint making that come into common use.

MAKING UP THREADED PIPE JOINTS

Coat the threads with pipe joint compound (Fig. N), then take a single strand of lamp wick and wrap it around the end of the thread

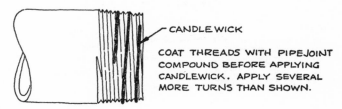

CANDLE WICK

COAT THREADS WITH PIPEJOINT COMPOUND BEFORE APPLYING CANDLEWICK. APPLY SEVERAL MORE TURNS THAN SHOWN.

FIG. N.

counterclockwise, crossing over the threads as you do. If you experience any difficulty starting the thread, "back thread" it. That is, turn it backwards, holding it in firmly as you do until it clicks. At this point the ends of the corresponding thread should be lined up. Then turn it clockwise to tighten it. If it still doesn't screw in properly examine both threads carefully for any damage, dents, or burns. These can be removed with a hacksaw blade or three corner file.

Threads that are seriously damaged must be cleaned up with a tap or die, or just thrown away in the case of a short nipple.

SOLDERED JOINTS

These joints are not difficult once you get the hang of it. First make sure the pipe is dry. Shut off the water, open all the faucets in the house, upstairs, downstairs, and outside, and flush the toilets. This will let most of the water in the system run out. All of it sometimes. However, water may be trapped because of pipes that are not pitched properly. Sometimes blowing down the pipe you wish to solder will push the water out the other end. If after you try to solder a joint you find that you still have a problem with water (symptoms: steam blowing the solder out of the joint or pipe not hot enough to melt the solder), take a piece of bread and push some of it down the pipe with a pencil packing it tightly. This will absorb small amounts of water and keep the end of the pipe dry. After the water is turned on, the bread will disintegrate and flush out the faucet.

Joints have to be dry and clean (see previous section). Both new fittings and pipe may be cleaned with steel wool and portions that are to be soldered—and a little more—should shine.

The inside of a small female fitting can be cleaned with a small piece of steel wool wrapped around a dowel or a piece of wood whittled to the right size. Old pipes can be cleaned with a strip of fine aluminum oxide paper or emery cloth and "shoeshined" clean. It is a good idea to clean up a section of old pipe before you cut the short piece off.

After the pipe and fitting are cleaned coat both with soldering paste and put them together. Assemble as many joints as is practical and solder them all consecutively.

A propane torch is used for soldering. To light the torch turn on the gas and strike a match. Bring the lit match up to the edge of the torch. If you turn the torch directly on the match it will blow it out. Adjust the torch so that the blue cone in the center of the flame is about 3/4 inch long.

Bring this cone in direct contact with the fitting end and hold it there for about ten seconds, then touch the hot pipe right at the edge of the hub with the solder. (Use 50-50 roll lead and tin solder.) If the solder does not melt right away remove it and wait a few more seconds. When the pipe is hot enough the solder will run and fill the hub, even if the hub is upside down. Just make certain that there is enough solder in the joint. Run the end of the solder wire all the way around the hub, then remove the torch and if neatness counts brush off the excess solder with steel wool. The joint must not be moved until the solder cools. However, you may cool it with a wet rag.

COMPRESSION FITTING

The compression fitting (two uses: valves on toilet tank and under sink) has a threaded hub and a ferrule that fits in the end of the hub and is held in place with a nut. (These fittings are more expensive than others but can be opened out of sequence and require no heating.) Cut the tube to fit in the hub, slide the nut and ferrule over the end of the tube and put the end of the tube into the hub. Then slide the ferrule down against the hub and follow it with the nut. Tighten the nut with an open end wrench or monkey wrench. Don't use pliers or a pipe wrench because these may crush the nut slightly—make it egg-shaped—and the joint will never be tight (see detail on Fig. L1).

THE BRASS OFFSET

This is used where a sink drain and trap don't align properly. A brass offset is used to link the trap and the tailpiece and can be cut to fit as needed.

To install put offset on the tailpiece dry. Turn it so it heads toward trap to get an idea where it will align. Then cut it with a hacksaw so it slips into other pipes at least 3/4 inch, but not more than 1-1/4 inches (won't fit in more than this). You might have to use extension drain pieces to make connection.

Note: When installing sink, if possible remove trap and clean out waste pipe. You may have to replace it. This collects a large amount of sediment.

MAKING UP A SLIP NUT

Slip nuts go together by friction rather than screw together and are used to connect drain pipes on basins, tubs, and kitchen sink to wall piping. Good alignment is the main thing necessary to get a tight joint.

There is a beveled plastic washer made for these joints that works very well. Just slide the nut up on the pipe followed by the washer (Fig. O). Slip the cut end of the pipe into the corresponding threaded end. Slide the washer down in place and tighten the nut up

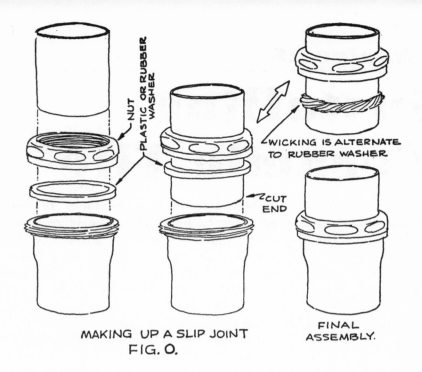

WICKING IS ALTERNATE TO RUBBER WASHER

CUT END

MAKING UP A SLIP JOINT
FIG. O.

FINAL ASSEMBLY.

over it. There is also a rubber washer for this that you use in the same manner. If you use this it is a good idea to also use joint compound around it.

If you find that you can't get a tight joint with either of these washers, or if you took a joint apart and destroyed the washer in the process, you can always fall back on candle wick or lamp wick. It looks like a ball of string but consists of multiple strands. First pull off about 12 to 15 inches of it. Coat the pipe with pipe joint compound, then wrap the wicking around the pipe clockwise and tuck it down against the threaded hub. Then coat the wicking with compound. Bring the nut down over the wicking. There should be enough wicking to make it hard to catch the threads in the nut. You will—or should—have to press down hard as you turn the nut.

If the nut won't catch because of too much wicking, cut off some and try again. On the other hand if it doesn't make a tight joint, use some more or use a longer piece.

One tip: Very often in making an offset, one or more of the joints do not line up properly. Sometimes lamp wick will make the joint tight when washers will not.

Chapter 26

Installing
Ceramic Tile

Years ago ceramic tile jobs were referred to as "mud jobs" because the tile was set on wire lath and wet cement. This was a difficult task. Today the job can be done with adhesive and is relatively easy.

A smooth surface is necessary for a good job. Waterproof Sheetrock is usually used in a bathroom. First rip out all the old Sheetrock if any and apply new, using the tips in the Sheetrock chapter.

Plan the tile installation with pencil and paper. Like floor tile, the idea is to avoid having to do a lot of cutting or ending up with many small pieces, especially where they'll be highly visible, such as in front of the tub or around a door or window frame. A certain amount of fitting will be necessary around the curved portion at the front of the tub. It is better to cut small pieces off whole tiles than to try to fit tiny pieces in here.

Use the top of the tub to set your first row of tiles. But first check the tub for level. If it is out of level start setting your first tile row at the high point. If it is more than 1/4 inch out of level use the low point and cut the tiles. Draw a level line around three walls as a guide for this row.

This will give you the height of horizontal rows. Figure the vertical rows the same way. Work off the front of the tub. Measure the width of one tile out from the narrowest part of the tub (usually the bottom at the floor) and draw a plumb line up from here. Figure the tile layout from this line. If necessary to avoid narrow tiles at back, shift the whole layout toward the back wall.

Before you begin actually installing tiles draw plumb and level lines as guides at the edges of one vertical and one horizontal row of tiles on each wall. You cannot trust the walls to be straight or plumb. Also draw lines to guide you as to the limits you want to spread the adhesive.

Begin installation by applying the adhesive. This is done with a notched spreader. These spreaders come with different size notches for different kinds of adhesives. Your tile dealer will help you to

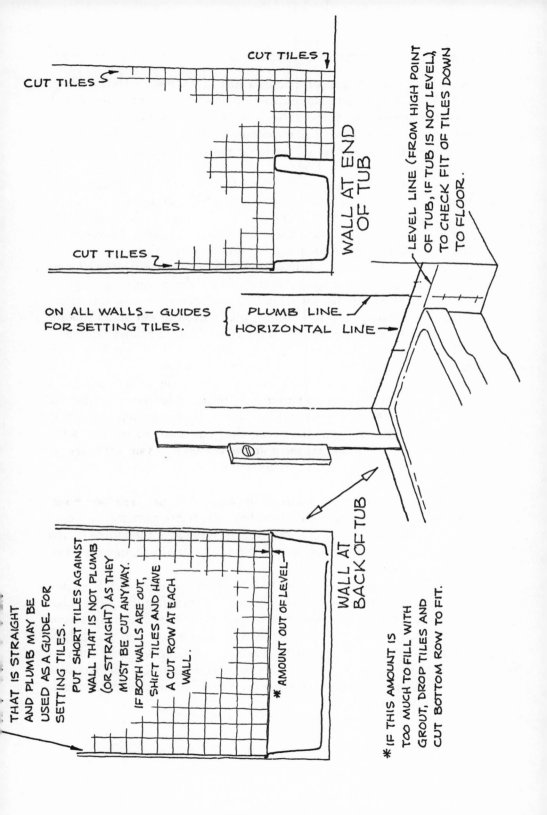

CUT TILES

CUT TILES

CUT TILES

WALL AT END OF TUB

LEVEL LINE (FROM HIGH POINT OF TUB, IF TUB IS NOT LEVEL), TO CHECK FIT OF TILES DOWN TO FLOOR.

ON ALL WALLS — GUIDES FOR SETTING TILES. { PLUMB LINE
HORIZONTAL LINE

THAT IS STRAIGHT AND PLUMB MAY BE USED AS A GUIDE FOR SETTING TILES.

PUT SHORT TILES AGAINST WALL THAT IS NOT PLUMB (OR STRAIGHT) AS THEY MUST BE CUT ANYWAY. IF BOTH WALLS ARE OUT, SHIFT TILES AND HAVE A CUT ROW AT EACH WALL.

WALL AT BACK OF TUB

* AMOUNT OUT OF LEVEL

* IF THIS AMOUNT IS TOO MUCH TO FILL WITH GROUT, DROP TILES AND CUT BOTTOM ROW TO FIT.

select the proper one. (Sometimes a spreader comes with the adhesive.) Usually, you cover an entire wall at a time but be sure to read the label directions; some adhesives must be applied a little at a time. When spreading, it is important to do it evenly—don't leave globs because this excess will ooze up between the tiles. Be careful not to cover your guide lines.

To install the tiles start where the plumb and vertical lines intersect. In the beginning use only whole tiles. Press them firmly in place along one line. Use a straightedge held along the guide line, pressing each tile tight against it to help you align them. Be sure that the straightedge doesn't slip while you are doing this.

After all the whole tiles are installed cut the remaining tiles to fit. This is done with a special tool made for the purpose, a ceramic tile cutter. Most suppliers will lend you one and show how it is used. Also, there is a special tile cutting pliers used to cut small mosaic tiles or to break small pieces off large tiles. Consider these more as a tool to crunch up the part of the tile you want to remove. They are inexpensive and it will definitely pay to get a pair.

If you have to cut a small square corner (say an inch or so) out of a tile to make it fit you'll find it virtually impossible to do it neatly. At any rate follow this procedure: Cut the tile all the way across the face in one direction and cut the piece that you want to remove with another straight cut and reassemble the tile on the wall. Of course it would be better to try to avoid this type of cut when you lay out your work.

Lastly, when the tiles are all in place the space between them must be filled with grout, which is basically white portland cement. Mix it up following the instructions on the package, then force it into the seams with a squeegee. Clean the tile faces as instructed on the grout package.

While standard ceramic tile is approximately 4-1/4 inches square, sizes vary from manufacturer to manufacturer—the tiles from one company and another are not interchangeable. If you have to do a repair job take a sample with you when you go to buy replacements so you can get tiles as close to same size and color as possible. If you can't get the exact color you might be able to use a tile with a pretty design or picture on it to fill so the design tiles look like planned accents.

Chapter 27

Adding an Electrical Receptacle

There may be all sorts of reasons why you may want to add an electrical receptacle. For example, you may need one in a certain spot because the existing one is hard to get at, say behind a couch in the living room.

Before you try to do the job there are a couple of things you should know about electrical circuits.

A circuit, basically, is like water pipe, but instead of carrying water it carries electricity. And like water pipe, which has different capacities, wires can carry just so much electricity. If you have too many electrical devices drawing power there will be too much pressure on the wire and it can heat up, overloading the circuit and the fuse will burn out or the circuit breaker will trip, shutting off the power. If this didn't happen the overheated wire would burn and possibly start a fire (a good reason, incidentally, for never putting copper pennies in a fuse to keep the circuit operating).

It is not necessary to go through a big complicated procedure to install and wire a receptacle. You can do it, in most cases, by hooking into an adjacent receptacle, perhaps that one behind the couch that's so inconvenient, or a switch.

Two types of wire are commonly used—Romex or BX. The first is a plastic cable with three wires inside—a black "hot" line which carries the current to the receptacle, a white neutral line, and a ground wire. The ground wire is a safety feature. BX is the same except that the cable has a metal armor around the wires instead of plastic. For living room and bedroom wiring, 14 gauge wire is recommended. Cutting the wire is shown in Fig. A1.

It is necessary, first, to determine if the electrical circuit the

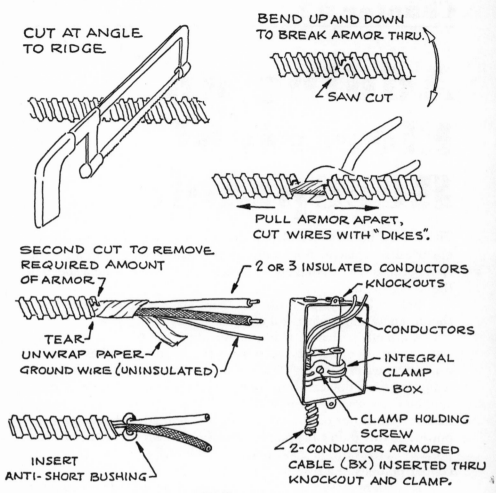

CUT AT ANGLE TO RIDGE

BEND UP AND DOWN TO BREAK ARMOR THRU.

SAW CUT

PULL ARMOR APART, CUT WIRES WITH "DIKES".

SECOND CUT TO REMOVE REQUIRED AMOUNT OF ARMOR

2 OR 3 INSULATED CONDUCTORS

KNOCKOUTS

CONDUCTORS

TEAR

UNWRAP PAPER

GROUND WIRE (UNINSULATED)

INTEGRAL CLAMP

BOX

INSERT ANTI-SHORT BUSHING

CLAMP HOLDING SCREW

2-CONDUCTOR ARMORED CABLE (BX) INSERTED THRU KNOCKOUT AND CLAMP.

FIG. A1.

existing switch or receptacle is on has the necessary capacity. In bedrooms and living rooms a good general rule is that you should not have more than ten receptacles drawing power off them. Kitchen and bath wiring should be left to an electrician.

To find out how many receptacles are on the circuit you want to use, first plug a lamp into the outlet. Trip breakers or pull fuses until the light goes off; when it does, you've located the circuit the receptacle is on. Then proceed through the house—upstairs and down —repeating the procedure. When you're through the entire house

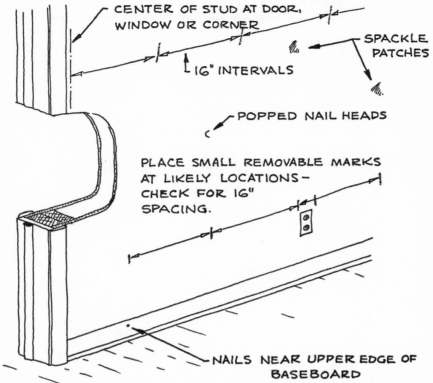

CENTER OF STUD AT DOOR, WINDOW OR CORNER

SPACKLE PATCHES

16" INTERVALS

POPPED NAIL HEADS

PLACE SMALL REMOVABLE MARKS AT LIKELY LOCATIONS – CHECK FOR 16" SPACING.

NAILS NEAR UPPER EDGE OF BASEBOARD

LIGHTBULB HELD CLOSE TO WALL WILL SHOW UP SIGNS OF STUD LOCATION (IF SHEETROCK). TAPPING WALL WILL ALSO REVEAL APPROX. STUD LOCATIONS.

INDICATIONS OF STUD LOCATION

FIG. A.

you'll know exactly how many receptacles are on that particular circuit and if less than ten, can proceed to hook on the new receptacle.

Before beginning the job the first thing to do is to turn off the power to the receptacle. Just remove the fuse or trip the circuit breaker that controls it.

Next decide exactly where on the wall you want the receptacle, then use a drill and keyhole saw to make an opening 2-1/4 inches by 3-5/8 inches at the same height as other receptacles. You want to avoid hitting a stud, which will be difficult to cut into. To find out where the studs are there are a variety of ways (Fig. A). Normally,

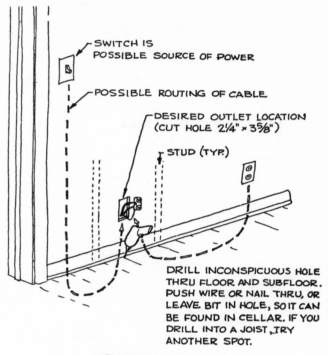

SWITCH IS POSSIBLE SOURCE OF POWER

POSSIBLE ROUTING OF CABLE

DESIRED OUTLET LOCATION (CUT HOLE 2¼" × 3⅝")

STUD (TYP.)

DRILL INCONSPICUOUS HOLE THRU FLOOR AND SUBFLOOR. PUSH WIRE OR NAIL THRU, OR LEAVE BIT IN HOLE, SO IT CAN BE FOUND IN CELLAR. IF YOU DRILL INTO A JOIST, TRY ANOTHER SPOT.

FIG. B.

they're 16 inches apart, though in some homes, mainly older ones, and some very new ones, 24 inches from center to center. You can check for nails in the baseboard—studs are normally where they are. Another way is by tapping the wall with a hammer. Sometimes you can feel the solidity and possibly hear it at the same time—it will sound dull rather than hollow. One other way: hold a lamp near the wall and observe the texture. Sometimes you can make out where the tape joints in the Sheetrock are.

Whether you hook up into a switch or receptacle you'll have to bring the wire down from either and then go through the shoe, loop it under the joist and then come up through the shoe again for the connection at the new receptacle. This is far more practical than going on a direct line horizontally, because you'd have to go through studs.

To make the two holes required for the wire in the shoe depends on what's beneath the floor you're working on. If the ceiling below is finished—say you want to add an outlet in a finished attic —forget it. It's too big a job. If the joists are exposed though, as in a basement, you can do it fairly simply.

The holes must be drilled from the underside of the shoe. To determine where they should be, check to see if antenna wire, pipes, or the like run directly down near where you want the outlet. Then you can go downstairs and use these as guides to where to make the holes. If there are no pipes or wires, drill a small hole in the floor near the baseboard below the outlet, then stick a piece of wire through it. You can use this as a guide downstairs (Fig. B).

With holes located use a long 3/4 inch diameter bit to drill up through the shoe. After drilling, if there is insulation in the wall, reach through the hole in the wall and push it out of the way with a small stick. You're going to have to fish wire up inside the wall and you don't want the insulation interfering.

Push the wire through the hole in the shoe under where the new receptacle will be. Go upstairs, reach in the hole and pull the wire up and out. The wire should be long enough to extend from one box to the other with an extra foot or two for safety.

The other end of the wire, as mentioned, must then be run beneath the floor up through the wall and connected to the existing receptacle or switch. If possible, staple the wire to the sill under the joists (Fig. C). If you can't do this you'll have to drill holes in the joists and run the wire that way (Fig. D).

Next take the existing receptacle out of the wall. This can be done by simply unfastening the screws that hold it on. Examine the box and look for an extra knockout disc—these are small discs in the box. If you see an unused one knock it out with a screwdriver, first removing the clamp above it.

Next aspect of the job requires a snake. This is a relatively rigid length of metal you can buy at a hardware or electrical supply store. Feed the snake through the hole in the knockout, then down to the shoe, probing for the hole you drilled. The snake has a natural curve so it is best to place it so the curve helps to keep the wire between the wall and the insulation. When it hits the shoe rotate it to find the hole.

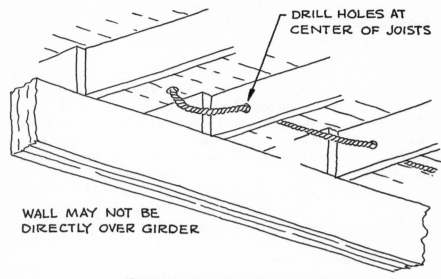

DRILL HOLES AT
CENTER OF JOISTS

WALL MAY NOT BE
DIRECTLY OVER GIRDER

WIRE RUN THRU JOISTS
FIG. C.

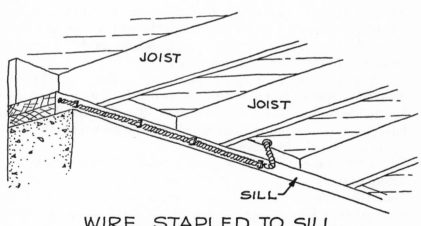

JOIST

JOIST

SILL

WIRE STAPLED TO SILL
UNDER JOISTS
FIG. D.

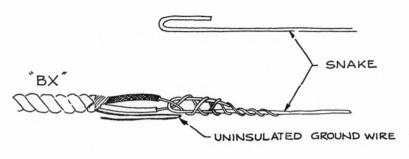

"BX"

SNAKE

UNINSULATED GROUND WIRE

PLASTIC TAPE

PREPARING CABLE TO BE PULLED
THROUGH HOLE
FIG. E.

When it's through (and this can take quite a while to accomplish), bend the snake end into a hook and attach wire to it as shown in Fig. E. The idea is to get the wire compact enough so it can fit through the 3/4 inch hole you drilled. Then draw the snake back; it may be helpful to have someone feed the wire at the same time until it comes out through the knockout hole in the box. If you don't luck out and can't get the snake through because there are no open knockouts, you have to remove the box from the wall to get the wire through so you can see down to the shoe where the hole is. Removal varies. Some boxes have a metal mounting bracket that nails on the face of the stud and is plastered over. If that's the case make a hole in the wall to get the box out; chip away carefully. Some boxes have a mounting bracket nailed to one side of a stud. This can probably be pried loose but you'll still end up making a little hole in the wall to get the box out. Other boxes are nailed with two tenpenny nails that go through holes in the box. In this case pry box loose a little, getting the nails far enough out so you can pull them with pliers. If existing wires have no slack to allow box removal you may be able to locate

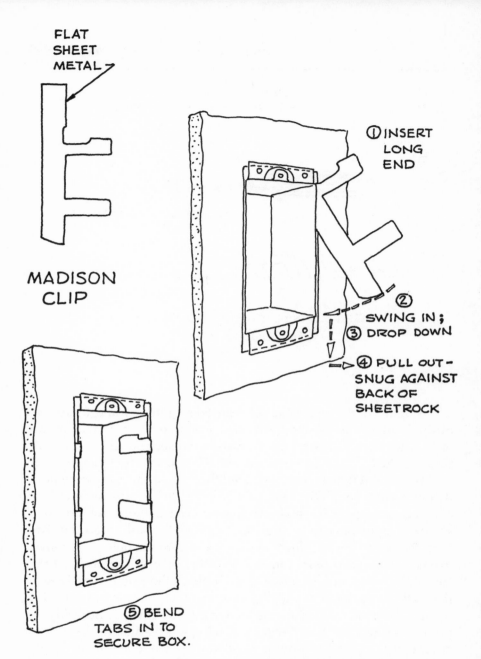

FLAT
SHEET
METAL

MADISON
CLIP

① INSERT LONG END

② SWING IN;
③ DROP DOWN

④ PULL OUT-
SNUG AGAINST
BACK OF
SHEETROCK

⑤ BEND
TABS IN TO
SECURE BOX.

INSTALLATION OF ELECTRICAL BOX
WITH MADISON CLIPS

FIG. F.

where they are stapled (usually a foot or so above the box) and pry the staples out; or you may have to remove the clamp on the wire and pull the box off the wire to get it out.

With the box removed you can get the wire up the same way as you did through a knockout. If you mutilated the box during the removal process throw it away and get a new one. A Gem type is best.

A handy way to reinstall a box is with Madison clips. This is shown in Fig. F.

Final step is to connect the wiring.

The cable, as mentioned, will have a black wire (covered with black insulation) and a white and a bare ground wire. Use a sharp knife to skin about 3/4 inch off each wire, then connect them to the new receptacle. The black wire goes on the brass screw on the receptacle, the white wire on the silver screw; the ground wire is turned under the ground screw on the receptacle. Incidentally, some receptacles don't have this ground screw but for safety you should buy one with it.

The existing receptacle or switch will have four screws on it. If two are free simply connect black and white wire to each as above. If there is an existing ground wire twist the end of it together with the

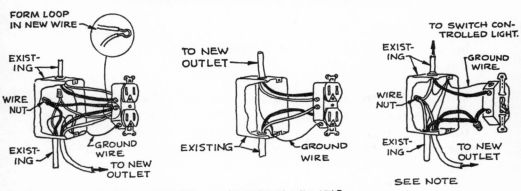

IF ALL SCREWS HAVE WIRES ATTACHED   IF SCREWS AVAILABLE

IN A RECEPTACLE   IN A SWITCH BOX

ADDITIONS TO EXISTING WIRING

NOTE : CONN. SHOWN IN SWITCH BOX IS ALTERNATE TO FORMING LOOP IN NEW WIRE, AS AT FAR LEFT.

FIG. G.

end of the new ground and attach both under the single ground screw on the receptacle, or on the box.

If the existing box has wires connected to all four screws you take a different tack for attaching the new wires. Remove one pair of black and white wires. Snip off the ends about an inch, then skin them back 3/4 inch; do the same thing for the new pair of wires. Also on the new wires skin off an area about 3/4 long two inches or so from the ends. Form a loop at these points and attach wires under the loop to the screws. This will leave you with four bare ends. Twist each pair of ends (white with white and black with black) together, then twist wire nuts over each securely. If you found when you opened the old box that there were three pairs of wires in the box, it's best to find a new box—one with four wires or less.

If you are connecting wires to an existing switch the procedure is the same. The power must feed through the box. If the box has only a black and a white wire, both attached to the switch, you cannot use it. Fig. G has details on making wiring connections.

INSTALLING A LIGHT FIXTURE

A light fixture is installed very much like a receptacle. The fixture itself is fastened to the box with two screws or a nut in the center of the canopy of the fixture. The screws either go directly into tapped holes or there is a metal bar fastened to the box with holes that match holes in the fixture.

Wiring.   The fixture has white and black wires that are connected to the house wires either by wire nuts, or they may be simply twisted together and taped. If they are taped discard the tape and use wire nuts to make new connections. Sometimes the wire nuts will not cover all wire that is exposed. Either use a larger size nut or tape over the nut to cover the wire.

Chapter 28

A New Concrete Driveway

Your concrete driveway may be in bad shape or you may have no driveway at all. Either way, if you're contemplating a new one, concrete is the way to go. The other common option, asphalt, requires use of a steamroller and is simply too big a job for a do-it-yourselfer.

BREAKING UP CONCRETE

The first thing to do is to break up any existing concrete. If the concrete is in bad shape it probably won't be hard to do this with a sledgehammer. These come in various weights starting at about six pounds. Use one that's not too heavy for you to lift, and let the sledgehammer do the work. Lift it up and let it fall mainly of its own weight, guiding it and using a small amount of muscle power to deliver a good healthy clout. Work at the edge of broken up pieces, sort of nibbling away at it, rather than trying to attack in the middle.

If you discover while working with the sledge that a big root is the cause of your problem, cut it out. Sever the largest part of it completely rather than just chopping a chunk off. You want to make sure it can't grow again.

Move the concrete with a wheelbarrow designed for the purpose. Disposal will vary depending on your situation. If you are hooked into a sewer and have an old cesspool handy, dump the material down there. If there is no easy place to dispose of it you can arrange to have it hauled away. Don't be tempted to haul it down to the dump by car. That's a good way to damage the car.

VARIOUS WAYS TO BUILD A DRIVEWAY

There are various ways to build a driveway, but many of them represent really haphazard craftsmanship and is why one often sees concrete driveways that are cracked. The one described here will take a little longer to build, but it won't be cracked five or six years after you build it. It consists of a two-inch base of sand and four inches of concrete reinforced with wire mesh. The concrete "floats" on the sand; in time of heavy frost when the ground swells and applies pressure the slab will yield with it and not crack.

The driveway should run as straight as possible from the garage to the street and pitch slightly downhill for drainage. If your land is naturally sloped this will not be a problem. If it is not, but is almost level, you can either pitch the driveway downhill or crown it up. That is, make the concrete rounded and higher in the middle than at the sides so water runs off to the lawn on the sides.

First step is to install the form boards in rough positions. These can be 2 by 4's, as straight as you can buy. Sight down them from one end to the other to determine that they have no twists or warps.

Assuming you're using the dimensions of an existing driveway, use a square-edged shovel or spade to dig out the sod on either side of the driveway to the depth of the 2 by 4's, forming ledges. Save the soil. Then lay them in place end to end.

Next fasten a mason's string on both sides of the driveway, to the top of the form boards at one end, and to stakes driven into the ground at the sidewalk end. Level the string with a mason's line level.

Next install the forms permanently (Fig. A). They should have their inside or outside edges aligned wtih the strings and be pitched at a minimum rate of one inch for every ten feet. By measuring between the string and the tops of forms you can tell if they're descending at proper pitch. Use your foot to hold each board in the proper position, bending it up or down slightly if necessary for pitch and secure by nailing it to 18-inch stakes driven into the ground. Use a stake every three or four feet and joint the form boards where they butt.

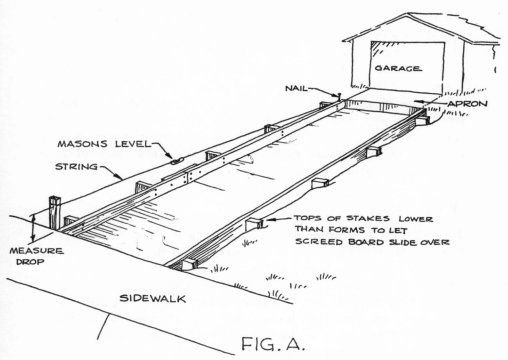

FIG. A.

Once the boards are staked in place, pack soil behind them so the poured concrete, which exerts pressure, will not push them out of position.

EXCAVATING

Remove the soil to a depth of six inches from the tops of the form boards over the entire driveway. Use a large rake to smooth the ground. Then fashion a screed board to check the depth (Fig. B).

Following this the sand base is added. To find out how much you need you can give the dimensions to a building supply dealer —so many square feet at a two-inch depth. Have it delivered to the site by truck.

When the sand is dumped on the driveway, spread it out, then use another screed to level it to the required depth (Fig. C). To use, grip it in the middle and push it back and forth as if you were taking excess frosting off a cake.

The easiest thing to do as far as concrete is concerned, is to have it delivered to the site by a transit-mix truck. A good strong mix is three bags of sand to every bag of cement or four bags of "concrete sand" (sand with rocks in it) to every bag of cement. Give the driveway dimensions to the dealer and let him figure the amount you need. These proportions, by the way, will be good for any concrete job you have (patio, steps, sidewalk, etc.).

WIRE MESH

The wire mesh placement is calculated next. Obtain a sufficient quantity of 1/8 inch wire (6 inch squares). Cut them to fit over the driveway in a neat patchwork (Fig. D), then lay them to one side in the arrangement you put them in. After this you should decide where to put the expansion joint strips. These are 4 inch wide strips of asphalt impregnated material that are installed across the driveway to segment it into sections; one very long monolithic mass of concrete is more susceptible to cracking.

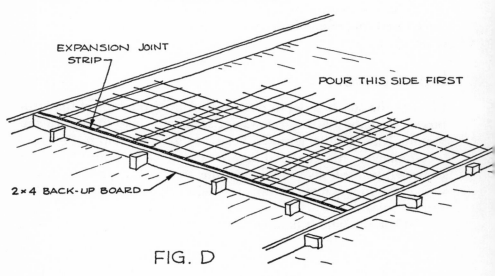

EXPANSION JOINT STRIP

POUR THIS SIDE FIRST

2 × 4 BACK-UP BOARD

FIG. D

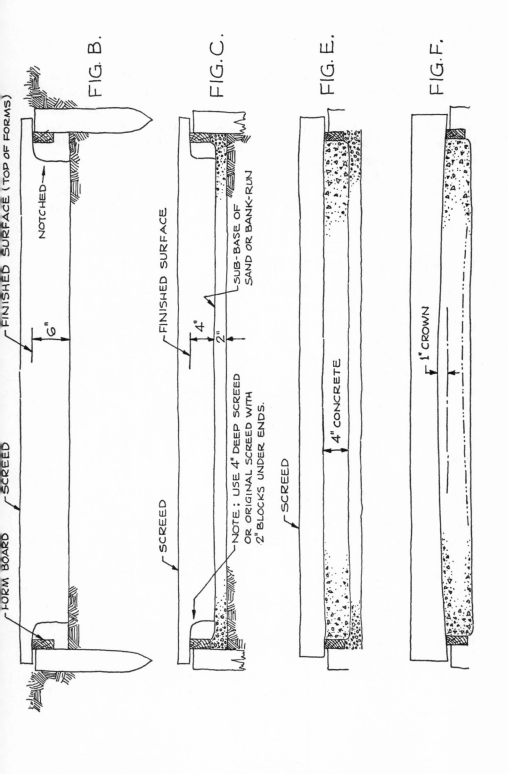

FIG. B.

FINISHED SURFACE (TOP OF FORMS)

NOTCHED

SCREED

6"

FORM BOARD

FIG. C.

FINISHED SURFACE

SCREED

4"
2"

SUB-BASE OF
SAND OR BANK-RUN

NOTE : USE 4" DEEP SCREED
OR ORIGINAL SCREED WITH
2" BLOCKS UNDER ENDS.

FIG. E.

SCREED

4" CONCRETE

FIG.F.

1" CROWN

A general rule is that you should not have more than 30 feet of unsegmented concrete. The garage slab, since you will pour next to it, should be part of your calculations. For example if the garage slab were 20 feet long, you would only be allowed to go another 10 feet before making another joint. Here, you could use one strip at the edge of the garage floor or apron.

Once decided install each strip (for most driveways one plus the apron strip will suffice) backed up by a staked-in-place 2 by 4. The 2 by 4 will prevent the concrete from knocking the strips over and keep them straight (Fig. D).

POURING THE CONCRETE

There are a couple of ways to do it. First lay bricks and blocks on the sand two inches high. Lay the mesh on in proper positions, then pour the concrete. Wear rubber boots and work with a shovel to spread it and to make sure there are no air bubbles. Then use a screed to level it with the tops of your forms.

The other way is to pour the first two inches, lay the mesh on, then make the final two inch pour and level off. Either of these ways will serve you well. Remove any braces for the expansion-joint material after the final pour and fill in with concrete. Use a straight board as your screed to level concrete with tops of form boards (Fig. E).

FINISHING THE CONCRETE

Some skill is needed to do a good job finishing off the concrete. You might practice for it by first doing a section of sidewalk. However, if you don't feel that you can tackle it, hire a professional mason for just this part of the job. It will take him only a short time and will insure a good job.

There are two types of finishes, or textures, commonly given a concrete driveway: smooth and rough. The smooth finish is done with a steel trowel; the rough finish is done with a wood float which looks like a big wood trowel.

When using either you have to do the job when the concrete is just right, when it's neither still soupy nor too dry. If it's too wet your tool will gouge furrows in it; too hard and you'll have to exert too much pressure.

Your best bet is to start troweling when all the water has *just* disappeared from the surface. If using a steel trowel make semicircular half moon sweeps with the front or leading edge of the trowel raised. If using a float use the same motion; you needn't raise the leading edge.

When the body of the driveway is finished go over the edges. There are special small edging tools for this that you run along the edge to round it off.

LET CONCRETE CURE

In order to give concrete its maximum strength you need to let it cure, or dry, gradually. To do this let it harden overnight. The next day you can remove form boards with a pick, then give it a fine spray from a hose and keep it wet for three or four days by spraying occasionally.

Finally, fill the gaps left by the form boards with soil and sprinkle on some grass seed.

NEW DRIVEWAY DIMENSIONS, CROWNING UP

If you don't have a driveway now you can follow the same procedure described. A one car driveway should be about 10 feet wide.

If the grade of your property is such that pitching it to the proper dimensions is impossible, crown it up. Cut a screed to the shape of the crown to the depth of one inch (Fig. F). Pour the concrete and run the screed over it as usual. It will leave the concrete higher in the middle than at the sides and when dry, water will run off easily to the sides. It will be necessary to feather, or blend, the crown into the sidewalk and garage slab or apron.

Chapter 29

Installing
A Sump Pump

A sump pump consists of a motor which powers a vertical drive shaft connected to a pump set in a hole you make in the basement floor. The hole is lined with a piece of chimney flue lining. The pump has a float mechanism. When the water table rises the hole fills with water. The float mechanism senses this, starts the motor, and the water is pumped out through a discharge tube which terminates some place outside the house. In effect, the pump lowers the level of the water table under the house.

The first step is to dig the hole for the sump pump. The hole should be as close to the center of the cellar as you can make it. Dig the hole when the water table is down. Otherwise the hole will keep filling with water as you dig.

Hole size is based on the size of the flue lining, which should be 12 inches square by 2 feet long, on the average. Dig slightly deeper and larger than the lining so you can slip the lining in place easily. The lining should have a series of holes drilled in it through which water can pass. Drill these carefully.

To break through concrete use a sledgehammer (8 pound size is usually best but you can get larger or smaller sizes), hitting the middle of the hole first, then chipping away at the edges. You can use a manual posthole digger to get dirt out, but a shovel and a square edge spade to define hole sides are also good.

When the hole is dug fill the bottom of it with gravel, enough so that the water will flow freely into the hole to the pump. On top of this put a piece of slate just big enough to stand your pump on. (Say 8 inches by 8 inches.) Anchor the motor to any convenient support you can, perhaps a pipe or a board.

You also need a discharge pipe. The easiest thing to hook up is flexible plastic pipe or, if you want a better looking job, you can use

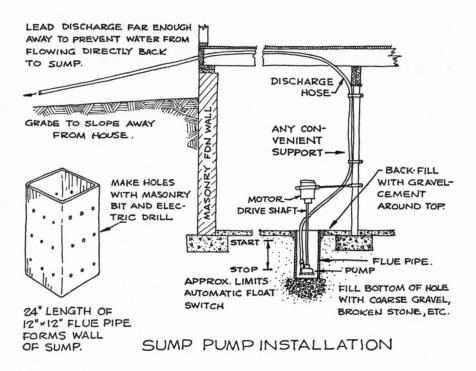

LEAD DISCHARGE FAR ENOUGH AWAY TO PREVENT WATER FROM FLOWING DIRECTLY BACK TO SUMP.

DISCHARGE HOSE

GRADE TO SLOPE AWAY FROM HOUSE.

MASONRY FDN WALL

ANY CONVENIENT SUPPORT →

BACK-FILL WITH GRAVEL-CEMENT AROUND TOP.

MAKE HOLES WITH MASONRY BIT AND ELECTRIC DRILL

MOTOR-DRIVE SHAFT →

START

STOP

APPROX. LIMITS AUTOMATIC FLOAT SWITCH

FLUE PIPE.

PUMP

FILL BOTTOM OF HOLE WITH COARSE GRAVEL, BROKEN STONE, ETC.

24" LENGTH OF 12"×12" FLUE PIPE FORMS WALL OF SUMP.

SUMP PUMP INSTALLATION

rigid plastic pipe. The diameter of the pipe will depend on manufacturer's recommendations.

As mentioned, the tubing has to terminate outside the house. Depending on your house, you may be able to run it out a window without any problems. Or you may have to go through the foundation wall. For this make a hole with sledgehammer and star drill, chisel, or electric hammer you rent. The hole in the wall should be 1/8 to 1/16 inch larger than the pipe diameter.

The water should be routed where it can run downhill on the surface. In most cases running it down the driveway is best. The pipe could be routed inside garage first. But you may be able to run it into a nearby stream or use the water in a garden. In some localities it may be necessary to install a drywell. If you do, keep it at least 12 feet away from the house.

For power you need an electrical connection in the vicinity of the pump. You shouldn't have the switch on the pump. The pump goes on and off automatically and could be switched on inadvertently. Just have the pump hooked up to a wire that plugs into the wall. To shut off power simply pull the plug.

Chapter 30

Painting

EXTERIOR PAINTING—PREPARATION

Properly preparing a house for painting is the most important part of the job. Here are some of the problems you may run into, and how to handle them.

Blisters.   There are two kinds, temperature blisters and moisture blisters. The first are usually caused by painting in the sun or high heat. Paint dries rapidly trapping the thinner or solvent underneath before it has a chance to evaporate. The blisters that form a few hours after or within a day or two of painting are usually temperature blisters. Darker paints are more prone to the problem because they absorb more heat than lighter ones.

Moisture blisters can be diagnosed by puncturing them—a little water will most likely run out. Causes of this type of blister vary. Excess water vapor generated inside the house from cooking and bathing, that tries to escape through walls to the outside may push the paint right off the wall, causing blisters. Eventually these blisters crack and you get peeling.

To decrease or solve the problem you can take a variety of steps:

1. Vent high-moisture areas (laundry, kitchen, bath, etc.) to the outside—let that moisture escape.
2. Vent the walls. You can do this with miniature vents that are inserted into drilled holes in the siding about five inches below ceiling level and windows. Instructions come on the package.

Moisture can also sneak behind paint through openings in the seams of the house—missing caulk at joints, around window flashing, missing shingles, etc. Another path is siding that is too close —within six inches of the ground. The siding soaks it in by capillary action.

The answer to open seams is to plug them up with caulk. When caulking don't overcaulk. Try to fill in spots where water will run, such as top and side of windows, leaving other spaces, such as beneath the sill, open for ventilation. If you have cedar shingles don't caulk at all. Also if brick is the siding, don't caulk it if joints are tight.

To remove blisters or peeling paint you can use sandpaper or a hook-type scraper (the latter is very useful). Or you can obtain or rent an electric paint remover that softens the paint so you can scrape it without causing a fire hazard, or a powered siding sander you rent. In any case get all loose paint off, then "feather" the edges of the resulting "craters" by rubbing them briskly with coarse (No. 36) sandpaper.

Alligatoring.   Here the paint segments and resembles alligator skin. It often occurs when paints are incompatible, not designed to be used with one another. If the segment lines are fine, you may be able to get by with a coat of compatible paint. If not the only solution is to remove the paint to bare wood. If you don't the paint will ultimately peel off the wall and take off coats of paint on top of it.

Chalking.   Chalking is the process whereby some of the paint washes away from rain and snow. A certain amount of chalking is normal with oil-base paints; indeed the paint is formulated to chalk. It keeps the paint fresh and clean looking and prevents paint build-up. However, excessive chalking is not desirable. There are three reasons for it: (1) the surface was badly weathered and was not adequately primed (first-coated) so it absorbs the "binders" in the paint and the pigment or color washes away, (2) the paint was applied below the recommended temperature, (3) the paint does not have enough binders in it. (Above all, on any paint job, use good paint.)

The solution, in any case, is proper priming with a good paint that is compatible with the one you have on now (check with your dealer). If chalking is severe brush or hose it off.

Crawling.   When paint draws up into globules like water does on a greasy plate, you have crawling. The cause is greasy, oily dirt. Usually, you'll get this condition in protected areas—on eaves or under the porch. To solve the problem scrub away all the grease.

Spotting.   Here, the paint loses color and gloss in spots. You may see the problem from a few hours to a few weeks after the paint is applied. It's usually caused by skimpy application of paint, overly porous spots in the wood, or poor priming.

There's no real solution to this problem, but you can try another thin coat of paint. As the paint weathers it should go away. You shouldn't apply another coat of paint right away. This may cause a too-thick buildup, which can lead to serious problems.

Cracking.   Here, the paint also breaks up into segments, like alligator skin, but not to the same degree. Usually, it's caused by using a paint that dries to a too-hard finish, such as applying trim paint over house paint.

The answer is to take the paint off down to bare wood. Of course this can be a massive job. If you want to take a chance just wire-brush or scrape away any edges that are curling up and repaint.

Wrinkling.   Here, the paint looks as if it were crumpled up, then pressed out flat on the wall. Common cause of the problem is applying the paint too thickly, then not brushing it out.

To handle it, use a belt-sander and a so-called open coat (the grit is far apart) sandpaper, 60 or 80 grit, and remove the spots. Take care to keep the sander moving—it's easy to make gouges if you're not careful.

Before starting to paint you should cover up properly. It's best to take down screens and storm windows, if any. To cover doors simply drape newspaper over the top and then close the door to hold the paper in place. Concrete driveways, walks, blacktop driveways, patios, and other areas that are susceptible to paint spotting, can be covered with newspapers weighted down with bricks or boards or 9 by 12 drop cloths. The best kind are the canvas type but these are fairly expensive (though they can be used indoors also). If they're too costly, you can get less expensive ones for one- or two-shot use.

Be certain to follow instructions on the paint can regarding what temperature to paint at and the like. It's also a good idea to time your painting so you paint only in the shade. In addition to problems with paint, working in the sun is tiresome.

The simplest scaffolding to use is a two-segment, rung-ladder. Far better, though, are either ladder jacks or A-ladders; both can be rented. Ladder jacks hook onto the rungs of the ladder segments, then you string a couple of boards (2 by 12) across them and work off the boards. In other words you can paint a large area before having to move your scaffolding, and you don't have to have the rungs digging into your shins. The A-ladders are even better. These are ladders shaped like the letter A, with a straight rung ladder running vertically through the top of the A that can be raised or lowered. You simply string the boards between ladders and work off them.

MIXING THE PAINT, PAINTING

If you can, obtain your paint in two gallon buckets and make certain it's fresh—it's easier to work with. It's also a good idea to get it agitated at the store; less mixing for you. To mix the paint first pour the contents of one can into an empty can. Then proceed to box the paint—that is, pour it back and forth between cans until it is a smooth, uniform consistency. You can also stir it. To do this stick the paint paddle all the way into the can and move the stick in a figure eight motion rather than round and round. It's best to have all your paint and equipment in one spot, either set on layers of newspaper or a drop cloth.

Painting Procedure   Start painting at the top of the house. First do the gutters, then the eaves, then the high windows, and then the upper siding. In this way if paint drips—and it will—the drops won't spot an area that's already painted, as would happen if you did the siding all at once. When the top part of the house is done do the windows and trim below, then the siding. Following are techniques you should use.

Siding.   If right handed start on the left hand side of the house at the top; if a southpaw start on the right side. Use a four inch brush. Dip the brush one-third into the can, then tap off excess. Do not wipe brush on the rim of the can. This can create bubbles which do not brush out easily.

If painting clapboard, apply the paint to the bottom edges of the top boards as far as you can easily see and easily reach. This usually is three or four feet. Then come back and paint the face of that board for the same distance. Paint the edge of the next board down, then paint the face. Continue on down until you can no longer easily reach the boards. Use plenty of paint but not so much it sags—most nonprofessional painters skimp, and it's a mistake. And paint from what the pros call the "dry into the wet." Apply the paint for a distance of eighteen inches or so, then start about a foot from one wet edge and paint back towards it. The idea is to cover the maximum dry area with each stroke, and not be brushing and rebrushing an area already covered with paint. This lets the paint do the painting, not the painter. As each board is painted smooth off excess with long even strokes. Final stroke should be light and the brush lifted as you end the stroke to blend the paint evenly into the previously painted area.

Next paint an area adjacent to the one you just painted and about the same size (three to four square feet high and wide). Continue along the side of the house this way until you come to the end. When you get to the end of the house you'll have a horizontal band three or four feet deep painted. Go back to below where you first started and small section by small section paint another band across the face of the house. Continue like this until finished. Tip: Paint sides of windows and doors with siding paint so you don't have to "cut in" with trim paint.

One other tip. As you paint, every now and then smack the brush against the clapboard to remove excess paint. If you smear the windows or trim just wipe the paint off with a rag moistened in the solvent you're using.

Shakes.   Shakes are particularly difficult to paint because they have vertical grooves or striations in them and you can't make broad, sweeping brush strokes as you can with clapboard. To paint these it's a good idea to use either a 4 inch brush cut down about an inch so the shortened bristles will be stiff, or a pad-type applicator. The latter is just a foam pad with short bristles on it with a handle. Whatever you use shakes are painted with a wiping motion. You jam the bristles up under the edge of the shake and wipe the paint on with a downward motion. Follow the same small-section-by-small-section procedure as with clapboard.

Composition Shingles.   Here you can use a regular brush following the same procedure you used for clapboard. However, make your final strokes vertical rather than horizontal, removing excess paint as you do.

Trim.   When doing this, be certain to follow the "dry into the wet" method discussed—you want to cover the maximum dry area you can with each brush stroke.

Windows.   Windows seem to scare a lot of people. It's as if the glass was going to bite you if you got some paint on it. Actually, the way to paint windows is to be bold. Concentrate on getting paint onto the wood. If you get some paint on the glass, and you will, just wrap a cloth over your finger and wipe it off as you go. No problem.

Paint the windows from the inside out; that is, the small pieces of wood framework the glass is set into and work out towards the sash—the wood on the perimeter. If you can, approach framework from the side rather than straight on. More of the framework surface is visible and therefore easier to paint.

A relatively recent development in exterior painting has been the airless spray gun system. Unlike regular spray guns which atomize the paint and may send it floating across the street in a cloud onto your neighbor's car, the airless spray gun does not atomize the paint. You merely need to cover up areas as you normally would with a brush. The system that I tested was advertised for painting siding, trim, and windows (you cover them up with cardboard cutouts) but I found it useful only for painting narrow areas and the cardboard masking cutouts didn't work properly. However, I do recommend that you try the airless spray on siding. It really does beat a brush—it is much faster. Of course you have to pay a rental fee for the gun and it uses about one-third more paint than ordinarily used with a brush.

Cleanup. If you wear long sleeve shirts, a hat, and long pants, cleanup of yourself will be minimal. Best thing I've found is Quickee, a pink lanolin cream that you wipe on, then wipe off with paper toweling or a rag. It removes paint spatters easily and does not irritate the skin.

Cleaning up around the house will be easy if you have covered up properly, and have wiped spatters away while still wet. Beware of getting paint on shoe soles, then tracking it into uncovered areas.

A particular bugaboo can be getting paint on a concrete driveway or path—it doesn't wipe away easily. You can remove it with paint remover. Apply it with a stiff wire brush or steel wool. If you use it soon after the spillage you should remove it without any problems. It does work on paint spots that have been dry a long time but it is more difficult.

INTERIOR PAINTING—PREPARATION

The most important part of an interior paint job as with an exterior one, is preparation. Walls and ceilings in living rooms, halls, and bedrooms will be soiled in varying degrees. While many painters will tell you to wash the walls and ceilings I have found this unnecessary. All you really have to do is make certain that dust, spider webs, and the like are removed. Today's paints are good—they'll do the rest. However, the kitchen is another story. Here grease from the stove forms on walls and really must be removed before painting. Any non-sudsing household cleaner you like can do the job. It's also a good idea to scuff-sand the walls with medium-grade sandpaper to take off a little of the gloss so that the new paint will stick. Don't forget to wipe off your sanding dust with a damp rag, or tack rag available at hardware stores.

Patching.   Patching is another important part of preparation. You may encounter holes ranging from hairline cracks to those you can drive a Mack truck through. There are various patchers that you can use. As far as I'm concerned the primary patcher you need is painter's plaster of paris. A five pound bag of this can be gotten for around sixty-five cents and it will do all the patching required in the average house. Of course plaster hardens rapidly—ten minutes. To get around this you can use an old painter's trick. To every coffee can full of plaster you mix add a dash of vinegar. This keeps the plaster soft three times longer.

Hairline Cracks.   These look like veins, and normally occur when the walls or ceilings are made of plaster rather than plasterboard. As the house settles it expands and contracts and the stress on the walls and ceilings make them pull apart a little. If you can get a fingernail in a crack you should enlarge it. Best tool for this job is an old fashioned beer can opener. Starting at the top of the crack, put the hook of the opener in the crack and draw it down along the crack digging out all loose, unsound material in the process. Then, using an old brush, brush out all loose material. Next mix your plaster. The best way to do this is in a coffee can. Pour the water into the can, filling it about one quarter of the way. Add plaster to the water, letting the plaster soak it up. Don't mix plaster. When you are ready to use it, scoop it out and work it together on the palm of your hand using a 3-1/2 inch scraper. It should be about the consistency of mashed potatoes. If plaster from the bag is lumpy, return it. It's no good.

Wet the cracks down with a brush or a rag. The idea here is to have the wall, which is dry and absorbent, suck in the moisture you apply rather than the plaster which would weaken it. Scoop small amounts of plaster off your hand and pack it into the crack. When the crack is completely filled, smooth off flush with the wall by drawing the scraper straight down the crack. The big idea when patching is to smooth the plaster with the scraper; don't rely on sandpaper. You'll sand until the cows come home and never really get it smooth. To do this you need a scraper with a flexible, springy blade. If you have trouble smoothing it with a scraper, a trick you can utilize is to go over it with a folded, soaking wet rag, running it down the length of the crack. The plaster is still soft and this will smooth it pretty well.

If the crack is so small you can't get a fingernail in, use Spackle as your patcher. This is something like plaster. Instructions for use are on the package.

Small holes in plaster.   To repair a small hole in plaster, first thing you do is remove any loose material from the hole or the crack with the end of your scraper, an old chisel or screwdriver. Brush out loose crumbly stuff with a brush. Then wet the hole down, or brush. Pack plaster into the hole, then draw your scraper across it.

Large holes in plaster.   Here I'm talking about a hole that goes all the way through the plaster. Sometimes there will be lath or boards to support new plaster that you put in a hole. Other times you'll have just a hole with dead air space. At any rate, first step is to cut away loose material from the hole edges. If there are laths to support the plaster follow this procedure: Mix an extra thick mixture of plaster. Pack it into the hole, mostly filling it, and covering edges.

Let dry. This will form a base upon which you can put your finished coat of plaster. Wet base coat with water, then apply finish coat of normal consistency. Smooth it out following the technique described for small holes. If there is no lath in a hole, in other words just dead air space, you need to put something into the hole first to support the plaster. Best thing for this is a piece of hardware cloth, a cheap metal material that you can buy at the lumberyard. Cut a piece of this material an inch bigger all around than the hole, and slip a twelve-inch string through its center. Slip the hardware cloth (it bends) through the hole so it overlaps the hole equally all around on the back side of the wall. Pull the string out and tie it to a thin stick of wood that overlaps hole. This will hold the hardware cloth in place. Now fill the hole three-quarters with a stiff mixture of plaster, covering edges; let dry, remove the stick of wood and cut off the string. Then finish off the hole with a finish coat of plaster. If the hole is especially large a trowel rather than a scraper is handy for smoothing. When smoothing plaster with a trowel you smooth it with the back edge of the trowel, moving the trowel across the patch with the front or leading edge slightly raised.

Very large hole.   The problem here is also to have some sort of base for your patch. The answer is plasterboard. First cut a piece that is slightly smaller than the hole all around. Nail it into the cavity with plasterboard nails, sinking the nails into studs or lath. Then apply a thick mix of plaster all around the edges at the seam of the patch. Let set. Then apply finish coat of plaster over the entire hole. For this you must use a trowel. If at any time you see that your plaster patch on any of these holes is starting to crack, you can recombine the plaster by drawing a wet rag across it.

PLASTERBOARD

Plasterboard hardly ever develops cracks. Far more likely is that an errant foot or fist will make a hole in it. If the hole is less than three inches in diameter you can repair it with the hardware cloth method outlined. If the hole is very large the best thing to do for repair is use a piece of plasterboard the same thickness as the existing wall, usually 1/2 or 3/8 inch. Enlarge the hole with a utility knife into a rectangular shape until 1/2 of each stud is exposed, on each side. Then cut the patch to fit inside the hole and nail it at the edges to the studs. Cover the joints around the hole with joint compound and perforated tape as described in Chapter 5. The tape-joint compound method can also be used on large holes in plaster—you'll probably find it easier.

PAINTING

The painting procedure used depends on what you're painting. For painting living rooms and bedrooms, the first step is to move as much furniture as you possibly can out of the room. Move the rest of the furniture into as close a group as you can in the center of the room. You should be able to reach the middle of the ceiling above the furniture from your ladder with your roller. In this way you won't have to move anything once the job begins.

To save wear and tear on yourself it's a good idea to move the furniture the night before you paint. You can use store bought drop cloths for covering furniture and floors but it's just as easy to use overlapped newspapers on the floors and cover the furniture with thin 9 by 12 plastic drop cloths, then cover the plastic with old sheets or blankets. Old sheets and blankets are not enough alone because paint droppings can seep through these porous materials onto furniture. Plastic is not enough because it's lightweight and has a tendency to lift from the slightest breeze. To avoid tracking paint on floors of other rooms make paper paths from the room you're painting to wherever you expect to go during the job.

Paint the ceiling first. Start in the end of the room which is closest to the light source; that is, the window, and paint away from it. The ceiling is painted in three foot wide strips. Start in a corner and "cut in" the areas that the roller can't reach with a brush. Paint only what you can easily see and easily reach. This might be an area three to four feet wide. Run your roller into the paint pan, roll off excess on the grid, then apply paint one way over the three to four foot wide area. Then come back and paint the other way over the same area. In other words, crisscross. Then come back the original way with a fairly "dry" roller and smooth out the paint. Paint across the ceiling in these three to four foot wide areas until you reach the end. Cut in with the brush, then come back and roll another strip adjacent to the first, overlapping it. The idea is to do one small area at a time. And do use plenty of paint. As with exterior house painting let it, and not you, do the work.

Every now and then look at the freshly painted area against a light source. This will tell you immediately where you have missed spots. Touch up right away. These missed spots won't be shiny —wet.

When the ceiling is painted, do the walls.

The walls are also painted in strips about three feet wide, and going from ceiling to baseboard.

Starting at any wall, cut in a three to four foot wide area at the ceiling with a 1-1/2 to 2 inch brush, then cut in the corner going from ceiling to the top of the baseboard. These cut-in lines should not be more than an inch wide—brushes and rollers leave a different texture that can be noticeable and you want to minimize the difference.

Then, starting at the top and using plenty of paint, make a V-shape with the roller, as wide as the cut-in line and about one third the depth of the wall, concentrating on going into the maximum dry area with each stroke. Crisscross back across this V-shape with horizontal strokes, then make vertical strokes over the area to flatten and smooth the paint.

Make another V in the middle of the wall, crisscross horizontally, then flatten and smooth vertically. Do the same thing on the bottom portion of wall, cutting in at the baseboard with the roller. Then, using a "dry"—undipped—roller, make vertical baseboard to ceiling strokes to smooth the paint. Immediately follow by painting the baseboard to the width of the strip just painted. If using trim paint on baseboard, paint after walls are done. When cutting in at the floor it's best to sight along the floor to the baseboard bottom: it gives a better view of things and makes painting a straight line easier. One strip finished, proceed down the wall the same way, strip by strip. Just before you get to the end of the wall, cut in the corner, then paint in the strip.

Proceed around the room as above. If you intend to stop at any point, stop in a corner, not in the middle of the wall. Otherwise you could get lap marks. If touching up is necessary do it right away while the paint is wet. If touchup is needed after the paint is dry just dab the paint on—don't brush. Brushing it out can lead to a texture change that will show up.

With walls painted using the procedure just discussed, come back and paint the windows. A 1-1/2 inch sash brush with angled bristles will be good here. As with exterior windows, paint from the inside out and try to see as much of the wood as you can while painting. In other words don't approach the framework head-on.

PAINTS FOR WALL AND CEILING

There are basically two kinds of paint for walls and ceilings of living rooms, bedrooms, and halls—latex and oil base. The former thins and cleans up with water; the latter thins and cleans up with mineral spirits. There's debate as to which is better. You would probably get better coverage overall using an oil base paint but it really isn't that much better than latex in this area, and the advantages of latex (namely, thinning and cleanup with water) should make it your choice. Above all when buying paint buy good paint. Bargain basement paint gives bargain basement results. The paint is harder to apply, takes more to cover, and will fade quickly. Good quality paint covers easily, is easy to apply, and has good color retention.

KITCHEN

For painting a kitchen the best type of paint to use is enamel, because it dries to a hard, shiny film that is easier to clean than flat paint. Oil base paint comes in gloss or semigloss form. Latex is also available in these forms. The latex semigloss paint does not cover as well as the oil base. The average kitchen will require about two gallons of paint, including the insides of cabinets if they are painted.

Preparation.   When painting the kitchen first patch all cracks and holes. You can proceed as discussed elsewhere except prime the plaster patches with shellac base coat rather than paint. This will prevent the patches from bleeding through the finished coat which would happen if you used paint.

Mix the paint as described using a 2-1/2 to 3 inch brush to paint the insides of the cabinets including the inside of the doors. Then, starting in one corner of the room, paint the ceiling. Use plenty of paint, painting small 3 by 3 foot areas from each ladder setting. In other words only what you can easily see and easily reach. Apply the paint in random strokes, holding the brush lightly, covering the maximum dry area with each stroke. And use planty of paint. When the area is completely covered with paint come back and smooth it all out with strokes that go one way. Continue like this painting one small section at a time until the ceiling is finished. Be sure to make your last strokes lift gently upward to blend paint properly.

Then paint the walls, also with a brush, following this procedure of painting one small section at a time, making your last stroke smooth out the paint vertically. Every now and then rap the brush flat against the wall, knocking out excess paint. When all the walls are done paint the cabinet doors, then the windows.

BATHROOM

The bathroom is painted like the kitchen. Start at the ceiling, finish that, work your way down the walls. Again, use enamel paint, either gloss or semigloss. To save cleanup, protect the tile with masking tape before you begin.